PENGUIN MODERN CLASSICS

Nomenclature

Dionne Brand is the award-winning author of twenty-three books of poetry, fiction and non-fiction. Her twelve books of poetry – *'Fore Day Morning: Poems* (1978), *Earth Magic* (1980/1993/2006, for children), *Primitive Offensive* (1982), *Winter Epigrams and Epigrams to Ernesto Cardenal in Defense of Claudia* (1983), *Chronicles of the Hostile Sun* (1984), *No Language is Neutral* (1990), *Land to Light On* (1997), *thirsty* (2002), *Inventory* (2006), *Ossuaries* (2010), *The Blue Clerk: Ars Poetica in 59 Versos* (2018) and *Nomenclature for the Time Being* (2022) – have won the Pat Lowther Memorial Award for Poetry, the Governor General's Award for English-Language Poetry, the Trillium Book Award and the Griffin Poetry Prize.

In addition to poetry, Brand has published six works of fiction and five works of non-fiction. The fiction is *Sans Souci and Other Stories* (1988), *In Another Place, Not Here* (1996), *At the Full and Change of the Moon* (1999), *What We All Long For* (2005), *Love Enough* (2014) and *Theory* (2018). Her non-fiction work is *Bread Out of Stone: Recollections, Sex, Recognitions, Race, Dreaming, Politics* (1984/1985/2019), *No Burden to Carry: Narratives of Black Working Women in Ontario 1920s – 1950s* (1991), *A Map to the Door of No Return: Notes to Belonging* (2001), *A Kind of Perfect Speech* (2006);and *An Autobiography of the Autobiography of Reading* (2020). Brand is the co-editor of two books: *Rivers Have Sources, Trees Have Roots: Speaking of Racism* (1986, with Krisantha Sri Bhaggiyadatta), and *Luminous Ink: Writers on Writing in Canada* (2018, with Rabindranath Maharaj and Tessa McWatt); and co-author of *We're Rooted Here and They Can't Pull Us Up: Essays in African Canadian Women's History* (1994, with Peggy Bristow, et al.).

Brand is the recipient of the Toronto Book Award (2006 and 2019), the Blue Metropolis Violet Prize, the OCM Bocas Prize for Fiction and the 2021 Windham-Campbell Prize for Fiction. In 2017, Brand was named to the Order of Canada. She was poetry editor at McClelland & Stewart from 2014 to 2021.

Christina Sharpe is a writer, professor and Canada Research Chair in Black Studies in the Humanities at York University. She is the author of: *Monstrous Intimacies: Making Post-Slavery Subjects* and *In the Wake: On Blackness and Being*. Her third book, *Ordinary Notes*, will be published in 2023 (Knopf/FSG/Daunt). She is currently working on a monograph called *Black. Still. Life.* (Duke, 2025). She has recently published essays in *Art in America*, *Brick: A Literary Journal*, *Alison Saar: Of Aether and Earthe*, *Grief and Grievance: Art and Mourning in America*, *Reconstructions: Architecture and Blackness in America* and *Jennifer Packer: The Eye is Not Satisfied with Seeing*.

NOMENCLATURE

New and Collected Poems

DIONNE BRAND

PENGUIN BOOKS

PENGUIN CLASSICS

UK | USA | Canada | Ireland | Australia
India | New Zealand | South Africa

Penguin Books is part of the Penguin Random House group of companies whose addresses can be found at global.penguinrandomhouse.com

First published in the USA by McClelland & Stewart 2022
First published in Great Britain in Penguin Modern Classics 2023
001

Printed and bound in Great Britain by Clays Ltd, Elcograf S.p.A.

The authorized representative in the EEA is Penguin Random House Ireland, Morrison Chambers, 32 Nassau Street, Dublin D02 YH68

A CIP catalogue record for this book is available from the British Library

ISBN: 978–0–241–63979–5

www.greenpenguin.co.uk

Penguin Random House is committed to a sustainable future for our business, our readers and our planet. This book is made from Forest Stewardship Council® certified paper.

CONTENTS

NOMENCLATURE

New and Collected Poems

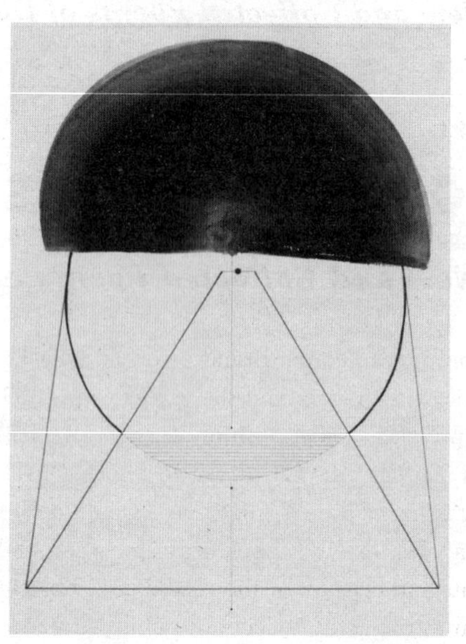

CRITICAL INTRODUCTION

Nomenclature: New and Collected Poems of Dionne Brand

CHRISTINA SHARPE

A NOTE ON THE TEXT

This critical introduction traces Dionne Brand's work, political engagements, commitment to experiments with form and shape, her place in Diasporas, her influences, and the beauty and radical push of her poetics. Neither *'Fore Day Morning: poems* (1978) nor *The Blue Clerk: Ars Poetica in 59 Versos* (2018) are included in *Nomenclature: New and Collected.* The former book is omitted because Brand considers it her juvenilia, and the latter book resists inclusion both because of its recent publication date and because of the very kind of object that it is—an essay poem. In addition to the eight collections published between 1982 and 2010, *Nomenclature: New and Collected* includes *Nomenclature for the Time Being* (2022), a new, long poem which appears here, in print, for the first time.

"THE ABACUS OF HER EYELIDS": *NOMENCLATURE: NEW AND COLLECTED POEMS OF DIONNE BRAND*

> You cannot be an artist if you don't have one foot on the ground and the other outside the planet.
>
> —Jacques Coursil

In her 2020 R.W.B. Jackson Lecture, "Nomenclature for the Time Being," a reading and conversation with professor, writer and theorist Rinaldo Walcott, Dionne Brand speaks about her long poem *Ossuaries* (2010). She says: "In it there are two speakers, one in the present and one in the future. The speaker who is in a future time looking back to ours—she calls our time our wingless days when even dreams are full of prisons, when every waking is incarcerated—describes the present as eroding, it lies in bones in an ossuary that speaker looks at in the future. And the speaker, in the present, has sent a note to that future—it contains disintegrating gigabytes of violent news—and the speaker in the present hopes the news will not reach the speaker in the future; will not reach the future. The poem is a letter from one hemisphere to another, one time to another . . ."[1]

Dionne Brand's poetry makes scalar leaps from the "eroding present" and the "intimacy of history" to "unknown galaxies" and "as yet / unarmed moons," as her work threads multiple temporal worlds—past, present, and futures. With a consciousness that is attuned to this world and open to some other, possibly future, time and place, Brand's ongoing labours of witness and imagination speak directly to where and how we live and also, and necessarily, reach beyond those worlds, their enclosures, and their violences. Brand is, in other words, a poet *engagé*, and hers is a poetics of liberation; she does not "write toward anything called justice, but against tyranny."[2]

This commitment to liberation is clear across twelve books of poetry that span more than four decades. Giving rise to whole new grammars and vocabularies, Brand's work cuts through and sounds beyond "our" implicatedness in narrative, which is to say "our" implicatedness in *this* tyrannical present carved out by nation, by borders, by militarism, by multiplying and intensifying global conflicts over resources and their extraction, and by attempts to firmly locate nations' insiders and outsiders.

all around, and creeping

self-righteous, let's say it, fascism,
how else to say border,
and the militant consumption of everything,
the encampment of the airport, the eagerness
to be all the same, to mince biographies
to some exact phrases, some
exact and toxic genealogy

When, for example, the woman at the center of the long poem *Inventory* (2006) is faced with the choice to watch *Law & Order*'s endlessly reproduced and globally circulated formula of selective crime and punishment, to go to bed, or to bear witness to the wreckage of never-ending atrocities and disasters (war in Iraq, war in Afghanistan, suicide bomb after suicide bomb, "targeted assassinations," Hurricane Katrina, Morecambe Bay), what should she choose but to witness, even as that witnessing is, and must be, partial, incomplete, ongoing.

There are seven inventories in *Inventory*, and the work of observation and witness in the poem is subtended by the making of language to bear the weight, and to sound the word against the self's calcification to registering the order and scale of disasters, a hardening made clear in a line like: "all this became ordinary far from where it happened." The woman in *Inventory* is sleepless, she has been collecting. Her inventory is long and deep—Middle Passage, Darfur, Toronto, Grenada, and Louisiana. Her lists are *bristling*.

> *What the chronicler sees: things animate with excess, people animate with excess, and riven by despair.*

"Restless collecting" and "an abacus for eyelids" are other designations for a kind of attentive gathering for which "inventory" is simultaneously one name and also form, mode of inquiry, politics, and method. Collecting is accounting, but this reckoning is not for reconciling. In Brand's corpus, words, sounds, places, references accumulate feeling and meaning, and one enters the space of Édouard Glissant's relation. When, for instance, the ocean and the earth appear in Brand's poems, they are not a poet's empty praise of the natural world. They appear because the world keeps at its hard work of remaking and we, too, keep at ours, animate, fracturing, disappearing *and* here. There is the body and then there is what can be done to the body; what composes it and what cleaves it. This poet's task is to try to hold all of this and to work toward some pellucid understanding of those materials that others might want to forget, or have to forget, or need to put aside. The poet works memory, she works the news, she works the everyday—violence, sunsets, sirens, sidewalks, and oceans—and she returns them to the reader utterly transformed by her lapidary attention.

II. *TO UNDO AND UNDO AND UNDO*

Appointed Toronto's third poet laureate (2009–12),[3] Dionne Brand brought poetry into the streets of the city with Poetry is Public is Poetry—a literary legacy project for the people of Toronto. "We want," she said, "to have poetry in that moment between the doughnut shop and car dealership, speaking through the cacophony of consumerism."[4] As laureate, she mounted poetry installations at the main Reference Library in downtown Toronto and at a suburban reference library. Brand was commissioned to write several poems that appear in locations across the city of Toronto. I draw attention to two in particular. First, on a wall in Islington Village, there is a mural based on Article 13 from the Universal Declaration of Human Rights; it was commissioned in 2010 by Louise Garfield, then executive director of Arts Etobicoke. The murals in that part of the city were largely idyllic Anglo nineteenth- and early twentieth-century scenes that did not reflect the people who were actually living there. This thousand-square-foot mural stands against that particular imagining and recuperation of idyllic whiteness—and Islington Village was and is home to many Somali Canadians who, in the year of the mural's commissioning and after, were subject to police raids and criminalization. It is fitting that in this poem appears the line "we are heartsick for the true world": "Inalienable nomads, global citizens / unfettered limbs, we are heartsick for the true world, / compelled to place we search for place, / there in the growths of black wild alders."

Second, in 2015 a poem was installed across the backs of two concrete benches at the Dufferin subway station in the West End of Toronto. Here is poetry at a busy intersection at Bloor and Dufferin—where people line up several deep waiting for the Dufferin bus, which is often late and usually packed, a bus that riders nickname the Sufferin' bus. Poetry appears here as beautification, not gentrification; this is a poem from and for the surrounding community. The poem begins, "Walking here . . ." and ends, "waiting, I felt the world coming toward me." This is poetry in the streets to cut commerce; this is poetry as another way to engage the world, not mediated by the demands of capital. Indeed, Brand has "always taken poetry's project to be . . . reflecting, intuiting, making sense of and undoing the times we live in. And doing that at the core of where the world gets made and articulated—language."[5]

From *Primitive Offensive* (1982) to *Chronicles of the Hostile Sun* (1984) to *No Language is Neutral* (1990), *Land to Light On* (1997) and *Nomenclature for the Time Being* (2022), a consistent quality of Brand's work is its intimacy: she observes and she is involved; this is a poet who is participant in that sense-making work of contemporary life not collapsible into but certainly shaped by histories (and presents) of slavery, colonization, war, and revolution. Her poems have air.

On any page of Brand's work, one encounters the intimacies and the estrangements of histories ("how come, how come / I anticipate nothing as intimate as history"), the radical inventiveness of communities, the glottal endeavours of sound and language, the ways that one is held in and by enclosure. To attend to her inventiveness is to trace lineages in Brand's work, to map her political commitments alongside and indivisible from her continued and rigorous attention to the line.

It bears repeating, then, that the aesthetic and the political are inseparable in Brand's work. Poetry is a leap into language, a leap into possibility, and Brand is always working at language's fibrous root. In an article that appeared in *The Black Scholar* in 2017, Brand writes, "We wait for narrative to do what war should or might do."[6] We might well read this as another iteration of her sense that "the reader interrogates narrative, but poetry interrogates the reader."[7] This is not the ascription of magical properties to poetry but an insistence on poetry's radical break with representation, its alchemical work of "meaning displacement."[8] Brand's poems model all that poetry is capable of doing and making; alert us to what is at work in a line and a form, to how a line breaks open understanding, arrests time, ushers in new meaning and propels a reader/listener to a different kind of knowledge. And one of the many gifts of her work is that as histories and presents of war, the ravages of capital, slavery and its residuals appear in various forms in her work, they are also animated by the possibility of revolution, love, and world (re)making. This is, to say, alongside Robin D.G. Kelley writing about Césaire, that it is "poetry and therefore revolt."[9]

The eponymous clerk of Brand's 2018 essay poem *The Blue Clerk* is searching for a new language. Her studied and desirous probing brings her to a language of colour (blue, lemon, violet, black) that is, precisely, a distillation of the kind of meaning-making that poetry allows. "Blue tremors, blue position, blue suppuration. The clerk is considering blue havoc, blue thousands, blue shoulder, where these arrive from blue expenses . . . The clerk hears humming in her ears; blue handling, she answers; any blue, she asks the author, any blue nails today? Did you send me, as I asked, blue ants? The author asks, blue drafts? Perhaps blue virus, blue traffic would make a sense, says the clerk . . . The blue clerk would like a blue language or a lemon language or a violet language. Blue arrivals. Oh yes."[10]

Visit with the lists in *Inventory*, the epigrams of *Winter Epigrams and Epigrams to Ernesto Cardenal in Defense of Claudia,* the cantos of *Primitive Offensive.* Read the six pages of verblessness in Ossuary I, in which the poet/speaker says, "after consideration you will discover, as I, / that verbs are a tragedy, a bleeding cliff-side, explosions, / I'm better off without, with vermillion, candles."

That "you" who will discover (that brutal language-logic of conquest) meets the "I" with the verb stripped away—the bleeding cliffside of war, occupation, refusal, and resistance. That bleeding cliffside spans centuries. It recalls the site of the resistance of the Caribs who, in 1651, jumped to their deaths in the town of Sauters rather than submit to European colonialism. The cliffs recall the 1983 coup, the executions of Maurice Bishop and Jacqueline Creft, the U.S. invasion, and the death of the dream and reality of the New Jewel Movement's socialist government in the English-speaking Caribbean. Without the intrusive verb, what space might be cleared or held? "What poetry allows," Brand says, "is the removal of parts of speech so that a life may make sense to itself."[11] And, in an interview published in the journal *Border Crossings* in December 2020, Brand returns to verblessness, saying, "I found that [it] addressed a particular philosophical problem that I'm trying to work on. Traces. How to lift traces to lines, to tangibility. The Americas are full of traces that have been erased by regimes of governance or regimes of power. So, where I find myself located as trace, trace becomes vocabulary."[12]

III. *TRACE BECOMES VOCABULARY*

Brand's influences are many and catholic. Among them are poets; fiction and nonfiction writers; poets of left movements in Latin, Central, and South America; feminist and anticolonial theorists in Africa and the Americas and revolutionaries: Martin Carter, Margaret Walker, Kamau Brathwaite, Derek Walcott, Wilson Harris, C.L.R. James, Amílcar Cabral, Eric Williams, George Padmore, Kwame Nkrumah, Taban Lo Liyong, Dennis Brutus, Mongo Beti, Nikki Giovanni, Gwendolyn Brooks, Countee Cullen, Sonia Sanchez, Frantz Fanon, Mahmoud Darwish, Aimé Césaire, Walter Rodney, Manning Marable, Cedric Robinson, Adrienne Rich, Muriel Rukeyser, Elizabeth Bishop, Rita Dove, Chrystos, Audre Lorde, Langston Hughes, June Jordan, W.E.B. Du Bois, Roque Dalton, Claribel Alegría, García Lorca, Alejo Carpentier, Pablo Neruda, and Ernesto Cardenal. Each of these poets, writers, and thinkers is important as an interlocutor, and together they form a cosmology of influence, a company of thought. In *A Kind of Perfect Speech*, Brand recalls reading Countee Cullen when she was in her late teens and recognizing in it something in the co-relation of Black and poet—"to make a poet black and bid him sing."[13]

Just as important to Brand's formation, just as important to the range of her work, are the musicians and visual artists who have accompanied her and given her sound and also shape and theory: Calypso Rose, Lord Kitchener, the Mighty Sparrow, Growling Tiger, Nina Simone, Sarah Vaughan, Jacob Lawrence, Sun Ra, the Shadow, Miriam Makeba, Betty Carter, Remedios Varo, Thelonious Monk, and always Coltrane's horn and Rashied Ali's drums on "Venus," making a new mythology, a mythology of the not yet. We hear and sense in Brand's return to "Venus" (it appears across works, in the novel *What We All Long For* and in the poems *Ossuaries* and *The Blue Clerk*) that trace vocabulary lifted to tangibility and with it, all of the poet's aspirations for how to sound Black life on the page and then out in the world.

"We are not simply up here in the north," Brand says, "we belong to a network of people thinking liberation (Canada joins Nairobi, joins Durban, joins Cleveland, joins Kingston joins Atlanta joins Manchester, Salvador, Bahia to New York, Chicago, Lagos, London . . .), our intellectual and geographic borders are porous and not patrolled in the ways that nation states would have them patrolled, and weakly try to embarrass or stymy our efforts to think through and beyond theirs."[14] Brand is like Yasmine, one of the two speakers in *Ossuaries*, about whom we read: "this genealogy she's made by hand, this good silk lace, / Engels plaited to Bird, Claudia Jones edgestitched / to Monk, Rosa Luxemburg braids Coltrane."

Brand's handmade genealogy brings all of the above influences (and more) with her. Her poetics were shaped by growing into a Black consciousness deeply informed by Pan Africanism, anticolonial movements, African liberation movements, and Black Internationalism. Reading works by Caribbean and African poets and theorists and African American poets and theorists as she began to write in earnest, Brand counted herself lucky to have come of age during a time when poetry was seen as essential to making new worlds. "I wanted," she said, "to show the utter joy of collective political resistance, the way in which its marvelous aspect is also an aesthetic pleasure. I wanted to show that liberation was political thought, and liberation is aesthetic power."[15]

Her fourth book of poetry, *No Language is Neutral* (1990) takes its title from Derek Walcott's *Midsummer* (1984), and in it "she addresses both the weight of language she inherits and the weight of language she makes. 'I have come to know something simple,' she says. 'Each sentence realized or dreamed jumps like a pulse with history and takes a side.' Neutrality is not possible, and her pulse turns again to the process of metallurgy when she talks about 'the heat of meaning-making' and about the lines in *No Language Is Neutral* that 'burn to a close.'"[16]

Then, there is Césaire's anticolonial, recombinant languaging: "I should discover once again the secret of great communication and great combustions. I should say storm. I should say river. I should say tornado. I should say leaf. I should say tree." When Brand encounters Césaire's *Notebook of a Return to My Native Land* she says, "I read him as if I was finding a new dictionary."[17]

Brand's work comes out of and writes into Black Liberation, it is constituted by and constitutes a community for liberation. This is the audience of her poems. And this orientation is part of what leads Brand to Grenada and to her participation in the revolution there. This is the largeness of blackness that gives heft to Brand's work—not nationality but that which exceeds nation. Reading, listening to, and studying the work of all of those great poets and thinkers, Brand wanted to sound it all, she wanted to bring it all with her into her poetry. And she does, from Brooks to Brutus to Okot p'Bitek to Lorde and Coltrane—the sounds reverberate in her writing; so too, their political commitments.

Trinidad and Tobago, Dominica, Burnt River, and Toronto figure regularly in Brand's work, but it would not be accurate to position her as, or solely as, a Canadian poet or Caribbean poet. The Caribbean is not the location of the writing poet (by which I mean she does not write from the Caribbean; she left Trinidad at seventeen years of age) nor is the Caribbean, usually, the place of the poetic consciousness of the poems. It is more precise to say that the Caribbean is deeply important for Brand as place and aperture, location and schema. (We might think of two works here as examples: Derek Walcott's *Omeros* and Kamau Brathwaite's *Middle Passages*, each of which begins in the Caribbean and moves out, back, and in multiple directions across time and space.) Brand is a major poet in Canada, and Canada has been the locus of much of her work. The city of Toronto, in particular, is a repeating character in Brand's work—as a city coming into being, changing, disappearing as people come and go, come together, are displaced, made into shadows of themselves, or grow large on the misery of others. Brand writes in *thirsty* of the "invisible breasts, in the shrinking lake / in the tiny shops of untrue recollections, / the brittle, gnawed life we live." All of her work is informed by a deep knowledge of these metropolitan and postcolonial spaces and by her commitments (writerly and otherwise) that are not amenable to anything called nation. Brand knows those spaces and the ways that they are continually being made, unmade, and remade. In fact, she began her writing work in the middle of Canada's national literature-making processes—processes in which Brand and many other Black writers troubled the very claims of nation. Put another way, Brand is in no way involved in that project, initiated in earnest in the 1970s and ongoing, of writing a national literature, of revivifying nation. The nexus of her work is Diaspora.

Many of Brand's references to the world are to a dispersed or diffuse populace who are connected by condition and not by nation; they are those who make up what Anne Winters names as "the displaced of capital"[18] and Sylvia Wynter the "global archipelagos of poverty." Brand is a poet who speaks to Black people in Canada and the Caribbean but is not a Canadian poet and not a Caribbean poet, she is a poet who thinks each location as part of a larger geography. As Wynter is a philosopher of the Americas, so is Brand a poet of the Diaspora and the Americas.

IV. *IF I AM PEACEFUL . . . IS NOT PEACE*

'Fore Day Morning, Brand's first book of poetry, was published in 1978 by Harold Head's Khoisan Artists. Although it is not collected here because Brand thinks there are, at most, two poems in it worth revisiting, it is important in her formation as a poet in terms of what she will come to write and because of the nexus of people, that earlier referenced cosmology of influences, whom she names as her interlocutors. The small press Khoisan Artists was established by Harold Head (ex-husband of the great writer Bessie Head) circa 1976, when he arrived in Toronto after being banned as a journalist in apartheid South Africa, via the twisted routes of exile: first to Botswana, then the U.S. and finally Canada. There was a swell of Black organizing in Toronto, and the establishment of Khoisan Artists was part of a corresponding new wave of Black publishing that included *Contrast* newspaper and *Spear: Canada's Truth and Soul* Magazine. Publishing, writing and the arts more broadly were directly connected to freedom struggles and Black Liberation movements. Together Harold Head and poet Ayanna Black would establish Great Black Music, a group that brought jazz musicians like the Art Ensemble of Chicago, Leroy Jenkins, Randy Weston, Anthony Braxton, and Cecil Taylor to Toronto. These connections deepened Brand's attention to jazz—an attention that finds itself in her poetry. Around this same time, Brand

and Black would organize an event at the Royal Ontario Museum called Poetry and Pan, with readings by poets and music by the pannist Ian Jones and his steel ensemble. The 1970s in Toronto were, as everywhere, a time filled with the work of Black political organizing done with people who were active in civil rights movements and anti-colonial and anti-imperialist struggles. This struggle work happened on local levels and also across borders, and it bears repeating that it included the work of artists, dancers, musicians, and writers.

In the mid to late 1970s Brand began to work with the Black Education Project in Toronto and with Marlene Green, who was one of its founders. In the early 1980s, Brand, the dub poet Clifton Joseph, and Makeda Silvera (novelist and, later, the founder and publisher of the groundbreaking Sister Vision Press) published the short-lived literary pamphlet *The Harriet Tubman Review*. That work with Green and the BEP was key to Brand's left political formation and commitments. (Brand's friend and comrade, Green appears in several poems; Inventory III, which begins, "The day you left the air broke / into splinters," is dedicated to her. Brand would follow Green to Grenada to work for the revolution.) This is the crucible of Brand's formation. "It was," she says "in the raised fists of the leather-jacketed, defiant-faced women and men that [she] recognized poetry's true language—transformation—personal and political. Not stasis and abjection."[19]

Five years after the appearance of that first book and before she moved to Grenada to work as communications officer for the Agency for Rural Transformation, Brand published what she considers to be her first two books of poetry, *Primitive Offensive* (1982) and *Winter Epigrams and Epigrams to Ernesto Cardenal in Defense of Claudia* (written 1979–82, published in 1983). Brand wrote the third book, *Chronicles of the Hostile Sun*, in Grenada and published it in 1984 on her return to Toronto. Each of these three books was published by Williams-Wallace, a Black press started in the late 1970s by Ann Wallace, who would also publish the great poets Claire Harris and M. NourbeSe Philip. When Williams-Wallace went out of business, Brand's friend Ted Chamberlain, the writer, professor, and trusted first reader of many of her manuscripts, showed the manuscript of *No Language is Neutral* to Michael Ondaatje, who would, in turn, recommend it to Coach House Press. Coach House Press also published Brand's first book of essays, *Bread out of Stone: Recollections, Sex, Recognitions, Race, Dreaming, Politics*.

But to return to that first book, *Primitive Offensive*, in it we encounter dispossession and repossessing, Middle Passage and its afterlives. It is a long, desolate, and raging poem in which a young poet observes the treatment of Black peoples in the Americas, in Europe, and on the street. The poet sees the world's inability to recuperate that which might allow her (and by extension Black people) to really live. And yet find a way to live she—we—must. *Primitive Offensive* is an excavation of the stuff of history, of what might be lost spiritually and of what is remembered. What is history? In the name, *Primitive Offensive*, the poet registers a kind of strike against the label of "primitive." The poem begins with ancestors enumerated, and then three sentences beginning "the name of our tribe" appear, and then the poet goes searching all over, through the Americas and Europe, where one encounters Black people, remnants, other possible iterations of oneself, on corners.

These are the histories of the Americas. And reading *Primitive Offensive*, one feels the influence of Neruda, especially *Canto General* (1950), in which Neruda writes a history of colonialism, a poetic history of Latin America. One should also feel the influence of Ernesto Cardenal writing about Nicaragua and all of the dictatorships and the history of struggle—in particular, his *Zero Hour*. In form and intent, *Primitive Offensive* meets Neruda's recounting of history in *Canto General*. Canto XI begins, "we die badly / always / public and graceless" and continues "on Atlantic river banks / black thread tangled up / embroidering sinister." Those bodies in the city and on the shore appear there—sinister—left there because the law that has written this outcome embroidered it. The language of these three collections, as the poet and critic Shivanee Ramlochan writes, "seemed to spark off the page, to incandesce."[20]

When Brand read Neruda's *Memoirs* and arrived at his realization that "the poet cannot be afraid of the people,"[21] his declaration on how he intended to write stayed with her, it hailed her—it was an instruction. So too his "Letter to Miguel Otero Silva, in Caracas" and his *Residence on Earth*. Each one exemplary of Neruda's ongoing commitments to write about and from the world in which he lived and the lives of "the disenfranchised of the world"[22]—a dedication to writing beyond something called individual experience. (Think of Neruda's scathing poem "Celestial Poets" in *Canto General*.) Likewise, of Brand's allegiances, Ramlochan writes, "You couldn't separate this political animus from Brand's work if you tried—in every genre, her commitment to her peoples, her places, would shun any smaller analysis."[23]

The poems published in Brand's second book, *Winter Epigrams and Epigrams to Ernesto Cardinal in Defense of Claudia*, are more playful than those in *Primitive Offensive*; they perform both political and aesthetic agility. The epigram is a form that is quick, tight, and witty. Written at the same time as the cantos in *Primitive*

Offensive, the epigrams balance those longer poems' length and tone. Where the lines in the cantos of *Primitive Offensive* are spare, the thought is sustained—in the poem there is a long, sustained breath, followed by a pull through from one line and one poem to the next. The epigrams are short, pithy, and observational—often humorous. They seem to answer the questions: How could one use irony? And how, after tragedy, could one learn, again, to laugh at oneself, even a little bit? One sees that form has never been limiting for Brand—she has always worked form to see what weight and pressure it might bear and what it might make possible. Brand is interested in what form might do when stretched. Here are two epigrams, the first from *Winter Epigrams* and the second from *Epigrams to Ernesto Cardenal in Defense of Claudia.*

> 40
> *Reading the Corporate Pages*
> I was thinking
> that it was a waste to have a moon here
> a moon is not cost efficient

and

> 54
> Cardenal, the truth is that
> even though you are not a country
> or my grandmother
> or coconut ice cream
> or Marquez' Autumn of the patriarch
> or Sarah Vaughan
> or Cuban music
> or Brazilian movies
> or Kurosawa
> or C.L.R.'s Black Jacobins
> or Angela
> or Guayaguayare
> I love you for the same things.

The first is devastating in its diagnosis of capital, the latter in its stitching of genealogy.

In his review of *Winter Epigrams*, Kamau Brathwaite writes of the poems and the poet who he calls "our first major exile female poet" that "the epigram form helps too; getting her . . . closer to the nerve, to the bone, to the clear wide integrated circuits of her meaning; circuits of blood, that is, not stereo. And what else, what more a fitting form, we ask at the 'end' of the reading, for exile, for loneliness, for such bleak loveliness, the winter of the IIIWorld's sense of present discontents and that quick radicle of green from which the poems spring."[24] In the epigrams, Brand inhabits politics broadly and works with a kind of aesthetic pleasure the challenges of the world, the line, and the form.

In his *Memoirs*, Cardenal writes about the pleasure and surprise of coming across "a little poetry book written by the Canadian poet Dionne Brand": "Nada ha quedado, sino unos epigramas que muchos han leido, especialmente muchachos y muchachas. Y un librito de la poeta canadiense Dionne Brand, *Epigrams to Ernesto Cardenal in Defense of Claudia*, en el que con un simpatico feminismo finge unos reproches de Claudia para mi; ficciones de una ficción, porque Dios hizo que la historia que aquí he contado fuera una realidad ficticia."[25]

In the foreword to *Chronicles: Early Works*, professor and critic Leslie Sanders notes that Cardenal sent Brand a copy of an anthology of his work and signed it: "Para la buena amiga Dionne Brand, que ya me escribó muy bellamente."[26]

One year after the publication of *Primitive Offensive* and the *Epigrams*, Brand published *Chronicles of the Hostile Sun* (1984). *Chronicles* is a poem in three sections—"Languages," "Sieges," and "Military Occupations"—and many of the poems are for and to friends, comrades, other poets, revolutionaries. There is a series of conversations between and among poets Pablo Neruda, Martin Carter, Adrienne Rich, and poems that take the form of dated entries of the days before, during, and after the deadly U.S. invasion of Grenada.

In, "October 19th, 1983," when Brand writes, "this poem cannot find words / this poem repeats itself," what appears is the horror of the during and aftermath, the afterlife of the U.S. invasion. She writes: "there isn't a hand large enough / to gesture this tragedy / let alone these words / dead insists itself on us" and "betrayal again, ships again, / manacles again / some of us sold each other."

In "On American numeracy and literacy in the war against Grenada," and about those logics of deaths that the U.S. engineers elsewhere, we read:

Counting in american
you start with 600 cubans,
the next figure in that numeracy

> is 1100 cubans,
> trouble ascending, move to 200 cubans,
> Pi equals zero grenadians
> which accounts for the resistance in the hills;
> when deploying troops
> or actually in most cases, thugs,
> send 15,000
> if 100 dies it's friendly fire
> and anyway that's less than if you
> only send 500 (percentage wise you know) . . .

Numeracy is the ability to reason using numbers; this is the logic of imperialism, invasion, foreclosure of possibility. And these poems are filled with the emotional and intellectual weight of these multiplied deaths, the end of the revolution, the brutal mathematics of genocide.

No Language is Neutral (1990) appears after those series of defeats of the left on the African continent and in the Americas, the corresponding deterioration of an articulate left politics in the metropole, and the enlargement of the flaccid (il)liberal democracies that emerged to fill the vacuum. It refuses nostalgia. The poet writing *Land to Light On* is one who inhabits that aftermath and the presents it ushered in. This poet truly is rent from nation. For this writer, amid the need to balance the possibility of defeat with the work that needed to be done as third world solidarities were imperiled in Grenada and Nicaragua and elsewhere, all nationalisms are thrown into question. This is a poet who is working through, in language, how to speak toward liberation in the absence of a political movement; this poet is working out, in language, what has survived the death of her politics. As she will write seven years later in *Land to Light On* (1997), "I don't want no fucking country, here / or there and all the way back, I don't like it, none of it, / easy as that. I'm giving up on land to light on, and why not, / I can't perfect my own shadow, my violent sorrow, my / individual wrists."

I am thinking with Brand here. To return to the poems in *No Language Is Neutral*, perhaps part of what survives the death of Brand's politics is sensible in her work's attention to a *poetics* of liberation, to the work that words do, to memory as rage and as mourning, to something like recognition—or regard—and the way that each is reciprocal and lit with care. The poet Souvankham Thammavongsa writes of the effect on her of encountering *No Language*'s multiple languages, the effect of the demotic and the play between and amalgamation of languages. "*This is you girl.*" "One of the first poetry books I owned," Thammavongsa writes, "was Dionne Brand's *No Language Is Neutral*. I read it over and over and over until those words on the page became a voice in my head. *This is you girl*, it said. This was a voice I had heard in the school hallways at the corner of Keele and Eglinton West, but I had never read it in a book . . . These words, *this is you girl*, that voice set me going."[27]

That sound hailed Thammavongsa, it ushered her into being through language. It was the sound through which she began to language herself on the page. There's an analogous moment, I think, in *Inventory*, when the litany of terror and the targeting of people, by those who imagine them as other than the self, is interrupted by Inventory IV, ii, a poem that begins "something else, more happened there." And then in the second stanza a voice, "familiar like the sound of water," speaks a common word, *cousin*. *Cousin* there performs a kind of echolocation, it is a way to name or make relation, a deep sounding of connection, that Brand identifies as a "wide open moment of utter recognition."[28]

Brand's next book, *Land to Light On*, is a poem in seven sections. Again, we recognize the defeat of a Black Socialist state in the English-speaking Caribbean and the work to make language suitable to the necessity of speaking into and out of the vacuum in radical left politics. The poet is conscious of how one is positioned and how race, sex, gender, sexuality may shape how one speaks—conscious that she is not a single-voiced poet. This is not the poet as mouthpiece for some kind of individualistic liberal or right-wing democratic discourse. No. Brand is aware of "the hard gossip of race that inhabits this road," and this poem speaks to that, to the landless and nationless, and as such, much of the poem is engaged in the work of undermining British imperialism.

In the penultimate section of *No Language Is Neutral*, we read:

A hidden verb
takes inventory of those small years like a person
waiting at a corner, counting and growing thin
through life as a cloth and as water, hush . . . Look I
hated something, policemen, bankers, slavetraders,
shhh . . . still do and even more these days. This city,
mourning the smell of flowers and dirt, cannot tell
me what to say even if it chokes me. Not a single
word drops from my lips for twenty years about living
here. . . .

I return to that once
grammar struck in disbelief. Twenty years . . .
I became more secretive, language
seemed to split in two, one branch fell silent, the other
argued hotly for going home.

In her E.J. Pratt lecture, Brand said, "the figure who emerges in these lines is someone who is watching and making notes about the proceedings of the world."[29]

V. *WE ARRIVED SPECTACULAR*

Brand's poetic worlds are filled with people whose ordinary and extraordinary lives signal collective moments of our past and present and also move toward what futures are possible. She does not spectacularize Black people in her work. Her attention is not the one in which—"they shoved microphones into our bawling mouths / and grief looked like archaeology." If, for example, we look at the women who appear in and across Brand's poems, those women, who are often or even usually the "I" and the "we" of her poems, do not appear in the register of the spectacular, but as forces making life-worlds in which Black women, Black people, are allowed the possibility of a full range of being.

Recognition interrupts the spectacular.

In "Blues Spiritual for Mammy Prater," there are two women: the narrator, filled with Brand's attention to photography and capture and the colonial gaze; and the woman, a woman who was once enslaved, and who is 115 years old when she sits for the photograph in question. This is a poem that in its untelling enacts precisely what it is to evade capture. It begins:

she waited for her century to turn
she waited until she was one hundred and fifteen
years old to take a photograph
to take a photograph and to put those eyes in it
she waited until the technique of photography was
suitably developed
to make sure the picture would be clear
to make sure no crude daguerreotype would lose
her image

would lose her lines and most of all her eyes
and her hands

The repetition of the word *eyes* here, eye (vision) and I (subject), brings with it the capture of Black people by the technology of the instrument (the camera) and the white gaze itself as technology. One thinks of the many enslaved people whose photographs (and daguerreotypes) were commissioned by, for example, Louis Agassiz in Brazil and before that in South Carolina in the U.S., where those seven enslaved people, some of them fathers and daughters, were also stripped and photographed, imaged without their consent. In *The Sovereignty of Quiet*, Kevin Quashie returns to this poem several times. Here is part of what he writes: "Brand's poem illustrates at least two different examples of waiting: the first is what the narrator imagines for Prater, that she waited for the right moment to take this photograph. In the narrator's mind, this waiting is robust—it has anger and impatience, is intentional and not, is a mark of strength and despair. But there is a second quality of waiting exhibited by the form of the poem—the way that the repetition of the few details of the poem slowly produces a distinct but complete image of Mammy Prater."[30] This is a pedagogy of looking. In the words of Glissant, Brand allows Prater the right to opacity.

There is a conversation here with Audre Lorde, perhaps, in particular with the poem "Martha," where Lorde's language is close to the ear, and the poem, in its duration, keeps opening up as you read. It is a poem that has internal integrity and intimacy, a poem, "a catalog of days," in which a speaker watches her former lover's recovery over time. The poem begins:

Martha   this is a catalog of days
passing before you looked again.
Someday you shall browse and order them
at will   or in your necessities.[31]

Brand has charted landscapes and whole geographies. In the final section, "Hard Against the Soul," we encounter a woman in her body, her language, her life, facing history, in Havana and Grenada, the present and the future:

I want to wrap myself around you here in this line so
that you will know something, not just that I am dying
in some way but that I did this for some reason . . .

> language not yet made . . . I want to kiss you deeply,
> smell, taste the warm water of your mouth as warm as
> your hands. I lucky is grace that gather me up and
> forgive my plainness.

And later: "I have become myself. A woman who looks / at a woman and says, here, I have found you, / in this, I am blackening in my way."

Rinaldo Walcott writes, "Brand's queer sexuality and sensuous writing have never stood out as surprising or attempting to write/right some wrong, or fix up Black community, or register an inventory of queer abuse; rather, she has penned for us the beautiful ordinariness of queer life simply occurring."[32]

thirsty (2002) is a poem set in the city of Toronto. It is filled with descriptions of the city that is and also the city that hasn't yet come into being—the city that does not yet appear on the retina of the establishment. These poems are finely attuned to time, to space and geography, and possibility—even if, and I repeat, that place of possible living does not yet exist. Entering this poem, one finds oneself in place, in a sweep both intimate and large. In the city, houses are connected to people, people live in the space of tragedies small and large, porous walls, time standing still. The very air is elegiac; there is the amber stillness of grief: "The walls of a house can sense like skin," and "since that day which they are still standing in, / skinless."

Albert Johnson was murdered by Toronto police on August 26, 1979. Johnson's terrible death was not the first or the last incident of police murder—it was exemplary of how Black people were going to be considered and treated by the city. In response to Johnson's death there a was massive uprising of Black people against continued state violence. It had become clear to Black people in Toronto that in the fabric of the everyday, from moving through the city, to the yearly Caribana festival, that the state was going to approach you with violence. In other words, Albert Johnson's murder was a signal moment in Black life in the city. In its wake, police brutality became the focus of much Black organizing in Toronto and elsewhere in Canada. Albert Johnson is the model for Alan in *thirsty*, a poem that is a forensics of a city and of multiculturalism's failed neoliberal policy. Brand takes us into the streets and also inside of skin and walls. "Consider the din of beginnings, this vagrant, fugitive city" and "A house in this city is a witness box / of every kind of human foolishness." In its attentions, the poem brings to mind Abderrahmane Sissako's film *Bamako* (2006), in which, in the midst of everyday life, some residents of the Malian capital put the World Bank and the International Monetary Fund on trial for their immiseration of the country, carried out under names like fiscal responsibility and structural adjustment.

> This city is beauty
> unbreakable and amorous as eyelids,
> in the streets, pressed with fierce departures,
> submerged landings,
> I am innocent as thresholds
> and smashed night birds, lovesick,
> as empty elevators

thirsty's opening stanza brings us into a city, Toronto, that is always touching those who live there, shaping them and being shaped by them. A city and an "I" almost pulsing with expectation. When we encounter beauty in that first line, we too are at a threshold, poised to meet in the poem all of Brand's understanding that beauty is "not uncomplicated . . . beauty is the ability to see everything; to confront everything."[33]

> breathing, you can breathe if you find air,
> this roiling, this weight of bodies,
> as if we need each other to breathe, to bring
> it into sense, and well, in that we are merciless

As the poem shifts subject from an I, to you, to she/her, to Julia, to he/him, to Alan, portraits of Alan and Julia, his wife, emerge. Those portraits are counter to the newspaper accounts, which amount to thefts, and to those photographs, even of the grieving, that are never taken with tenderness.

When Black grief is currency, we appear in newspapers as spectacle, so much matter for sales and narratives, wreathed in glyphs of grief. Framed, in other words, in and by stock images, a whole obscuring photographic vocabulary. But here the poem, unlike the newspaper, tells us that "it would matter to know him as a child," he was one who "would weep at a trail of ants spurning his friendship."

Seeing the paper, Julia thinks:

yet she too had glimpsed herself,
an unrepentant cheekbone, those fingers
brushing glyphs of newsprint away
the extraordinary emptiness of the woman
emerging from clusters of dots on the front page
then the second page, then the last page
then vanishing all together, but not vanished

Julia is haunted almost as much by her photograph (she wonders, if it is really her, she does not recognize herself) as she is haunted by Alan's murder. To Julia, both are thefts.

No one prepares for how he died,
no one had a diagnosis beforehand
unless you count the mere presence of him,
his likeness, unless you count that
as a symptom of what he would die of,

The poet Asiya Wadud distills a similar feeling in *Syncope* when she writes of those African people fleeing terror and purposefully left to drift and die in the Mediterranean: "You may die a brutal death / the brutality being the happenstance."[34]

Julia wants it back—she wants her face back and her blue skirt back, not just from Alan but from the city itself.

lust she had lost along with the things
in her suitcases that morning, and the things,
the slivers of seconds in between.
fallen, all of it, tinted, sunken, all of it,
that, she wanted back . . .

once she wore powder blue skirts and embroidered
Indian blouses,

In Brand's work, Black people, in death, in struggle, in life, are not written in the register of the explanatory or the pathological. By which I mean it always seems to me that Brand writes Black life (and the lives of the disenfranchised) how Roy DeCarava photographed—for each, the photographer and the poet, that life is textured, and blackness is not taken up through the logics or the register of what Césaire named "thingification." There is instead, always an attention to the world and to power. Brand refuses to concede Black humanity, she refuses the sense-making logics of anti-blackness.

With the repetition of the titular word, *thirsty*, we encounter a desire for time not only to slow or halt but also to hold, as in "there, in time, transparent, / held and held, she had been held, why." There are more words that appear across a number of Brand's books—*blue* (the colour), *bristling*, *inventory*, *held*, *police*—and with each encounter they carry with them the traces of their prior appearances, and . . . trace becomes vocabulary. Can you read "bristling" and not think of the exonerated cop's moustache, and then the witnessing watcher's lists in *Inventory*?

> So, a cop sashaying from a courthouse,
> his moustache wide and bristling,
> his wool coat draped across his body
> and carefree, his head centred in the television
> cameras against
> scales of justice, he would strike
> a match on the bottom of his shoes,
> light a cigar in victory of being acquitted
> of such a killing, and why not

The article *a* marks this scene as one produced by *any* cop, at *any* courthouse—it is simultaneously particular and distributed. His mustache is alive, it is bristling; the person he murdered is not. And then, in a devastating connection, Brand links the cop and the catwalk; he strikes a match and a pose, "this élan, law and outlaw, SWAT and midnight rider, / history and modernity kissing here".

What are cameras against scales of justice when we arrive spectacular? When media conglomerates in the West conspire in their spectacularization of Black life and their romanticization of those who wield terror (back to the always-on *Law & Order*). The cops swagger and the city and its many inhabitants keep going, both producing the conditions for more terror and grief and also the possibility of something that exceeds that terror and that grief.

"We believed in nothing." So starts Inventory I. With this first line, Brand is not summoning nihilism, and this is not despair. Rather, "we believed in nothing" articulates one of the major ideas in the poem; that what is now a past belief that planted itself in the body, in chests, lungs, hearts, minds, and limbs, is the *nothing* of the *idea* of America (the U.S.), the *nothing* of capitalism and the financialization of "each square metre of air" and sea and land. The nothings are the deadly myths of freedom, with their particular innocence, and its perfection that take root in the chest—and crack it open with violence.

At the point of *Inventory*'s writing and publication, the end of the second decade of the twenty-first century was approaching; the U.S. wars in Iraq and Afghanistan and the obliteration of entire groups of people continued apace. When she was asked about her motivation for writing *Inventory*, Brand replied: "What would a poet write historically, in this moment, in these times that we are living, the call by some for a kind of endless war. Endless war is . . . what we've been promised in recent history. And the bodies pile up and the images pile up, for us who live in the west, of these bodies and this terror."[35] Diana Brydon writes of *Inventory*, "The poem lays its hand on the reader's shoulder with a power of the imagination that is almost physical."[36]

Brand writes again and again into that dilemma that is witnessing—she writes into that gap between what has been done and an accounting of it. What happens in thresholds, doorways, and on street corners? What is registered in flesh, in bone, in viscera? What accumulates in lungs, chests, hearts, skin, and eyelids? These words repeat across Brand's work, and as they do, they enumerate the ways that violence (capital, globalization, extraction, unending accumulation and immiseration, witnessing) and its traces lodge there in a place and in a body, and then the work that that body must or might do to excavate something from within it itself—something that survives these onslaughts.

With "We believed in nothing," the poet names her, names our, implicatedness in those carceral systems that explode lungs and grind bone and sinew to dust and grit. We are implicated from that "we" of the first line to the "I" and the "you" of the closing stanza:

besides the earth's own
coiled velocities, its meteoric elegance,
and the year still not ended,
I have nothing soothing to tell you,
that's not my job,
my job is to revise and revise this bristling list,
hourly

The absence of a full stop after the poem's final word, *hourly*, alerts readers that this list keeps getting longer; at poem's close, the poet is still at her witnessing task.

The correspondence between two parts of an utterance appears in syntactic and rhythmic repetition, and the build-up of parallel lines becomes a litany. The inventory is a ritual and an estranging device that is filled with surprises, repetitions, synthesis, and accumulation.

Black life is riven by inventory; cleaved by it. Black writers, thinkers, artists have been repeatedly drawn to the ledger, as *one* iteration of the inventory in order to undo its logics and render palpable what we know about living. In working this material, we are once again in the terrain of the questions: What does it mean to bear witness? What is the work of the poet? What is a poetry of witness? The poet insists, again, that there is a life, there are lives, being lived there—and that capital and the war makers are intent on obscuring that living. The poet witness answers: "At least someone should stay awake, she thinks / someone should dream them along the abysmal roads." A call to disrupt the normalization of brutality. To refuse the commodification of freedom dreams and chants, recorded in the italicized verses of civil rights and anti-capital singers whose lyrics are now used to sell cars. Another poet, Charlotte Delbo, wrote about the impossibility and the necessity of witness, "Try to look. Try to See."[37] Brand's work is always at least an attempt at an affirmative—a Yes to that call to witness, to attend. In *Inventory* she writes:

> let us all deny our useless names in solidarity
> with these dead dinner guests and pedestrians,
> and anonymously dead mechanics, and desultory
> children and passengers, and those faceless cosmeticians

Brand is, as Adrienne Rich wrote, "a cultural critic of uncompromising courage, an artist in language and ideas . . .".[38] She does not memorialize and monumentalize that which is not over. This is not to use these "anonymously dead" in order to declare, "Never again." This is not to instrumentalize their suffering. Instead, knowing and facing this wreckage, what is there to do but to make the language capable of sounding a different future. Calling Brand "a magician of language," the poet Canisia Lubrin says that in *Inventory*, Brand "takes words, turns them, anew . . . revealing things about power . . . and considering again and again and again what the value of a human life is."[39] For

Lubrin, *Inventory* is perfection. George Murray called *Inventory* "one of the single most perfect books of poetry written in this century—in its craft, honesty, and terrible beauty—it's also one of the most important, and rewarding."[40]

The poem is relentless, because the time is relentless, and the lamentation, and the time of the lamentation continuing, but that does not mean that there is no breath and no respite. Indeed, the last inventory both anticipates and dismisses such a response: "On reading this someone will say / God, is there no happiness then, / of course, tennis matches and soccer games, / and river song and bird song and / wine naturally and some Sundays." Brand has said that after she wrote *Inventory,* she needed a new language, that English was weighted with that violence and by that witnessing and list-making of atrocity. English was laden as well with the explaining away of atrocity, and the domestication of atrocity by those who perpetrate and perpetuate it through phrases like "shock and awe" and "collateral damage."

VI. *WHO COULD HAVE LIVED EACH DAY KNOWING*

Ossuaries (2010) begins with a consciousness that is summing up and looking back at the accumulating wreckage—"I lived and loved, some might say, / in momentous times, / looking back, my dreams were full of prisons"—and soon falls away into pages of verblessness. The poem is fifteen ossuaries, in tercets, and there are two speakers stretched between a present which is eroding and a future time; stretched between a current time and a possible time. The tercet, as a form, is elastic and tense, it produces tension and alleviates it—it is triangular and always moving. The pages of *Ossuaries* are urgent, incantatory, spellbinding, they have weight and elasticity, motion and force. Brand says of the poems' two speakers: "Think of this artist reaching out of his time, composing small moments of sound, and somehow these compositions—whether this is the intention or not—they speak a speech made up of more than what can be contained in that particular historical or cultural moment. So, Yasmine thinks that is the speech she should have been making, and there are parts of her speech which propel themselves to that point. But she is trapped in that particular historical or cultural moment."[41]

There is a time and an "our" and a "we" that the poem speaks from and into. But those our[s] and we[s] are specific and particular. There is Yasmine, and then there is an "I" that is the poet and not Yasmine. Yasmine is going through her underground itinerary, and she is interrupted by the shortwave radio and the newsreader saying Manhattan is under attack. Yasmine knows that she is not in Manhattan, and she refuses preemptively the question that one will be asked to answer—"Where were you?"—and the answer, one form of which will refuse history in order to speak that bromide "we are all New Yorkers now." In a line that recalls the beginning of *Inventory*, we are told that "she believed in nothing." Here *Inventory*'s "we" becomes particularized in Yasmine's "she."

In *Ossuaries* we are deep in the wreckage of modernity. As Césaire said, "Europe is responsible before the human community for the highest heap of corpses in history."[42] It is this "malicious horizon" that "made us the / essential thinkers of technology." *Ossuaries* is a choral dirge, a threnody filled with Brand's fine-honed attunement to how power is exercised on the flesh and across geographies and technologies: photography, human zoos, in war and philanthropy, in philosophy, newspapers and newsrooms, the "stone pits," and in all of the apparatuses of capture. Here is power's effect on bones, eyelids and eyelashes, lungs, and ribs. What is the language for this? How does one reckon with this? How does one live in this? Observe it?

In *An Atlas of the Difficult World*, Adrienne Rich writes,

if you know who died in that bed, do you know
who has survived?
. . .
What does it mean to say *I have survived*
until you take the mirrors and turn them outward
and read your own face in their outraged light?[43]

Here is Brand in Ossuary I: "what brutal hours, what brutal days, / do not say, oh find the good in it, do not say, / there was virtue; there was no virtue, not even in me".

In each poem, the internal repetitions are demonstrative of an overturning of a posture of innocence. A revelation of innocence's monstrosity, qua Baldwin's "'People who shut their eyes to reality simply invite their own destruction, and anyone who insists on remaining in a state of innocence long after that innocence is dead turns himself into a monster."[44] Rich and Brand both write with an intimacy that is large—this intimacy takes the measure of the world and the self in relation to that world. In 2020–21, *Ossuaries* was selected by the National Book Foundation as one of five books for its Literature for Justice reading list, which highlights books that speak to abolition and imagine otherwise.

Writing for all of the judges, the poet Natalie Diaz says that: "From within one of many ossuaries of American punishment, these visible and invisible architectures, designed to ravel a body of its flesh and touch, prophesies of an impossibility 'to live and love at the same time,' Brand asks, 'who could have lived, / each day, / who could have lived each day knowing' and the answer is: All of us—we know, and now, how are we prepared to live, what are we willing to wage and wager to make one another free."[45]

"Let us begin from there . . ." This line is an invitation, an opening, a declaration, an ethics.

There are two voices in *Ossuaries*. One is Yasmine, a revolutionary, living an underground life, moving from Algiers, to Havana, to upstate New York, and Canada. Yasmine is recollecting the past, her past of active struggle; she is alert to violence and committed to liberation. "I've always been interested in that kind of woman," Brand says, "that was politically engaged in the late 60s, 70s, how they became women of action."[46] The other voice in *Ossuaries* is the consciousness that diagnoses the ecocidal world.

We see Yasmine with "her back alert like paintings to its usual ache," an unlikely simile that opens up into all kinds of new meanings, especially when read in relation to Jacob Lawrence's War Series, which appears in Ossuary XI when Yasmine, in the museum, sits "with Jacob Lawrence's war, / his 'victory,' red and drenched, looked like defeat, / of course."

Many paintings appear in these ossuaries, from Lawrence's War Series to José Villegas Cordero's *Lucia Monti*. Lawrence offers relief from the paintings of crucifixions, relief from God and that mythos and that aesthetic of flagellation. The sitter wonders what comes from that aesthetic both visually and psychically. There are rooms and rooms of these paintings, and they produce the rooms and rooms of violence and sacrifice and evisceration in the West and the places the West brutalizes. (One need only think of the Prado in Madrid—so many rooms of torture and suffering.)

When Brand writes in Ossuary XI,

"shipping out"
who could not see this like the passage's continuum,
the upsided down-ness, the cramp, the eyes compressed

to diamonds,
as if we could exhume ourselves from these mass graves,
of ships, newly dressed

what emerges is a rendering of something closer to the scale and reach of planetary brutality and of what might survive it, or not. The accumulation here is different than that in *Inventory*, by which I mean that here nothing and no one appears to interrupt the damage; here there is no leavening connection as with the word *cousin.*

they ask sometimes, who could have lived,
each day,
who could have lived each day knowing

some massacre was underway, some repression,
why, anyone, anyone could live this way,
I do, I do

anyone, I'm not unique, not shy,
someone goes out for milk and butter,
and returns with gashed face, wrung larynx

practically ancient,
I'm not fooling myself, I've tried,
this regime takes us to the stone pit every day

we live like this,
each dawn we wake up, our limbs paralyzed,
shake our bones out, deliver ourselves

VII. *COLLECTED OVER THE TIME OF BLACKNESS*

There is something being worked out in relation to time in Brand's poetry, over time, in time. This inhabitation appears in different registers made through the knowledge that time is lived not only differently by different beings, but also by the same being at different moments in a life. "Even as a poem is a record of time, it is also a record of possible time."[47] Brand's work is always cognizant that Black people have to be simultaneously ahead of time and outside of it. "Clinically aware"[48] that they have had to notice and watch with anxiety and accuracy everything that happens in the world—that it has been necessary to really try to understand the uses of violence in the world. (This is a different kind of numeracy—this is that "abacus of the eyelids.") In *Nomenclature* we read:

There was that time in a room on Calle Nueva

when the world crushed my chest
like the world, like a boulder

as if the world were a boulder, as if gravity knitted sternum to finger, to hill
to lip, to thread, to floor, to chair, to boat, to gull, to Calle Nueva Alta
to thought, to hem, to a bus, to three note pencils, to umbrella, to foot,
    to insect

To jaw, to stem, to M8 Lagoon Nebula, to Deneb, to fish

to velocity, to sheet, to wing, to light socket, to
metal rail, to postage, as if gravity melted oxygen tank, to grief, to hip

to shoreline, to chair, to drinking glass, to green light
to xiphoid, to November
to tailpipe, to insect, to transcriptome, I know everything, I'm not innocent[91]

What kind of time is this? It is not the clock time of capital. This is another inhabitation.

Part of Brand's attention is an attunement to forms of knowledge—as when music (keeping time) weaves through a work like *Ossuaries*, both in the poem's musicality and also in the ways that musicians and painters and poets appear and reappear, providing, as I wrote earlier, shape and sound, feeling and theory.

Each ossuary begins with a single tercet on the page. Ossuary I begins with the personal pronoun *I* and then moves the reader into the poetic consciousness that wants to begin from there, without illusions, having taken a measure of the carceral world.

Because of the nature of the social forces at present, one is continually responding to time with repositionings. The "I" in this long poem is constantly recalibrating its register against all of the forces of war and violence as well as against the internal stagnation of a community in the face of those forces. That voice becomes more and more wrought. Brand says, "I hope, in some kind of way that voice doesn't have to do some other things anymore; it doesn't have to describe some other things any more. . . . It simply has to keep sounding, it has to keep reckoning with what can and cannot be reconciled."[49]

In *Nomenclature for the Time Being*, a long poem published here for the first time, Brand continues these explorations. The speaker here asks: "What is it to talk as if the world you know is the world?" As if the world "you" know is *the* world. There are different, disaggregated yous being summoned here. The you who speaks that way is not the you of these lines: "Understand, you cannot skip playfully away / down a highway from death, who are you? they asked. Death". That latter you summons Laquan McDonald, seventeen years old and skipping down the street when he is struck by sixteen bullets, assassinated by the police in Chicago. There is a whole entire world, a galaxy, between these yous.

Early on in *Nomenclature* the speaker wonders:

> what is it to lament this, I am not really lamenting, I am hating this, I am
> loving this
>
> I am turning into the something
> necessary to live this

What is between lamenting and hating, between hating and loving, between loving and turning into the *something* "necessary to live this"? What is this relation? The poet is finding the words to say this. For Brand, "Poetry's major proposition is that it will turn language over—that it intends to reorganize how a thing is thought or may be thought." The poet wants to record everything. She says, "We are all struggling to live wonderfully. I certainly am, and I assume the person living in the most ravaged of places is too."[50]

"We did everything not to kill you," the speaker says in *Nomenclature*. "The monsters are talking all over the world." That first line reappears in the poem transformed to "We tried everything / not to kill you, we even tried not living."

We are in need of words that make new worlds. The work of the poet is ceaseless, and it is partly the work of accumulation and juxtaposition, certainly the work of imagination, and certainly the work of "putting pressure on verbal matter." It is the precise work of witness and, also, the precise and expansive work of wonder. What appears again and again is time, as flow and movement (revolutionary and temporal), as history, the present, the galaxy, music, and the earth. "The only thing that amazes her now is the earth." And yet, "amazement at the natural world . . . How does that all just keep going? It's the smallest of wonders—it's not a big wonder but it always repays itself."[51] Now, presently, that amazement and what occasions it are both threatened: "This is the region called surmounting / this is the volcano called evidence." We are in that place—"our country moving closer to its own truth and dread, / its own ways of making people disappear"—that Adrienne Rich described in "What Kind of Times are These?"[52] We are, as Brand locates us, in a worse place, facing "creeping capitalization" and financialization and the accumulating catastrophes that keep arriving: "This does not seek a remedy / this does not need a balm / This needs an ending." The "this" (multiple and dispersed) that needs an ending is the regimes of violence, the tyranny of the human. But water, water which holds a perfect memory, that remains—"water doesn't end."

In that R.W.B. Jackson Lecture and conversation between Brand and Walcott with which I began, Walcott says, "There is, if you will, a pedagogy in *Nomenclature*. It is a pedagogy of looking, of seeing, of bearing witness. But it is also a pedagogy of how we see, hear, and even feel." Brand says that "the 'I' and the 'we' in the poem is an aesthetic consciousness who has moved about in the world experiencing, looking, acting in, thinking on, drawing on what it has lived and studied and absorbed; they have lived, have been immersed in, apprehended certain phenomena, observed, synthesized, and brought these phenomena into arrangements of feeling, arrangements of the senses. So, this speaker of the poem is that aesthetic that hovers, draws from the world and is an active seeker in the world. At root, this aesthetic consciousness is in search of what Robert Hayden called 'the beautiful needful thing' in his poem 'Frederick Douglass' and is drawn by that imperative into the world. The 'I' or 'we' of the poem is/are part of the register of accumulated observations, part of the archive of facts and truths, experiences collected over the time of blackness." She continues, "I was thinking of the courage, or the attention one must pay each day to keep oneself intact, to not become as depraved as that system, to wake up each morning, to recover the self, to breathe and to continue."[53]

Brand has given us words for continuing, for connection, and attention; for longing and revolution; she has taken risks; she has worked at the edge of things. She has gifted us words for our time being in languages attuned to the sound and the feeling *necessary* to our living this—even as the "this" and the "living it" are joined by the phrase "necessary to."

> How do we manage
>
> fear, he asked. We don't. Fear is a necessary reaction
> a good, good sign
>
> my thanks to all who gave me fear
> I know it now, molecularly
> don't worry, don't you remember, our life all along

By way of an ending that is really an opening and an invitation, I join this speaker's meditation on fear's elemental lessons, and "we are remainders of burning oxygen / we are just the end of helium, we are speeding / we are slow, water doesn't end," to the unnamed speaker in *Ossuaries*. The poetic consciousness in *Ossuaries* spans time, and the "I" who surveys the wreckage of the planet says, "I hope that you never remember, these ossuaries, these days and years filled with abattoirs and bones." That "I" declares that there is something like freedom in the possibility of forgetting, when forgetting means the making and inhabitation of a different world. The opposite of the process by which "memory's memorylessness functions in or is rather made into monument." Instead, "go on, go on," this speaker says, "the brilliant future doesn't wait."

Nomenclature: New and Collected Poems appears right in time.

1 Dionne Brand in conversation with Rinaldo Walcott, "2020 R.W.B. Jackson Lecture," https://www.youtube.com/watch?v=_wuBjTnWtiQ.
2 "Dionne Brand: Writing Against Tyranny and Toward Liberation," Barnard College, Caribbean Feminisms on the Page series, 2017, https://www.youtube.com/watch?v=ychlzoeeImo.
3 The position of poet laureate of Toronto was established in 2001.
4 Alec Scott, "Dionne Brand Releases Her New Collection, *Ossuaries*, While Serving as Toronto's Poet Laureate," *University of Toronto Magazine*, March 16, 2010, http://www.magazine.utoronto.ca/all-about-alumni/dionne-brand-toronto-poet-laureate-ossuaries/.
5 Dionne Brand.
6 Dionne Brand, "An Ars Poetica from the Blue Clerk," *The Black Scholar* 47, no.1 (2017), 60.
7 Ibid., 59.
8 Ibid.
9 Robin D.G. Kelley, "A Poetics of Anticolonialism," introduction to *Discourse on Colonialism*, by Aimé Césaire, trans. Joan Pinkham (1950, repr., New York: Monthly Review Press, 2000), 28.
10 Dionne Brand, *The Blue Clerk: An Ars Poetica in 59 Versos* (Toronto: McClelland & Stewart, 2018), verso 13.
11 Brand, "An Ars Poetica from the Blue Clerk," 59.
12 Dionne Brand, interviewed by Robert Enright in "Pressure on Verbal Matter: Dionne Brand and the Making of Language," *Border Crossings*, November 2020.
13 Dionne Brand, *A Kind of Perfect Speech* (Nanaimo: Institute for Coastal Research, 2008).
14 Brand, R.W.B. Jackson Lecture.
15 Dionne Brand in Conversation with Christian Olbey, Wordfest, Calgary, 2002.
16 Robert Enright, "Pressure on Verbal Matter: Dionne Brand and the Making of Language," *Border Crossings*, November 2020, 38.
17 Brand, *A Kind of Perfect Speech*, 20.
18 Anne Winters, *The Displaced of Capital* (Chicago: University of Chicago Press, 2004).
19 Brand, *A Kind of Perfect Speech*, 12.
20 Shivanee Ramlochan, "Dionne Brand: The Reinvention of Poetry," Closeup, *Caribbean Beat* 159 (September/October 2019), https://www.caribbean-beat.com/issue-159/dionne-brand-the-reinvention-of-poetry-closeup.
21 Pablo Neruda, *Confieso que he vivido; memorias* (Barcelona: Editorial Seix Barral, 1974).
22 Leslie Sanders, foreword to *Chronicles: Early Works*, by Dionne Brand (Waterloo: Wilfrid Laurier University Press, 2011), viii.

23 Ramlochan, "Dionne Brand: The Reinvention of Poetry."

24 Edward Kamau Brathwaite, "Dionne Brand's Winter Epigrams," *Canadian Literature* 105 (Summer 1985), 18.

25 "Nothing has remained except for a few epigrams that many have read, especially young men and women, and a little poetry book written by the Canadian poet Dionne Brand, *Epigrams to Ernesto Cardenal in Defense of Claudia*, in which, with a charming feminism, she pretends a few reproaches from Claudia to me. Fictions of a fiction because God willed the story I have told here from a fictious reality." Sanders, foreword to *Chronicles*, xii.

26 "For my good friend Dionne Brand, who wrote about me so beautifully." Sanders, foreword to *Chronicles*, xii.

27 Brick Books, "Celebration of Canadian Poetry: Week 71—Dionne Brand Presented by Souvankham Thammavongsa," May 5, 2016.

28 Dionne Brand, Teju Cole, and Madeleine Thien in conversation with Eleanor Wachtel, *Writers & Company*, CBC Radio, May 14, 2017, https://www.cbc.ca/radio/writersandcompany/teju-cole-madeleine-thien-and-dionne-brand-on-the-places-and-spaces-that-inspire-their-writing-1.4814555.

29 Dionne Brand, "A Hidden Verb Takes Inventory," E.J. Pratt Lecture, Memorial University of Newfoundland, St. John's, March 15, 2017.

30 Kevin Quashie, *The Sovereignty of Quiet: Beyond Resistance in Black Culture* (New Brunswick, NJ: Rutgers University Press, 2012).

31 Audre Lorde, *Undersong: Chosen Poems, Old and New* (New York: Norton, 1992), 57.

32 Rinaldo Walcott, "A Revolution on the Page: Poet Dionne Brand's Contributions to Culture Are Unparalleled," *Superqueeros!*, CBC Arts, 2019, https://www.cbc.ca/artsprojects/superqueeroes/dionne-brand.

33 Conversation with the author.

34 Asiya Wadud, Syncope (Brooklyn: Ugly Duckling Press, 2019), 32.

35 Dionne Brand, *The Arts Tonight*, CBC Radio, April 13, 2011.

36 Diana Brydon, "Dionne Brand's Global Intimacies: Practising Affective Citizenship," *University of Toronto Quarterly* 76, no. 3 (summer 2007), 994.

37 Charlotte Delbo, *Auschwitz and After*, trans. Rosette C. Lamont (New Haven: Yale University Press, 1995).

38 Adrienne Rich, back cover of *Bread Out of Stone: Recollections, Sex, Recognitions, Race, Dreaming, Politics*, by Dionne Brand, paperback edition (Toronto: Vintage Canada, 1998).

39 "Canisia Lubrin on Why She Loves Dionne Brand's *Inventory*," *The Next Chapter*, CBC Radio, 2018, https://www.cbc.ca/player/play/1308101187625.

40 George Murray, "Canada Reads Poetry: George Murray on Dionne Brand," Afterword blog, *National Post*, April 15, 2011, https://nationalpost.com/afterword/canada-reads-poetry-george-murray-on-inventory-by-dionne-brand.

41 Dionne Brand, interviewed by E Martin Nolan in "'To Promote Statements That Don't Have an End': In Conversation with Dionne Brand," *The Puritan*, 2010, https://www.puritan-magazine.com/to-promote-statements-that-dont-have-an-end-in-conversation-with-dionne-brand/.

42 Aimé Césaire, *Discourse on Colonialism*, trans. Joan Pinkham (1950, repr., New York: Monthly Review Press, 2000), 45.

43 Adrienne Rich, *An Atlas of the Difficult World: Poems, 1988–1991* (New York: Norton, 1992), 48.

44 James Baldwin, "Stranger in the Village," in *Notes of a Native Son* (1955, repr., Boston: Beacon Press, 2012), 178.

45 Natalie Diaz, Committee's Citation, National Book Foundation 2020–21 Literature for Justice Selected Reading List, https://www.nationalbook.org/programs/literature-for-justice-fund/#tab-4.

46 Brand, "'To Promote Statements that Don't Have an End.'"

47 Dionne Brand in "Literature for Justice: A Path Forward" (live-streamed panel event), National Book Foundation, December 2, 2020, https://www.youtube.com/watch?v=i5YYBwEqCKU.

48 Brand, *The Blue Clerk*, verso 16.6. 96.

49 Dionne Brand, conversation with author.

50 Conversation with author.

51 Brand, "'To Promote Statements that Don't Have an End.'"

52 Adrienne Rich, *Collected Poems: 1950–2012* (New York: Norton, 2016).

53 Brand, Walcott, "2020 R.W.B. Jackson Lecture."

NOMENCLATURE FOR THE TIME BEING

(2022)

The apocalyptic reports have come

true, dilute in our arterial solvent
the atrocities saturate our latent notebooks

we stay awake lambent
there are iridium rectangles under our tables
we meet languid, nauseous

Transfused presently

for a few decades, chronic, venous, insufficient
the intervals of talk speed to nothing

and we've become scientists of without
under force, out of water, across loading
with bearings, of us

Nothing will come from our innocence

you know that, after all, no
discoveries in old texts, no modern symmetries

no revelations, no wisdoms to be admired
messages to be deciphered, smuggled to each generation
or so prescient they require philosophers

These were not clandestine works

there are no secret hallways waiting for
the transcriber of great portents; it's simple

the wars they recorded were the wars they won
let me be plain with you
these portraitures are portraitures

Of what we suspect

the insoluble facts are these then
no one carried their writings across a river

in a ringed cloth on the head
or sewn into the precious fold of a hem, no one buried
them in a desert to wait for a coruscating time

The illuminated manuscripts are just the gaudy

sacredness of violence
the electronic leeches downloaded their data bulk

I, for one, understood this, eventually, my
tendons were xenolith by then of course
the tectonic plates zigzagging, shivering against us

There was that time in a room on Calle Nueva

when the world crushed my chest
like the world, like a boulder

as if the world were a boulder, as if gravity knitted sternum to finger, to hill
to lip, to thread, to floor, to chair, to boat, to gull, to Calle Nueva Alta
to thought, to hem, to a bus, to three note pencils, to umbrella, to foot, to insect

To jaw, to stem, to M8 Lagoon Nebula, to Deneb, to fish

to velocity, to sheet, to wing, to light socket, to
metal rail, to postage, as if gravity melted oxygen tank, to grief, to hip

to shoreline, to chair, to drinking glass, to green light
to xiphoid, to November
to tailpipe, to insect, to transcriptome, I know everything, I'm not innocent

It was 5 pm all day that day, the sky

if I say the sky's small arithmetic
its inscription, its echo

through one undone instance and the other
we discovered new diseases
travelling the floor of our tissue

We leathered these in catalogues

of our antigens
what with one thing and another, I

am only ever uttering every other word, skirting
all articulations shaped by ideology, wary of this
understand, it has been several winters to the next

We lost absorption

we broke this down into subtle molecules
we needed iodine, polyphenols, annatto seeds

the analytics of arriving, and the whole dictionary of
the knowledges of seabirds
not to succumb

The storekeepers set up as our guardians

and our friends and our comrades, they smiled
with us one day, they took whisky with our enemies too

we read their books, as I said earlier, took
in their alphabets like popsicles and lesion paste
it is a good thing that they don't know who we are

To begin with

there are dingy pictures of picturelessness
we saw nothing, nothing evaporated

the year was endless, the occipital lobe
driven, maximizing propylene yields, how
the cyclical literatures made our arteries theoretical

Which is to say, I myself, I'm sick, sick today, sick always

in the tetravalence in any specific quadrant
or the orbits, elemental and inorganic-seeming

a stellar career I have made of waiting, carbon, seeing
what they saw on the periphery they now see
in matter and resurrect and replicate the dayless days

The beautiful innocence of those

who live at the centre of empire, their
wonderful smiles, their sweet delight and

and their singular creation of the
word *hope*, when I am actually dying, but now
we enjoy them, their sweetness, their love of us

We envy their cuisine, their insouciance

no, truly, I am not being facetious
I am honest in my lovely amazement

it is like candy marbling in the mouth
it is an overview of the temporal lobe, misfiring
unrecognizably

The scrim of their philosophies

when they say, humanity, everyone, we
these are not lies, we, we misapprehend

the function of language and speech
how can I assure anyone
there is no rancour, trust me on this

With a world's gaze focused on reducing emissions

apply now, renewable hydrogen alliance
let us return

we never learned to be quiet
something coming though we could never get a hold of it
we've taken down the bookshelf, and we'll depend on any hour

And our razor-bladed veins, our cardboard signs

saying, “do not look at me”
we have our precious luggage in our hands all day long

our feet are against the ocean crust, palmate
with every intention to listen like moths and leaves
we freeze in summers on the mere thought of winter appearing

What is it to talk as if the world you know is the world

I admire that focus on these grubby economies, these narrow precipitous doorways
selling everything like hardware

with all my good, good life, in a mirror
years have passed, great day, good brief morning, again
all they’ve made of it is

Money and something named sex, made out of a

kind of self-hatred of their testicles, all they've made of it is the law of testicles made of
their hatred, how jealous

when I was happy, and when I was lonely, all they did was laugh
all I did was laugh
destitute all I did was

Stand up straight, stand fucking straight, they said

then I ate the antidote for living
I had the throat of living; all I did was living

thirty-one thousand reasonable weeks, they said. I
foraged living out of the garbage then, living
glistened on me, bioluminescent like algae

To atomize

they used copper, lead, aluminum, iron, and tin
cadmium and nickel for death's again and again

so, we were circuited by death
abbreviated
look how we hung heavy in our funereal clothing

Lead-antimony alloy encased in soft brass jackets

how we walked before the cameras
disguised in our tears as if we were that cruel

to ourselves, and wore hardened steel just to please them
they shoved microphones into our bawling mouths
and grief looked like archaeology

Understand, you cannot skip playfully away

down a highway from death, who are you? they asked. Death
is the chamber of commerce and the association of manufacturers

two hundred and nineteen thousand solitary days in the bureau
of death's war and supply department; sixteen
missions of the counter narcotics operations

Control of the maritime environments

the building of intimate security capacities, bodily
analgesic surveillance

of course, they would like a description from the corpse
the light pink death
at very least, the fixed interest

The wise drowning death

death's clack
clack, clacking of death

the green and blue uniform of killing
and how much appetite they have, I'm exhausted
but they are never tired of themselves killing

The how, how, how to get rid

of these people of death
and their constant self-portraiture, quotidian

the halt of the heart of killing, the
no tomorrow of their killing, the
how on earth to get leave of their tattoo of killing

The worst thing they said about me

was I had a vagina, they said it every time
in various tenses and many languages, and they wrote it in water

they drank the water, and they screamed hysterically
from the space shuttle and
the one-man submarines, through to the lithosphere

They made a prohibition called vagina and

you could breathe it under water and dip it in milk
and disodium bio chloride phosphorus

it became the logic
for their miscalculations, the reasoning
of their fungible lies, what to do

I notice the famished globe, I

do, the dead theory of humanity in Spanish, and in Italian
the Anglo-American prison of thought in a bookshop

on Calle Porvenir in Cartagena
I have seen the translations, and the instructional manual
On the economics of morphology and phonology, the worst things

They said about me, they said every time and I don't mourn this

I read their bulletins
I am measuring their temperature

I am making my diagnosis of their sentences
and their ailment, I take it by their syntax
they are not alive

The bandages I undid from these wounds

the sulphur thiazole we kept
in the glass cabinet, the poultices and salves

the ocular washes, the saline lacrimal
solutions I dispensed
they've all run out

This does not seek a remedy

this does not need a balm
this needs an ending

I'm not suggesting anything called human
that is a discredited theory
their most gentle imagining is bitter with expertise

They were allowed to walk around in newspapers

and have children and announcements of children
and their good life, they had the temerity to sell me

movies and portfolios and terabytes of their lousy activities
and I bought them, and it punished me to hear their awful news of their victories over
me that made me laugh and love them as they insisted

And there was stupid me in my fluffy slippers

thinking I was a lover
in the world, my address was 1791 Tulip Lane

Bois Caïman, I had a motorcycle and a car
the light bills were no worry, I am not
suggesting, but I could drink wine in the mornings if I wanted

A tattoo with a whale in Montreal, and

believe me I love concrete and believe me I love rubber but now that I am leaving
I will not miss their acidity, good luck to you I've left

homeless, there's a mauve cloud on its own along Boul. St-Laurent relentless
surveillance in the underpass until the yellow exit where a pretty baby appears in a
carriage, the usual cops are in the usual

Place on a cellular tower at Saint-Antoine with the

wedding on the beach, what in this nothing morning should we say, all the bicycles
all the runners, all the furious production, the steaming

snows, the containers vers Haiti voie de droit let us go east, the lined and last of
the Inca in Cuzco putting out her hand for cash
pragmatic with disgust

That dress, so fatal, you cannot meet the world

any other way now, when could you meet the world in any other way the deep sleep
of capital, the unbroken field, the crickets perhaps

the only sovereign things, even the birds have altered their flight and song, the medicos
will give oxygen and loneliness
for the microscopic adhesives in the lungs

The faecal planes, the drooling sky

not true the sky is the sky always the sky, wondrous the sky, under which, the acid
oceans

what is it to lament this, I am not really lamenting, I am hating this, I am loving this
I am turning into the something
necessary to live this

I'm wearing cardboard declaring "do not look at me"

my life is on the frequency of sirens
is on the risen contusions on the vendors

is on the parallel, is shift work
is on the lethal faces of the buyers
is the strangest, noisiest night in the rawest market

Here I notice resinous

the ones who keep people sleeping with their art
somnolent and private, gestural and fatal

do not distort the violence with any water
any love, any laughter, any ink
do not. It was 5pm all day today, the sky

There isn't the psychiatry yet

to take me out of my madness
when I played tennis with such sadness

when I drank wine with such sadness
when I watched the sea with such sadness
When I drove to the lake with such sadness

No branch of medicine still

diagnosed my sadness
with tests returning sadness

when aconite bloomed with such sadness
when pages read with this sadness
when sleep resigned its intervals to sadness

And all the things that happened with such sadness

these were the best days
and my friends held me with such holding

and they ate with me holding
and they laughed with me holding
we were in San José holding

And my chest was empty holding

we were in Santiago at the Plaza de Armas holding
and my arms with such sadness

we were in Phnom Penh at the Russian Market holding
55 storeys in glass buildings with such sadness
and I, still with my rough eyes, such holding

Disappearances, what is the nature of monument or memory

does it matter, or is it too a sentimentality, I experience it as both sentimentality and the fact, how a whole set of events must

sometimes be rescued from sentimentality
I do not have day and I do not have moonlight
I do not believe in time

I do believe in water

I cannot wait
for their unfortunate earth to dissolve, say what's obvious

that is a sentimentality too
I am recklessly here, to move forward is as the same as staying and going back, there is no forward, even that is optimistic

These people with their crude minds think they can love anything

think they can see anything
they think they can know the art of the world. All their lives are

spent clawing the grace of things, mangling the sheen of things
they lift their arms and displace millions
why am I on earth with these people

I am in hell, sister. Man from Ghana on a street in Venice

is this a protest, is this a protest, I asked
there is the only word for holding insufficiency of holding

no amount of euro, the neck of jacaranda approaches
then once in the post office meeting in transit, a holding, the time I lived on Calle de Donceles, and in the cemetery with books and satchel

We did everything not to kill you

turned ourselves inside out
the general hospital asked me to donate this ugly heart of mine

I said, no one should have it
let us leave it at that
no one should have it

The monsters are talking all over the world

they are talking an insane language
in this language we are inanimate, they are cytotoxic and happy

they are multidisciplinary macrophage, and we are finding
it hard to move our limbs again
the government sent me the results: my cervix was normal

The racial intrigues, spinning off local narrations

of stasis, the layers of inconceivability, intractable narrations, unforgivable narrations
that

may cause, at any moment, explosions that I suppress, but they detonate nevertheless
in me
in me the duration of stones

I owe my beating heart a debt for its endurance, its persistence, its

profound knowledge that is beyond any capacity to know its amplitude for taking
these detonations and insisting on living, on

beating . . . beating, jumping to the roof of the ribs. I cannot know
this latitude. I cannot know. I do not know its duration
I am destroying it, I am sure. I cannot conclude. This is in the region

Outside the geometry of other considerations. I do not know its

distractions, the scabs of its work. I interpret small signs of its breathless career and I know its weight

I try another language, I invent rhetoric, I think perhaps this will be intimate of the rate of killing, this will sustain, will wait out; but I know better. The simple volume of my breathing. The encroachments melt

Vein tissue. I know the rages I suppress. Close regenerative neurons

I am wearing away the inside of my mouth with acid saliva. All this my heart must contend with, must ignore, the absences, in these

hemispheres of lewd elevations; and how many dreams I have with the same obligations as the waking life; how these obligations have the same duty, the same amount of

Weight

as the ones admitted to reality; therefore, they cause the
same worries, they register in the same jurisdictions, they

are recorded in the documents of the veins, the durability of the
knees; they employ time, they account and they appear on the schedule of minutes
they take their quota of days and appointments

This is the region called surmounting

this is the volcano called evidence
why do I keep anything, sitting near a Tenochtitlan pyramid, forgetting

one language after another; some last evening after another; this
evening the crate of worries and intensions has a sonous echo of
musicians and sweet ice vendors

I refuse to reproduce whiteness

the innocuous procedures of good morning
and good evening, good night's malign debenture

the lien and mortgage in how are you today
oh so sorry, look out, oh dear
let alone the bailiff emergency

What time is it

we tried everything
not to kill you, we even tried not living

nothing worked
we even tried living our own lives, nothing
worked

We forgot us

our sleep is ideological
who sleeps well, I wonder

and capital sells time, and oxidates time, alloys
time, and gullets time
skins time, it wears time away, vacuum-packed with time

All the cities are violent with time

the pulvering light, the caked slivers
of our breathing, namely

on this done-killed the earth, the birds
are decorative, the other beasts, metastasized food
here is time ferrous in the mouth

There was that time coming to evening

when the world cut my face diagonal
as if the world were the aqueous path into worlds

into bleeding
into the unused interior, the advancing sunlight
as if it were the just before and never meeting

Of the sea

and the line of horizon
fractured my cheekbone into 300 million years

of ribbed argillite, as if my left side
is falling and falling, their fracturing
their securities, futures turned positive

As we learned to smell our raw gangster fingertips

but didn't you laugh with me in Montreal or Amsterdam
or somewhere with Audre. That time when we were ibises, and we flew

red feet across three continents; what is that cellophane over my sky, what
is that noise out my window, I can't sleep, here
"*the grey of Werner, without lustre is greyish . . .*" no fault of anyone

They don't account for their dreadful imagination

and this is how it went down, first
they persuaded us we needed technocrats, then

they persuaded us we needed businessmen and
then they persuaded us we needed fascists
then we all had the flu from which we never recovered

And this morning closer to French and smoke grey

the sky, up here, why every turn here is to birds, we
hate them so, they go on anyway, indifferent

on the road to the airport once, two egrets flew into the
wheel of a truck, one de-winged, dead, the other
landed looking in astonishment

Any being can be astonished, any bird

lose any bird
bewildered by violence, this feels like a day in 1983

a headache, a sound like planes
like metal on threaded metal
like the tingle of the word *thermite*

A Sunday in any known year, gloomy with rain and possibility

when the big world is leaning on me
so weighted with what I have not

done, simply, what I have been forced to do
walking through sentences, hate-gritty corridors of one word
then another, making my way through a meaning less

Meaning, and their certainty of the meaning less

meaning
let's leave it at that

I remember nothing, not childhood
not anything after I place it here, if I
come out of this with gentleness, I'm found

And lost, we left everything in these years' six eclipses

we lost almost everyone, the daylight hours elongated, chance
disappeared, triviality, the delightful disappeared

from the city. Life exhausted
intimacy's equations. The molecules of air decided
all this. Among the more distant objects of interest

The house tops were our horizon; not counting all the evenings

every day is lived in crisis, wasn't it always so
and we in all those coats, we look like past lives of our selves

as if we are looking at photos a century ago
and we were dressed in all the horrors, sanguine of our possibilities
and we, with all our knives with all our honeysuckle looks

Me? I don't have you to mind

I have my heart to take care of
if heart is what it is, if heavy is its leaf weight

and one afternoon in that assizes it felt enormous with
its own metaphor, as if its chambers and pipe work
understood the temblous assignment of living

I have its undone workings in my hands

in constant recalibrations
the sun went down in our orbit

I recall what we made of these inconsiderable kilometres
the way we dissolved into doorways' salvage
we calculated extraneous solutions

What we lifted open

when we lifted open the lids of mornings
and what we made of these inappreciable minutes

the way we eased into the provinces of window frames
not invertible
24.71 million km^2 plus 17.84 million km^2 plus 521,876 km^2 plus 324,000 km^2

Equals something, something, some thing incalculable

insubstantial, ancillary, piers, brick, extreme dirt, earth fast wood, clay and stick kettle
unrelieved iron, systems architecture, one door and posts

24.71 million km^2 with the addition of 17.84 million km^2 and the dividend of
521,876 km^2 and the advantage of 324,000 km^2
Preposition, adjective, noun, and conjunction, plus, piu, plus

Et al

parts of speech, summa de arithmetica: ampersand, mehr, plus equals
infinity. Particularis de computis et scripturis, each day

no one should take it, no one interpret
these signs yet, lit as they are in the everything of us
nothing of us, all this time, except

I am waiting

all this time, we were
living in the slightest "degree of inflammation"

how else would I index these kilometres, how else
would I keep a record of their exact parching, except
as anatomy and prologue

What awaits us

is disaster not justice, I will
weigh this for a long time, over many days

how it is to turn it over in your hand
over and over, and when we were going
with suitcases, the airport, the waiting room, the ledge to this world

When we spoke

it was of catastrophes, and when we arrayed all our
intelligence against them nothing happened

we came out each day with flowers, we had to do this
we denied the scabs and the waterlogged lungs, we
breathed water when there was no air, we grew gills and fins

What a strange, strange life I've lived

I tell you I don't know how I've done it but
it seems I've pulled it off

not anticipating anything, you know
but quite the interesting way I've gone about it
to be truthful, it was not at all interesting to me

If you were someone else you would find it so

perhaps
but not me

what I mean is, if I told you who I was according to this world
you would take too much for granted; and if I did not tell you
who I was you would assume too much

And if I did not tell you who I was

would I have denied who I was
which brings us to the question who am I

and in what context does who I am
or the question of who I am arise
and would I be betraying, in some way, that part of me

Whom I know intimately

to be who I am and was and want to be
suffice it to say then

no one could possibly know what to do
With the answers
let us say I don't know how I did it but I'm here

Any word I land on will surely tell who I am

it will contain who I am as well as who I am
which is who I reject and who I have been called

and who I embrace. These are not odd questions if we are to
begin. Two. Winged insects in the airplane window. Caught
anywhere. Three, we lived in the factory, no expanse

This is what I have heard said. Whole islands were whole continents, so

the topography we are living on, the plane
you cannot tell the depth of it because

that will mean that you are dead, you can only say enough
so that you yourself can continue in a kind of bad faith with yourself
knowing already that you have killed a part, if not all of you

But then there is forgetting, which is always durable

I went to those institutions where I entered like a person
but of course, those expectations were a cover for my expectations

the truth is
I had no expectations except running a life
I had to run life like a business, they said

The baby was familiar to me

she was eating with her mother in the outer room. I
thought it was my sister or someone I knew lying in the bedroom

I passed through, having gone downstairs with someone, in a jumble of building materials where I tried to be quiet renting the room toward the toilet. She said, Bring the baby I want to give her the medicine

I missed the plane to Dublin

I have my reasons. And I have my reasons there too
I don't like hypocrisy and maybe it's not hypocrisy but something more fatal

anyway, suffice it to say that style will kill us all. And you know exactly what I mean, the big kill-off will be down to them. Let me say that this is not a conceit of fiction or anything

There is no plot resolution, at the second microalgae summit

we ingested their sense of hopelessness, their ennui, their endings
their philosophies of hopelessness, their culpability in the state of affairs

we were always rediscovered flowering, surprise
I wish I could be fooled into living a life, it bears repeating
the point is here I am, I intend to last

There was that time, I spent decades returning

on rainy days it comes to me
beginning again, I spent decades weeping

work hard & reliable & trusty out of doors
an excellent ploughman. An excellent & well-disciplined workman
a good & industrious servant. Good milkmaid. Out hand

Chambermaid, seamstress & launderer. Not robust. Launderess. Generally

out hand. Lost the sight of one eye. Plain cook / milkmaid & Spin. Very healthy
healthy. Healthy

spinner—plain seamstress & would I think make a good nurse because smart &
out hand. Generally healthy but complaining this summer. & knitting
a milkmaid, washer & spinner. A plain seamstress & spinner (not strong)

Also carried away a gun

of uncommon large size, and a fiddle
dear All, short as my tenure has been, I have decided to resign

I have limited time, many demands. My time would be better spent
as an orphan. Took with me an iron pot, a narrow axe, a handsaw
moreover, I have some concerns about the document, Sincerely

Oil and water, cities, read in the times

showed little sign of letting up
around the world, the slowing death rate

led investors early Monday
opening 4 percent up, economists
fully functioning without a high risk of catching the virus

Now this. Empty

empty, empty subways, empty buses. We saw
empty stores, empty bars, shut restaurants

whole streets became quiet, and some desultory
bicycles and baby buggies seemed superfluous
there was no one to reference our casual greediness

We stepped into the open tentatively, we stepped into trains

tentatively. Our noise was extravagant. Our need was
extravagant. The expanses of fields and snows now only covered

in fields and snows and people-less, the empty
highways without the usual angers of bottlenecks and
drivers. Except for we who always fill the mornings and

Hospital gowns and factories

except for those who open the city each day and keep it open
except for those who lift bodies, who lift arms, who lift backs

who travel from one emergency to the other, one warehouse of
the human to the other. We saw
surprised birds flourish, their apartment-building nests

In many trees along particular roads, we heard

some sound we did not recognize since
there was no noise to cover it. Zoos reported happiness, we

took all sleeping sleeplessly. A rabbit appeared in our back
yard. A hummingbird I've never seen for fifty years found the
orange honeysuckle last summer. We saw the use of

Everything

the uselessness of everything. One era to the next, some of us take
self-portraits dressed in useless clothing, some of

us go to work as use. All of us suddenly became essential
since overproduction is
essential. Since all they had done until now was make

Commerce essential. We were apprised again of the catalogue of

being—the needed people who were the needed, were the un-
needed, and, only needed when needed but considered un-

needed, nevertheless. They were given an extra four dollars for
the unnecessary. Then the powerful started kneeling
until they took off in spacecrafts

It was frightening. We became depressed since if they

were kneeling what should we be doing. Then came the requisite
praying, and the politicians assured us they had hearts and that their hearts

were aching for us. This reminded us of the paper cut-out hearts from
kindergarten. Between the kneeling and the cut-out paper
hearts we suspected these people could not help us. We saw that

They could kill us

their interstellar innocence was astonishing
and obsequious

they were in charge they told us
something irreversible was in charge they said and there
were logistical functions to our hungers

Few of us recognize each other in photographs of

ourselves before this all happened, as
when we knew each other across streets and

after a while we knew we would not be
going back to those asphalt expanses. We would not meet casually
hypocritical

Smile that stricken smile we used to smile as we passed. We

watch films with scenes of where we used to be. Forms
of appearances, knives to cut our way through

appalled if only they could see us. We aged a lot in one year
farther away from use and exchange
as if we were all in another country, yet only streets away, only

Cities away. We cannot linger on embodiments, we

knew we had lost intimacy when we missed unintimate offices
when we missed unintimate bars. We do not miss unpleasant

people. We think of them with greater derision. In the beginning
a certain masculinity
vanished overnight

All

the sports pages lost reason. Pity, brutal
masculinity, the lethal skeleton crew of patriarchy kept

those vital analytics working. Women lost. And
some lost more
than others

Until it fully develops a discourse of complete unshaded

but until then it is necessary to point out
We must deploy more than pity

the south is not to be helped but to be repaid
for that matter we may apply expropriation indiscriminately
colonialism is a narrow concept albeit that we are all held in it

And so, what is beyond is greater

all season we calculated, without knowing, the Callan-Symanzik
equation, it's amazing to me how everything turned out

I was certainly happy with my life in the dragged scrim of electricity
there was a gravitational as if I were in a pot with a cover over it
the sound of the cover closing over me, as when back then there were iron pots

In the scrim today, there were two summers outside

and two wasps chasing or looking for something
in the air, I could not tell or know because I don't know their world

"The destruction of the colonial world is no more and no less than
the abolition of one zone, its burial in the depths of the earth or
its expulsion from the country," Fanon said

I won't feel better tomorrow

I have a possible hundred tomorrows where I will feel increasingly worse
but let me not predict what I can predict. And I will not mislead

I won't feel better until that's done and buried
of course, we drink glasses of wine to everything we possibly can. Cabral
said, ". . . our historic mission is to sanction all revolts, all desperate actions . . ."

That is where I began, and have built an oropendola nest here

to continue, my uncle came into the house
one mattress after another until all the rooms were filled. I lay in my delirium

suffocating under the weight. My grandmother raised her hands
telling him to stop. He kept coming in, one mattress after another burying us
Each time I was ill this is what would happen

All the films we saw were just tragedy

only tragedy
not even tragedy, we could never escape with simply tragedy

dear all, unbeknownst to everyone, I know
the arrangements of the disks
of asterales

The tradition of the oppressed

teaches us that the "emergency situation" in which we live
is the rule. We must

arrive at a concept of history which corresponds to this. Then it will become clear that the task before us is the introduction of a real state of emergency; and our position in the struggle against Fascism will thereby improve . . .

I am depending on this Benjamin paragraph, as

to explain where I am now but of course after I have said that I realize that while
I may have picked this paragraph up in a small bookstore one day a few years ago

I have understood its uncanniness all my life. All my life
but to complete this task would have meant some difficult decisions on my part
not the least of which was to live the statement out

Truly

so, I proceeded to forget the sense of it or keep that sense of it
in an adjacent life or room or merely as close to forgetfulness as possible

it would have required an action on my part that I neither had
the courage nor the wherewithal to commit
I'm again playing around and not saying what I mean

Each meridian is perpendicular to all circles of latitude

each is also the same length, being half of a great circle
on the Earth's surface and therefore measuring 20,003.93 km

how many and which cities do you live in and how
and what happens to the body in these cities and
who are you in these cities, walking

A road can also be a set of disappearances

whose toxic memories am I surrounded by called
monuments

I experience it as rancid sentimentality
how a whole set of events sit in their violent facts, how
memory's memorylessness functions in or is rather made into monument

St. George Station, the first place my sister took me, I recall

the glitter and the lights, of students, the motion
I thought it was going to be lovely

but of course, no one will discover it for a while. If at all. I think
that I will go to sleep now and figure something out
when I wake up

In this tumultuous history

being alive is rawness and alertness
brittleness

being here is inertia, being is inertia
inside a tumult
indicated here

This brief summary, circadian and curious

I leave here
I prefer rain, I prefer the gurgle of water

I do desperate thinking
what is it that I loved
what is it that I said I loved

What is that advent of blackness

that is the texture of lilac and barberry
Breakability. To be plain

to acquire the basic level of existence
all can be lost
in that particular resolve

Taxonomy then

I wrote everything down, you know
not that it matters. The notes won't survive the search

they won't survive the opposition to this living. Kingdom
hostage, Phylum hostage, Class hostage, Order
hostage, Family hostage, Genus hostage, Species the hostage

Kingdom ore, Phylum lenticular ore body, Class refractory

order refracting, Family lens
genus refractory ore, Species refraction

kingdom extracted, Phylum extracted, Class extract
order extraction, Family extracted, Genus extracted

species extracted

I won't tell you my exploits escaping this taxonomy

I am grateful to metaphor
I won't say what needs to be said, although

"contractile fibrous bundle producing movement"
I'll leave that there
it was the way the air felt, it

Was the autonomous gestures of a hand

a shoulder's discourse on effort, then
the paraphrase a bit of laughter does

someone walked the way a perfume walks
it was what was left after labour, after a time
after time itself, small, the implications

If I opened a door I could transcribe the technology

of a life, its pivot and breach, and joint
I know the skill of epiphytes

feet hanging, never touching the ground
eating air and grit and moisture, I do all these things
no attachment. Take this world

We do not know if we will meet after the pandemic

so here we are, still
we always meet after the pandemic, don't you

remember, we never know what is going to happen
now they don't know, that's the one good
thing

How do we manage

fear, he asked. We don't. Fear is a necessary reaction
a good, good sign

my thanks to all who gave me fear
I know it now, molecularly
don't worry, don't you remember, our life all along

We were surprised and unprepared

for each coming era
all we had were the febrile thoughts, crumbled membrane

for wing-flight. We had only summoned ourselves
for more of the same
we cannot provide any more bodies, however

The messages from the parietal lobe are alarming

we turned our senses and all our art
to these disappointing frequencies again

we had no hopes of ever getting out
we made litres of platelets from muddy water and dressed
in alarming suits as usual

What if I told you

our lies amazed us so
till we hated the beauty we made

we could not bear the thought of ourselves
we kept feeding paper to the apparatuses, the technologies
of which wore us down

We were used to the way of the world

and if we ever recalled what we might have been
we wept for days on end

the ledgers we kept of the chest-caved mornings
and our burnt-out fingerprints, with the electric headaches
all this

I used to dance, you know, there

are photographs, I lived in many apartments
the walls were of some intense unstable material

who lives there now, several and broken
in each instance. By 12:41am eleven thousand people
had been born and four thousand had died

Each year the group of us

offer jokes that bring more perfect unhappiness
plastic and viral, bacterial. Though and yet

we are remainders of burning oxygen
we are just the end of helium, we are speeding
we are slow, water doesn't end

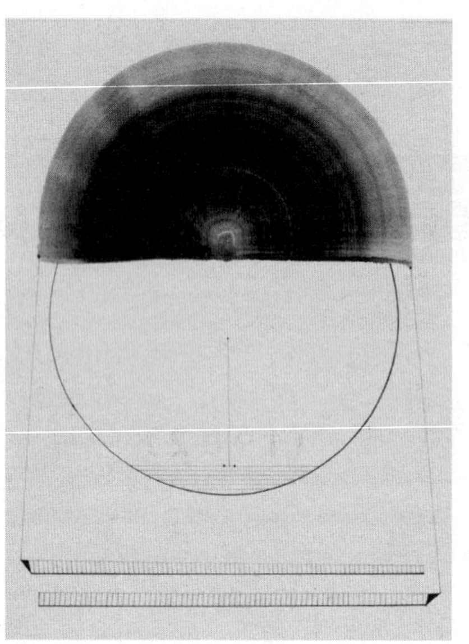

PRIMITIVE OFFENSIVE

(1982)

CANTO I

Ashes head to toes
Juju belt
guinea eyes unfolded impossible
squint a sun since drenched
breasts beaded of raised skin
naked woman speaks
syllables come in dust's pace
dried, caked rim of desert mouth
naked woman speaks
run mouth, tell
when the whites come they were dread men
we did not want to touch them
we did not want to interfere in their business
after the disappearances
many times there were dead men among us
and we cursed them
and we gave them food
when the whites came they were dead men
five men died in our great battles before
guns gave us more heads of our enemies
and those who disappeared were dead men
and the dead take care of their own
for things come and they leave
enemies were dead men and whites were
   dead men
and our city and our people flourished
and died also
naked woman speak
syllables come in water's pace
long river mouth, tell.

the skulls of our enemies
were the walls of our wealth
and we filled them with food
and palm wine for our ancestors
and everywhere there were skulls
white of beaten iron and guns and
white with the ancestors' praise and

white with the breath of the whites on our land
white as of eyes on sand on humid vastness
white as the tune of fingers, brisk on dry skin
not even pursed hungry lips were as white
and even the sorghum was as white as this
not even the dust of the goat's grounded horn
and each night became different from the next
and we stood by our fires
and left the places outside our compound
to the skulls and the disappeared and the whites
and the skulls stood on their sticks
and no one was born on the nights after
and no one joined their age mates
the disappeared stayed away and did not
help us to kill our enemies
and we ground our breasts and our teeth to
   powder
belly roped in ashes as the sky falters on the
   rainbow
naked woman speaks
syllables come in palm wine's pace
run mouth, dry,

CANTO II

ancestor dirt
ancestor snake
ancestor lice
ancestor whip
ancestor fish
ancestor slime
ancestor sea
ancestor stick
ancestor iron
ancestor bush
ancestor ship
ancestor old woman, old bead
let me feel your skin
old muscle, old stick
where are my bells?
my rattles
my condiments
my things
to fill houses and minutes,
the fete is starting
where are my things?
my mixtures
my bones
my decorations
old bread! old tamerind switch!
will you bathe me in oils,
will you tie me in white cloth?
call me by my praise name
sing me Oshun song
against this clamor,

ancestor old woman,
send my things after me
one moment old lady,
more questions,
what happened to the ocean in your leap
the boatswain, did he scan
the passage's terrible wet face
the navigator, did he blink or steer the ship
through your screaming night
the captain, did he lash two slaves to the
  rigging
for example?
lady, my things
water leaden
my maps, my compass
after all, what is the political
position of stars?
drop your crusted cough
where you want,
my hands make precious things
out of phlegm

ancestor wood
ancestor dog
ancestor knife
ancestor old man
dry stick
moustache
skin and cheekbone
why didn't you remember,
why didn't you remember
the name of our tribe
why didn't you tell me
before you died
old horse
you made the white man
ride you
you shot off your leg for him
old man
the name of our tribe is all i wanted
instead you went
to the swamps and bush
and rice paddies
for the Trading Company
And they buried you in water
crocodile tears!
it would have been better
to remember the name of our tribe
now mosquito dance a ballet
over your grave
the old woman buried with you
wants to leave.

CANTO III

one thing for sure
dismembered woman,
when you decide
you are alone
understand,
ugly faced woman
when you decide
you are alone
when you dance
it's on your own
broken face
when you eat
your own plate of stones
for blasted sure
you alone
where do you think you're going
dismembered woman
limbs chopped off
at the ankles.
when you decide,
believe me
you are alone
sleep,
sleep,
tangential face
sleep
sleeping or waking
understand
you are alone.
diamonds
pour from your vagina
and your breasts
drip healing copper
but listen woman
dismembered continent
you are alone

see
crying fool
you want to talk in gold
you will cry in iron
you want to dig up stones
you will bury flesh
you think you don't need
oils and amulets, compelling
powder
and reliance smoke
you want to throw people
in cesspits.
understand
dismembered one
ululant
you are alone
when water falls back
land surfaces

    they're like bottle-flies
    around my anus
    look at their blue mouth on my excrement
    when my face is bandaged up
    like war,
    white and cracked
    like war
    I know
    I am alone.
    You think I don't know
    I am alone
    When my foot
    is cracked and white
    like hungry people
    I have a stick for alone
    tell them to come for me
    and bring their father too
    fly will light on him before day finish
    my face will set up

like the sky for rain
for them
tell them to come for me
and bring their brother too
all that can happen to me
has happened
I have a big stick for alone.

I was sent
to this cave
I went out one day like a fool
to this cave
to find clay
to dig up metals
to decorate my bare and painful breasts
water and clay
for a poultice
for this gash
to find a map, an imprint
anywhere
would have kept me calm,
anywhere
with description.
instead
I found
a piece of this,
a tooth,
a bit of food
hung on,
a metatarsal
which resembled mine,
something else
like a note, musical
ting ting!
but of so little pitch
so little lasting
perhaps it was my voice
and this too

a suggestion
an insinuation
so slight
it may be untrue
something moving
over the brow
as with eyes closed to black
the sensate pole
the middle of a dance
no, I cannot say dance
it exaggerates;
a bit of image
a motion close to sound
a sound imaged on my retina
resembling sound.
a sound seen out of the corner of my eye
a motion heard on my inner ear
I pored over these
like a palaeontologist
I dusted them
like an
archaeologist
a swatch of cloth, skin
artless
coarse utility
but not enough.
yes enough
still only a bit
of paint, of dye
on a stone
I cannot say crude
but a crude thing
nevertheless
a hair
a marking
that a fingernail to rock
wounded scratch

I handled these like
a papyrologist
contours
a desert sprung here
migrations
a table land
jutting up,
artful
covert, mud
I noted these
like a geopolitical
scientist
I will
take
any evidence of me
even that carved
in the sky
by the fingerprints of clouds
everyday
even those
that do not hold
a wind's impression.

CANTO IV

dry water
brackish dust
base days hurrying base days
primordial journey
blistered, chafed,
let me through
let me up
whose is this in my hand
whose green purple entrails
veined, prurigenous, fetid
mine?
tote it?
through this place?
wet land
rotted wood
this humus body
plant and blood
excreta
dead things weigh me down
this obsidian plain
bald
dead things
dead leaves
dead hair
dead nails
tongue, a swollen flower
glottis, choked with roots
my teeth fall bloodless
a damp mange covers me
I cough a velvet petalled herb
my neck bleeds
ants sprout hills on my head
leave wings in my blood
red feast of my blood
fat leaves of my blood

pressed against me,
dead mud,
i have never lived,
this thing changes me
so often
obscene
dead clatter
sepulchral smell of my limbs
the sun embedded
in my skull
dung heap of my bones
my eyes are dead
they want to talk stone,
the lagoon is burning
green day of my death
there is nothing
that I remember
days collapse
fall on each other
hours collapse
days remain new
obscure primeval metaphor
hot faced labyrinths
stone and water
molten water
cannot clean my eyes
dead things
dead years contrive
secret dead windows
ah jewel of airs
sepulture of air
my veined face
gestates
mornings before
the day of my death,
each side of me
the dust smoke smell of days

i am lost again
wild for a wet rock,
blowing air through a stick
wild to grunt
wild to whistle
squeezing my feet
into my belly
wild to plummet,
spectral note
spectral buzz
spectral spider
laying eggs,
gnawing through my skull
lying there, picked clean
among other bones
in this eyrie
this place of clawed feet
I am bird's treasure
my ear against its wings,
imponderable
slate wings
fasten me to one day,
at every step
something falls,
legs about to leave me,
ephemeral dross
where am I
that I am transparent, blue winged
yet cannot move
where insect eyed in corners of dead sunlight,
light coffined in dust
long travelled shafts,
where am I
beetle legged, dust-crisp in rigor,
my arms are sand
twigs make my vertebrae
twigs and faeces

dust ensanguined
now I bleed water
soon I will bleed dirt;
my eyes
are pus bags
pus of anger
ground teeth
bitten bone
dry spittle
pus of my insides
sand of my insides
I cannot see
barren flower
lance of laughter
ghosts of things
scraps of propositions
bargains of mud;
hot stink breath
of the sun
my belly is wind
harsh
shine
corbeau's meat,
hegemon
of sticks
wet
acrid
bag ribs of rain
drought
jealous sweat;
of husks
pigs's mud
fibre, chicken feathers.
hegemon
of huts
bound with salt,
twine,

my belly is rope
bread of wood
chalk
teeth of chalk,
a stellate of chalk wings
on its distended point
i know that stone,
i've danced on it
often enough,
friend stone
friend foot
dead stone
i know that dance,
i've . . .
i know that stone,
dead stone
in my throat
that stone of spit
i've danced on it
often enough.
i eat myself
dance my smudgy dance
powder step
chalk move
paper leap.
hegemon
of adjectives,
kites, absences
feathers
guesses
chances, string
hats, tambourines
costumes, disguises
bells
dry seeds, powder
of dry leaves
glass pieces

paints
mules
octaves
rum, clarinet
arrow, oils,
hegemon
of receptacles
conveniences
baffling flags
gaping anthems.
rumour
of a day,
I move very lightly
in you,
day of tin rain
metal teeth
electric
configurations,
day
embroidered with cuts
flesh eating metals
sore glitter
ornaments of grief,
day of wire spit
you rise from my back,
this bed of ash,
as if
you want to kill me
press me into jade
grind me into blue stone
for a broken pot
if I could fall
charred breath
on my lips
dead bird of my lungs
flour bag wings
of my lungs

be sirens
yellow
and piercing
disturb
this place
gulp
glitter
break
take over
or be hard,
the present is empty
winds must have scratched it away since then.
I am too much weight for myself
too much breath
too much mourn
too little air in my chest
slave of my limbs
my mother's gestures
I precede myself
in bones
in hollows, basins
flesh of novena candles
juju
cemeteries in tree spines
Gods in big toes
bath of chicken blood
houngan, sing Oshun song for me
I need to talk to her, the only one I remember
give me a tongue
I've . . .
ta tat a, dip, de de bop
I know that stone
hands
growing worse
these votive cows
this gruel
this white ashes

to sprinkle me
with seriousness,
this dance
to tell lies to my legs
rigored twitch of my legs
this is no dance
rip de de bop
I've danced . . .
I know . . .
all that is left me
pulled back
to the shrubs
leafless baobab
murdering sun
red in my eyes,
waterless from seeing
seeing each night, each place
unrecognizable
red in my eyes
they cannot close
I don't have the belly for that
broken pot of a sun,
which place
am I trying to remember
like a tune, legato of ashes, nothing, iron
broad, dense ear
air of thick stone
wife to rock
daughter to fish
eye to stunned beach,
caves to hold my freeness
Spanish galleons lying off,
doubloons to fill caves,
two looks
one before, one behind
still
still dead air

battler of wind
of wind and rope
escaped feather
still
dead air,
there is a thing
I want to be
there is an endness
to it
a dreadful metal
to it
a greyness in its look
a writhing crack in its mouth,
shroud
my face is stone
shroud
my face is stone
broken into
cut and stained.
face of air
face of torn rag
workcloth of my face,
stone.

CANTO V

still
I can eat flour
I can eat salt
I can eat stone
and oil
I can eat barbed wire
I can eat whatever is left
I can grow fat
on split atoms
I can eat toenails
I can eat their toenails
and their flesh
and my own flesh also
I can eat galvanized zinc
and cockroaches
my mouth waters
for radioactive morsels
I can run like hell
to the bushes of
some continent
to Orinoco maybe or the Okigwe plateau
some room strangled by lianas
and tree lice
walled with indefinite
pungent weeds
some wasted stretch, eaten by snakes and bush
that no vulturine mouth
can pronounce
I am not frightened
I am dead already
I can run without
my sarcophagus
without my earth hole
without my bones, my grandmother's sheet
they know me,

they will follow,
I am a liar, I procrastinate,
my teeth
don't want to die
they want to chatter
something soft and bland
they want to chew hot peppers
my limbs don't want to die
don't want to feel the
slightest pain
they like to act
to bend and flex themselves
they like to take their lead
from the sky
they want to jump and bounce
they want to play that little
game with gravity
so I'll run
and maybe one thursday
in some year
perhaps 3050 p.n. (post nuclear)
if I remember and if
I stand just so
in some longitudinal
passage of light
and if it strikes me
and if the shadow I cast
sees a nude eye
before or after noon
and if the sun is on the ground
and if the ground is in the sky
and if a tree grows from my breasts
i'll come out
and then having become rough and short
and green, and brittle-legged
some solar-winged brutal contraption,
will surprise me

CANTO VI

you, in the square,
you in the square of Koln
in the square before that huge destructive
   cathedral
what are you doing there
playing a drum
you, who pretend not to recognize me
you worshipper of insolubles
I know you slipped, tripped on your tie
the one given to you at the bazaar where
they auctioned off your beard
you lay in white sheets for some years
then fled
to the square
grabbing these colors, red, green, gold like
   some bright things
to tie your head and bind you to some place
grabbing this flute
this drum
this needle and syringe
this far from Lagos,
and you, the other day in Vlissengen,
I was so shocked to see you
in your bathing suit
on that white beach in Holland
what were you doing there
and again the other night
I saw you in Paris near St. Michel Metro
dressed like that
dressed as if you were lost,
Madagascar woman, hand full of pomme frites
rushing to your mouth
looking at me
as if you did not know me
I was hurt

so hurt on Pont Neuf
so hurt to see us
so lost
maybe rushing
off to some
dog work in Porte de Vincennes
or maybe to press hair
in that shop in Strasbourg-Saint-Denis
that shop, already out of place
the latest white sex symbol was in the window,
                in corn rows,
and me too
here in this mortuary
of ice,
my face
like a dull pick,
I wondered if
If I resembled you,
did you get my dead salutation
I sent it
dropped it as a dried
rose at your feet,
me too
on all fours
in this decayed wood
waiting

but I stayed clear
of Bordeaux and Nantes,
no more trading me
for wine and dried turtles,
oh yes
I could feel their breath
on my neck,
the lords of trade and plantations.
not me
not Bordeaux
not Marseilles
not for sugar
not for indigo
not for cotton.
I went to Paris
to where shortarsed Napoleon said,
'get that nigger Toussaint,'
Toussaint, who was too gentle,
He should have met Dessalines,
I went there to start a war
for the wars we never started
to burn the Code Noir
on the Champs Elysees.
So hurt in Paris
Senegal man
trying to sell them
trinkets
miniatures of Africa
goat tail fly swatters
hand drums
flutes, toumpans
you didn't see me,
there was a hum between us
refractory
light about us,
you sold a few things along the Seine that night,
I hoped you read Fanon

and this was just a scam
but I knew it was your life
because your dry face
was my dry face.
your eyes were
too quick
too easy to become lovers
too urgent
it would be minutes
before they would be in our room
in our bed
touching our skin
like silk for sale
palms
wanting more
wooden
rhinoceroses
ivory
fertility gods
monkey tail
flyswatters
filling up our room
wanting
lion skins for mats
pricing our genitals
for tassels, victory regalia,
don't look at me, man
we need the business.

I saw what you did
gendarmes
what you did to the
old man on the train
you took him to the middle of the car
and searched him and squeezed him
and laughed
because he was afraid,

he could have been my grandfather
he tried to explain,
his passport
was in his luggage
the man with the other uniform
in Gare du Nord
but, I don't understand
but I am a . . .
the man with whistle
but I am a . . .
but I have money. . . .
what . . . you're touching me
look at my face
I am a . . .
corpse
I have met another corpse,
he was going to his son
in Heidelberg
his son
had a scholarship
his son was studying
german linguistics for negritude
in Senegal
he tried to explain,
he could have been my grandfather
but you jabbed his ribs,
he did not want to stay in your country
he said he had a shop
in Dakar, reflection, rhinestone
of France.
he was astonished
I will not forget you, gendarmes.

CANTO VII

guajiro making flip-flops on the wing tip of
the American airline
they decided,
hot,
carnival along the Malecon,
cerveza,
Jose, Miguel, Carlos,
I met them twenty years later,
Luis though, still dances for the turistas,
Havana twinkles
defiant, frightening,
all the lights are on,
this decision they made
so clear, so bright,
with everything so much bigger.
the wing of the plane dips,
aren't they afraid?
it could be a bomber,
and they in the street!
Jorge Roberto Flores is sixteen,
he speaks English and Russian,
Jorge Roberto Flores said,
that is the museum of the revolution,
there are many things in there
this thing I can't put my finger on
only now and then a quick look,
Granma
and every chicken truck turned
tank and armed convoy,
guajiro turning cartwheels on the wing tip of
my airplane
threatening Havana with its powerful steel
influence,
a woman, she, black
and old said,

somos familia,
I could not understand,
it was Spanish
so she touched my skin
todos, todos familia eh!
Yes, Si! I said
to be recognised

she knew me
and two others did too,
one night in the Amphiteatro de La Avenida de
  Las Puertas

and then in Parque Macco
recognized me
guajiro doing handstands on the nose of the
  airliner
with its uncertain purpose,
my friend thinks
socialists don't get drunk,
cerveza! treinta y cinco centavos
carnival along the Malecon
companeros, companeras
so certain
defiant, frightening,
all the lights in Havana are on.

1513, HAVANA

and when it was
Encomendero in Cuba
De Las Casas, the viceregent
drained
a continent of blood
to write the Common Book of Prayer
even as he walks
his quill drips
even his quill
is made of my tail feather
feather of balance
feather of gold
but this little pale viceregent
in his little pale robe
hail marys embroider his blue lips,
still he is not alone,
his acolytes bear his accoutrements
lingeringly, kindly, even now
his sperm atonement on his dry hands,
lizards eat on the latrine floor,
that left, soaks into the oppressed
ground
and brings up dead
bodies from the bush,
terrors legate
scribes a hecatomb of this Antillean
archipelago
scribes desert, Bantustans to a continent
still plundered,
condemned to these Antilles
fallen into the hell of them
De Las Casas
ecclesiastic nostrils
scent for gold
scent for sweat

scent delicate
keen
ecclesiastic nose hairs,
blood kisses
the cord around his vestments
the hem of his communion skirt
the edges of his communion slippers
the Romanesque set of the stone in this
communion ring
the light ric-rac braid of his
communion sash
the fawning glint of his communion chain
the host he consecrates in the eucharist
clot in his Eucharistic wine cup,
hostia
hostage in the vestry,
fingers of a counting house clerk
he counts me on this chaplet
for Ferdinand and Isabella
for Napoleon the little emperor
for virgin mother, child, and canon,
the cataclysmic murmur of his breath,
"we adore you oh Christ
and we bless you because
by your holy cross you have
redeemed the world"

Toussaint, i loved you
as soon as i saw you
on that weevil eaten page
in 1961,
i learned to read for you
from that book with
no preface and no owner
you waited for me
hundreds of years,
i learned to read for you

from that book with
no preface and no owner,
about how
a French courtesan
in Cap Haitien
threw
a black woman,
the cook,
into the hot oven because
the hens were not baked
to her liking;
about how
Dessalines was terrible
in war;
Toussaint, I loved you
as soon as I saw you
on that mice shit page
in '61.
Dessalines you were right
I can hear that cry of yours
ripping through that night,
night of privateers
night of fat planters
leave nothing
leave nothing white behind you
Toussaint heard too late
when it was cold in Joux.

CANTO VIII

a belly, elongated, balloons somewhere,
a hideous thing comes for me,
if I close the window
I'll stifle on the ratty air,
Stay! Leave off my throat
no calmness now, I'll rage
my hair will curl its tight ringlets
around your neck,
my teeth will wait for your flesh,
my breath
will scorch your bones to dust
leaving its stench in your wake,
I'll spew you into the sea
like the pit of a lime,
then be a scavenger bird craning
on a rock
to pounce on what is left,
Even then,
I will not leave you alone,
I'll scour the sand and stones
for your heart, strip it
with my gnarled toe nails,
till for the seaweed you are gone,
depending from which continent I spring
Europe, Africa,
It will be honour or savagery.

CANTO IX

What a morning, Rockefeller
What a morning!
when you and I
are the same
finally, dead
a morning when you ended
as I continue
but not really
you died, your stomach
lined with caviar
mine with barbed wire
what a funeral, Rockefeller
what a funeral!
you, dressed in your casket
me carrying mine
for days, I have counted
sometimes sparingly
deliberately miscounting
to avoid living them,
Now we can talk
dressed in the same uniform—
never mind you have attendants—
I count one year as one day, Rockefeller
it works out so that I have
less to go through
you count each day separately, don't you?
Savouring them I suppose,
I bet you even count nights
not me
nights are too dangerous
my hands get itchy
for Molotov cocktails
for rocks and knives
The noise of you sleeping quietly
keeps me awake,

I saw where they buried you Rockefeller
At night, I prance over your grave
like a stormtrooper
in my hobnailed boots
I prance until my legs are exhausted
but you know me Rockefeller
every morning I smooth your grave over again
I am your gravekeeper
I put fresh flowers
I stick them where I think your teeth are,
I prepare for another dance party
when I crush them
what a morning Rockefeller
what a morning!
You bought it
you bought what I get for free.

CANTO X

Then I find myself
rushing about, inadequately
knowing something
and part of something
never everything
or enough
and not yet
and only when I
remember
Then
I find myself
standing still
half deaf
or only hearing
half the thing
and each time
it is not the same half
but it is never the whole
then I find myself
not found
longer than ever
not yet
and then
shortly
I am dead
and you would think that it ended there
you would hope
you would think
it was enough,
instead,
I find my corpse
determined
ambivalent
contradictory.

come away
        this house is never quite right
        it always looks uncertain
        the walls
        their eyebrows are raised
        the room looks as if the rent
        has not been paid
        it is sure I cannot stay
        this house looks skeptical
        this room is so nervous
        I'm clearing off
        it scared me
        I don't like houses
        they're so . . . safe
        I don't like how they stand
        as if nothing is going to happen,

Finally, what I have suspected
all along is true
I am exactly who I thought
I was, dreamed I was,
mockingly
exactly what I seemed to be,
scarce, bare,
this time I should have
made no excuses,
this time I should have come home
and hung myself.

CANTO XI

we die badly
always
public and graceless
sixteen of us
bloods mixed in on a bus
bombed
without names,
in our mirrors, in our hands, in newspapers,
in stained rooms,
wrestling with piss and shit
in gutters
for room to die
on Cape town pavements
in contorted embrace with stone
stone the perverse
lascivious for flying lovers
we fall out of windows
as if we do not know how to use
doors
or perhaps there are no doors in Jo'burg
only windows
laid down as traps for us to fall
out of windows only ten feet below
we are not cats
we fall one hundred feet
particles of our hair and skin
on wooden clubs
and concrete banisters
in our houses
on Sunday mornings
in Toronto
if the police say we're wielding
machetes
on Atlantic river banks
black thread tangled up

embroidering sinister
and on the radio
in phrases
about innocent missionaries
and so many hundreds of us without lineage
without mothers to call us by name.

CANTO XII

goodnight from Pretoria
goodnight from Pretoria
the Professor answered the radio announcer
the Professor was skeptical about . . .
the national party would not be pressured
the national party was skeptical about humanity
the radio announcer would not be pressured
goodnight from Pretoria.
About four o'clock in the morning
when the door gets cold
and the glass wants to cake and crumble
as the bigness
presses against the house,
fills up the spaces
where it has pushed us back,
and the street shivers,
pees itself,
and something, some spot, some absence,
some resonance of it,
stings a stray mangy dog
into a yelp,
strings his tail in the air,
flings his jaw useless,
his nails dig into the asphalt
hopelessly,
running . . .
what difference?
the dog and me
in excruciating arabesque.

There between the bush
ingratiating. . . .
between the leaves
hanging cold opaque cloth
slender . . .

my exquisite improvisation
broken
a feeling of bowels and tissue
such softness, such flesh
now . . .
so close to being nothing
my etude
not done correctly
breaks the glass, opens
a morning in Pretoria
a morning nervous and yellowish
its guts ripped out
stuffed back into its throat.
The professor and the national party
and Botha
and Oppenheimer the diamond man
were skeptical about
the Bantu in Bothutapswana
goodnight from Pretoria
goodnight from Pretoria

CANTO XIII

I hated evenings like this
when I fall asleep
in the afternoon
and wake up when it has
already turned evening,
a smell of muddy oil
in the air
a scent of dirty water
trapped under the earth,
it would be damp
a breeze every now and again
got through
the grey watery sky,
and they would hang,
the clouds I mean,
there is no one else
in the world
on those evenings
those absolutely quiet evenings
waking up, looking across to the window,
hearing shoes on the pavement outside
hollow heeled, spiked, woman's
and those man's
flat, slap of leather,
slithering,
I know he has a smile
gold teeth in his mouth
perhaps,
rings on his index, middle
and little fingers,
I'm sure he's wearing tan
she, her face is tight
as the pavement and the
heel of her shoe
her mouth is full of sand

her legs are caught
in that hobbled skirt
and the leaves of the trees
above those sounds
of steps
made a deceitful silky sound
like that
there is no one else in the world
on those evenings,
that dog's voice
barking through,
that child screaming
surprised to be awakened,
astonished at the quiet,
so startling,
to wake up at the wrong time,
the man and the woman
knocking at my sleep,
I am afraid of them
I lie still
waiting for them to leave,
the man's smile, his gold
the woman's tight face
her armpits
tight with sand
they hollow and slither
in turn,
cover me like gauze
like a master-weaver spider,
no matter where I am
these unforgiving evenings
fallen asleep and forgotten
centuries in this huge and ruined
room.

CANTO XIV

naked skin woman, run,
legs to silence
bush to water, to snake's
evanescent legs to dark
water, tree unscaled, run
moss to creeping liana,
nothing grows here
nothing except everything
so green it blacks
so green it thinks
of crevices
to moist on, to ponder
things fecund
full breasts of things
naked skin woman, run.
Here I am
rough and green, as it were
brutal as they come
grubby as usual
where is my battle shoe
one boot and a bead
for my navel,
it's all I need,
here my shale skin
battle dress,
green jacket, protect me,
here again
sister dust, comrade water
here I am
ugly and ready,
hand down my juju,
my life stone, sister clay
wet me with some water
dash my breasts over my shoulders
come sister, hold me back

parry enemy!
Naked skin woman dance, run
belly full of wind
I dance, run
my arms then eloquent wisps
worn over this shawl of a face,
something of a poised mantis
so poised, turned to wood
wooden pall for a cracked face
that met itself in the look of
one million coral
naked woman run.
good day sister death,
let us get drunk
let us eat roses
let us eat newspapers,
what will it matter,
here I am
mercifully bare,
prop up my elbows,
my battle points,
throw water on my face,
give me rum,
show me the dog
let me at him,
houngan!
prepare my bier
put sticks and spit,
my back is like iron
there's blood on my forehead
put a cloth to my temples
come sister, hold my cowry
parry enemy!
Naked woman, run
aloneness comes in the end
it covers ground quickly
but to be a bright and violent thing

to tear up that miserable sound
in my ear
I run
my legs can keep going
my belly is wind.

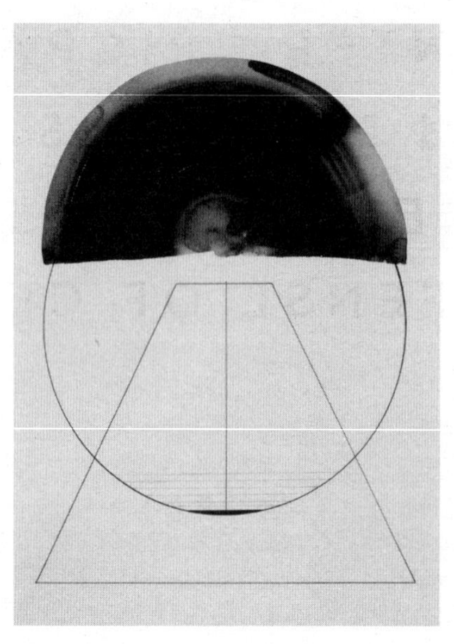

WINTER EPIGRAMS and EPIGRAMS TO ERNESTO CARDENAL IN DEFENSE OF CLAUDIA

(1983)

WINTER EPIGRAMS

1

A white boy with a dead voice
sings about autumn
who knows what he means!

2

no one notices
the tree in the front yard
of the next apartment building
is dead, again

3

ten months in the cold
waiting
I have forgotten, for what!

4

they think it's pretty,
this falling of leaves.
something is dying!

5

then months in the snow
dashed in this icy gutter
quartered by a Yonge Street wind
snowflakes, brutal as rapists.

6

sick song
for sick leaves
every September, about the first week
a smell of infirmity clasps the air,
it is a warm lake like an old hand
trying to calm a cold city.

7

a coloured boat
sailed on a frozen lake
at Harbourfront
two northern poets, thankfully rescued
by this trip to Toronto, read
about distant grass
about arctic plains
who wants to see, who wants to listen!

8

cold is cold is
cold is cold is
not skiing
or any other foolhardiness in snow.

9

I give you these epigrams, Toronto,
these winter fragments
these stark white papers
because you mothered me
because you held me with a distance that I expected,
here, my mittens,
here, my frozen body,
because you gave me nothing more
and I took nothing less,
I give you winter epigrams
because you are a liar,
there is no other season here.

10

I'm getting old
I know.
my skin doesn't jump any more
I am not young and in the company of people;
I am old and in the company of shadows.
things pass in the corners of my eyes
and I don't catch them,
what more proof do you want, look!
I am writing epigrams.

11

winters should be answered
in curt, no-nonsense phrases
don't encourage them to linger.

12

thank heavens
in the middle of it all
is 1348 St. Clair, Hagerman Hall,
Cutty's Hideaway, These Eyes
and El Borinquen,
where you get to dance fast
and someone embraces you.

13

I can wear dirty clothes
under my coat now,
be who I am in my room
on the street
perhaps there'll be an accident though.

14

I can pile a winter of newspapers
under my desk
cultivate mice which
would be a new twist in this
Vaughan road cockroach belt.

15

it's too cold to go outside,
I hope there won't be a fire.

16

I've found out
staying indoors makes you horny,
perhaps winter is for writing
love poems.

17

snow is raping the landscape
Cote des Neiges is screaming
writhing under
winter's heavy body
any poem about Montreal in the winter is pornography.

18

I've never been to the far north/cold,
just went as far as Sudbury,
all that was there was the skull of the earth.
a granite mask so terrible even
the wind passed hurriedly
the skull of the earth I tell you,
stoney, sockets, people
hacked its dry copper flesh.
I've heard of bears and wolves

but that skull was all I saw.
it was all I saw I tell you,
it was enough.

19

I can buy books
which I do not read and cannot afford
and make plans for them to
carry me through my depression,
winter solstice/flesh buckling,
I attempt various standing and sitting positions
until
sadistic February brings me to my knees,
then, I re-examine my life,
in a maudlin fashion,
conclude that I'm worthless
and spend March and April
in a wretched heap
beside the radiator.

20

going in to Sudbury,
brown and white mountains of rock stood up,
a sound like a dull weapon
going against the shield,
once in, you could never come out.

21

I had to leave that town,
that town in the north
where my uncle went for his asthma.
He bought me a guitar,
I had thought before of singing in a café,
I cried to come to Toronto/Yorkville—the Riverboat
where I thought it was hot and open
and my guitar would collect dust.

22

here!
take these epigrams, Toronto,
I stole them from Ernesto Cardenal,
he deserves a better thief
but you deserve these epigrams.

23

the superintendent dug up the plants again,
each June she plants them
each September she digs them up
just as they're blooming,
this business of dying so often
and so soon
is getting to me.

24

someone in the window
across the way
in the brick and red apartment
is drinking coffee,
smoking a cigarette:
the light is on
it is 3 o'clock in the afternoon.

25

In Resolute Bay
they sing better than I

(*Inuit song*)

26

If one more person I meet
in an elevator in July says to me
'Is it hot enough for you?'
or when standing, cold, at a car stop in November,
'How could you leave your lovely sunny country?
I will claw his face and cut out his tongue.

27

It was not right to say
her face was ruined by alcohol and rooming houses,
it was still there, hanging on to her

cracking itself to let out a heavy tongue
and a voice (if you could call it that),
her eyes opened not out of any real interest, not to see
where she was going, but out of some remembered courtesy,
something tumbled out of her mouth
a Black woman walked by,
one who could not keep a secret,
betrayed the drunken one's counsel,
I'm not crazy, I just want a cup of coffee,
the wounded tongue replied.
I had a subway token and eleven cents
gave her the latter, told her
I knew she wasn't crazy instead of embracing her,
she closed her hand over the coin
and called me 'sucker'.

28

one good day
if I lift the blinds
and the sun through the glass seems warm
and a woman passing wears a windbreaker,
I forgive you everything,
I forget the last hundred harsh white mornings.

29

if it's not out in the morning
then one day is lost,
if it's not seen for weeks
then months are lost,
with long dank spells as this
I pick up the stitches on my funeral shroud.

30

I feel wicked
when there's no snow in December
as if I've willed it so,
I say 'damn good there's no blasted snow';
I have no sympathy for skiers,
I say they enjoy other people's misfortunes,
snow plough drivers and other warm blooded creatures
as for ski resort owners—procurers and panders!
when there's no snow in December
I feel wicked and positively sublime.

31

Montreal is so beautiful
winter is unfortunate.

32

the first goddamn snow!
as usual it caught me
in my fall sweater.

33

Spring?
I wait and wait and wait;
peer at shrubs,
the neighbours don't know what to make
of this crazy Black woman

rooting in their gardens
looking for green leaves;
in only March at that.

34

comrade winter,
if you weren't there
and didn't hate me so much
I probably wouldn't write poems.

35

Bottles of brandy
beer and eggs for breakfast
jogging in 10 degrees below
past the all night donut shop,
marathon scrabble
going to sleep at 5 a.m.
shorten the days before summer.

36

For Filomena Maria

says she turns greenish yellow,
'infesada' in the winter,
far from an Azorian childhood,
cliffs the colour of roses,
language sounding like full kisses in warmer climes
tighten on the lips of this winter:
Saudade Agua Retorta.

37

I've arranged my apartment
so it looks as if I'm not here
I've put up bamboo blinds
I've strung ever green hedera helix
across my kitchen window
I've bought three Mexican blankets
to put on the walls
I've covered the floors in Persian rugs
(or some reasonable facsimile)
hung pictures of Che and my childhood
bought a rattan-chair—peacock throne
and I've papered my book cases with Latin American writers
I feel like I'm in Canton, Oaxaca, Bahrain and Cocale
now,
If only I could get York Borough to
pass a city ordinance authorizing
the planting of Palm trees along
Raglan Avenue—
my deception will be complete.

38

Only the sound of the light poles
only the sound of the refrigerator
only the sound of the stereo
only the sound of the stove
only, all the sounds seem to be connected by electric wires.

39

that a moon has to shine!
that a moon has to battle fascist street lights!
that a moon has to get mixed up
in that sordid business of car lights!
that a moon has to constantly watch for ingénue skyscrapers!
Enough to make a moon undignified.

40

Reading the Corporate Pages

I was thinking
that it was a waste to have a moon here,
a moon is not cost efficient.

41

Dec. 18th–20th, 1982

Just to sabotage my epigrams,
the snow fell,
these three days,
softly.
Throwing a silence on the streets
and the telephone wires,
whiffling against the north side of the trees.
Two days ago it began,
falling,
so slowly,
3 a.m., Sunday driving along Bloor Street,
Tony, Filo, Pat, Roberto and I

singing to Oklahoma, to a sailor in Valparaiso
and to Billie Holiday
with no wind to witness, to curse us
and this tender snow.
Walking down Greensides Avenue now,
I think someone sitting in a house this minute
and looking through a window at this silence,
cannot be a fascist,
Everyone is covered by this silence
no one can be thinking of how to oppress anyone else
they will have to think of how silent it is
and how to shovel this quiet snow,
no one can make a telephone call
or press a button
or utter a racist slur in this gentleness
they will be struck by their own weakness
they will recognize this silence,
this sphinx of a snowfall.
Just to sabotage my epigrams,
the snow fell,
these three days,
softly.

42

Monday: I am one of one hundred
against the United States
in a demo for Nicaragua
the snow, still falling, softly.

43

Oh yes, there it is
the kind that grows cruelty
there it is
what a wind!
the kind that gives a headache
that makes a Christian,
that sculpts a grim mouth
there it is
the one that blows on reservations
and Jarvis Street.

44

Charles Fowler—1981

Spadina and Baldwin—
the last time I saw Charles Fowler
the wind stung him as he took the corner
went straight through, cutting
his grey hair and his sallow skin;
he had spilled out of the Paramount
in a chain reaction to the twelve beers
pitched up by his stomach—gagging him,
trying to make it south on Spadina
his coat abandoned him, colluding
with the vicious wind and his fingers too,
escaping, just when he found them
buttons on his coat would disappear
London where he was born
Montreal where he met Rose
Toronto
eighty years of being mast and sail
to this wind.

45

—winter suicide—

shall I do it then,
now, here,
a riddle for Februarys,
shall I,
here, under this Mexican blanket
clutching my dictionary (Vol. II the shorter
Oxford Marl-Z),
Shall I do it before falling asleep
before the summer comes
before seeing the Chicago Art Ensemble again,
maybe if Betty Carter never sang,
or Roscoe Mitchell never touched a saxophone;
losing my life like that though,
mislaying the damn thing,
and right in the middle of winter,
me!
and it gone
flown
shall I chew the berries
which I collected before the freeze.

46

some one in the window
across the way
above the coffee drinker
stood
watching me
then he showed me his penis,
how quickly we've established this intimacy.

47

coffin of a winter!

48

sweet tyrone
don't fuck up my night,
Halifax to Toronto
in the dead of winter,
my hands are numb,
gimme back my gloves.

49

carabid of a winter
it chews my ears
and my toes
it gnaws on the extremities.

50

season of ambiguity
blinding sun, cold air
days imitating night
me, here.

51

I had planned the answer all my life
rehearsed my 'fuck offs'
practiced my knee to the groin
decided to use violence;
now, leaving the train at Montreal,
gone!
all my rebuttals,
all my 'racist pig'
nothing,
dried up!
iron teeth of the escalator
snickering like all of 'them',
my legs stiff as the cold outside,
my eyes seeing everything in blood,
a piece of cloth,
a white mound of flesh atop
like a cow's slaughtered head,
emitting,
'whore, nigger whore'.

52

at first I thought
it was because I had no money
and no job and no friends
and no home and no food
then I realized that it was because of February again.

53

Two things I will not buy
in this city,
mangoes and poinsettia;
exiled,
I must keep a little self respect.

54

comrade winter,
look what you've done,
I have written epigrams to you,
e'en poems,
can it be that . . . ?
No, no, I am not your lover,
Perhaps . . . your enemy.

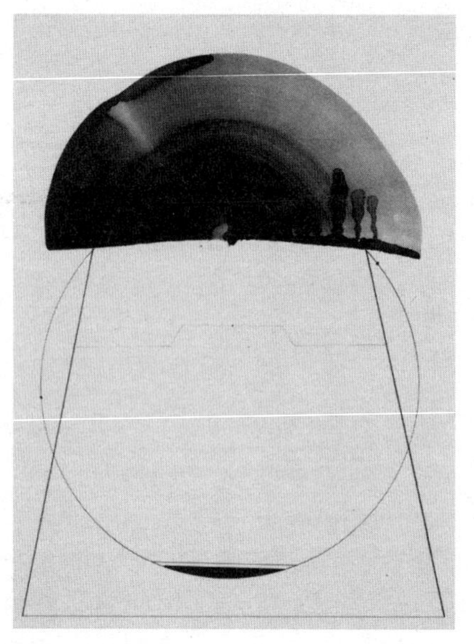

EPIGRAMS TO ERNESTO CARDENAL IN DEFENSE OF CLAUDIA

1

I've handed out leaflets at subway stations
crying death to the murdering policemen,
I'm sure the RCMP has my name, my picture,
my letters and now my poems.
You don't even return my calls!

2

These verses are for you Ernesto,
not for all my lovers
whom I bad mouth in these lines,
poor things, they were smaller than these epigrams,
but a poet's ego needs entire pages.

3

If you were there when I came home
after that poetry reading on Spadina,
if you were there when I needed no talking
after that man told me that he liked my poems
but not my politics (as if they are different),
if you were there instead of that empty fellow
I slept with,
you would have held my head, kept me warm
and asked me for nothing else.

4

that cold boy I slept with
believed stories
about cannibalism,
he woke up every morning
in the 19th century,
he wore a pith helmet
to hide his black face,
he didn't know Martin and he didn't know Malcolm
or Garvey or Du Bois or Angela,
he had been trained to be orderly and genteel
in little England,
not to give an opinion either way,
not even if it concerned him.

5

we could never talk, you and I.

6

one year and a half
I wrestled in the trenches
with opportunists, quasi-feminists and their government
friends;
a struggle like that in some places
would be revolutionary, empower a whole people;
here in Toronto
we get a community service
and a congratulatory letter
from the minister of immigration.

7

The other day
when France and England and America and Canada and West Germany
were deciding about south west Africa
I packed my things for Namibia,
the plane ticket would not have been a problem
if I only had a gun.

8

we could never make love, you and I
it always has an edge to it
a touch of disbelief.

9

poorest Claudia,
to the barrio
to bare feet
to a boy's sweaty hand
to lipstick from America
to the Hilton hotel
to the carnivorous neon signs
to the electricity shortage
to the banks
to a vulgar sunset
to the ocean.

10

oh! Why do you laugh?
so you think making cruise missiles
for human beings
is more sophisticated, more astute
than poison tipped arrows.

11

Often Ernesto,
little girls are quite desperate.

12

How do I know that this is love
and not legitimation of capitalist relations of production
in advanced patriarchy?

13

Often Ernesto,
women are quite desperate.
Often in your glance
we wish to be invisible.

14

so we spent hours and hours
learning Marx,
so we picketed embassies and stood
at rallies,
so it's been 13 years agitating
for the liberation of Africa,
so they still think, I should be in charge
of the refreshments.

15

the last time I fell in love
was 1972,
then there was Chile and Mylai,
all the Panthers were killed,
Angela was sent to jail,
the guy who did that in California
was rewarded in Washington,
Andrew Young gave up a martyr's day
for a corporate suit
and a lot of other betrayals.

16

I can't speak
for girls of the bourgeoisie,
but girls like me can't wait
for poems and men's hearts.

17

some Claudias are sold to companies,
some Claudias sell to street corners,
even debasement has its uptown,
even debasement has its hierarchy.

18

poorest Claudia,
to the love of a poet
to the singing of a madrigal
to the dictator's American shoes
to the wall
to the afternoon blossoms
to the escape across unknown borders
to the perfume of a freedom.

19

nights have waited for me also
hot and desperate, but cool
the weakened street lights
half of the coca cola sign blinking

another country
the boy leaning on the pole at the Esso station
—there's a flower's smell
which wraps around my face in the night
pale, a yellow-petalled whorl
stretched like a tongue
a taste for night insects
blind ephemera fly into the sweet murky smell—
there's an older woman waiting too
near a hibiscus shrub
the face, dark and knowing, her gaze
bigger than the weakened street lights
what had I given
the boy leaning on the pole at the Esso station
—nothing Ma—

20

Beauty for now, is a hot meal
or a cold meal or any meal at all.

21

so I'm the only thing you care about?
well what about the incursions into Angola,
what about the cia in Jamaica,
what about El Salvador,
what about the multi-national paramilitaries
in South Africa,
and what do you mean by 'thing' anyway?

22

If you don't mind,
can I just sit here today?
Can I not be amusing please?

23

when I saw the guerrillas march into Harare
tears came to my eyes
when I saw their feet, a few
had shoes and many were bare
when I saw their clothes, almost
none were in uniform
the vanquished were well dressed.

24

Carbines instead of M16s
manure explosives instead of cluster bombs
self criticism instead of orders
baskets full of sulphur instead of washing.

25

That is how we took Algiers and Ho Chi Minh city and Maputo and
Harare and Managua and Havana
and St. George's and Luanda and Da Dang and Tet and Guinea
and . . .

26

I wanted to be there.

27

Dear Ernesto,
I have terrible problems convincing
people that these are love poems.
Apparently I am not allowed to love
more than a single person at a time.
Can I not love anyone but you?
signed,
'Desperate'.

28

Of these soccer tournaments, Selwyn,
of this strutting,
of this herding in playing fields,
of this head knocking and ritualistic dirty talk,
of these decorative cheerleaders
and mannequined man-hunters,
of these incantations over smelly socks, jock straps and shorts,
why so grim?

29

you're lucky I have a bad memory
or I'd remember that red hot arrow
in my ribs,

that feeling of turning to water,
I'd recollect that stupefied look I carried
on my face for three years,
all the signs, they said,
you're lucky I have such a bad memory
for names, faces
or I'd remember that I loved you
then.

30

Ars Hominis/the manly arts

Since you've left me no descriptions
having used them all to describe me
or someone else I hardly recognize
I have no way of telling you
how long and wonderful your legs were;
since you've covetously hoarded all the words
such as 'slender' and 'sensuous' and 'like a
young gazelle'
I have no way of letting you know
that I loved how you stood and how you walked,
and forgive my indelicacy,
your copulatory symmetry, your pensile beauty;
since you've massacred every intimate phrase
in a bloodletting of paternal epithets
like 'fuck' and 'rape', 'cock' and 'cunt',
I cannot write you this epigram.

31

At least two poets,
one hundred other women that I know, and I,
can't wait to become old and haggard,
then, we won't have to play coquette
or butch—
or sidle up to anything.

32

Have you ever noticed
that when men write love poems
they're always about virgins or whores
or earth mothers?
How feint-hearted.

33

Ars Poetica

Yes, but what else was done
except the writing of calming lines
except sitting in artsy cafes
talking artsy talk.
what else except marrying three wives
beating them, flying into tantrums,
except tonal voices, bellicose sermons,
self-indulgent dulcimer expurgations
about fathers and women
what else was done, except
a disembodied anxiety, anger unable
to find a table to bang or a door to slam

what when the chance to speak is only taken
when it is not necessary, past,
what when the chance is lost,
what when only doodlings mark a great stone
visits to the asylum mark a great poet
and freedom is personal
yes what then was done except a poser
worse, a mole has infiltrated poems.

34

Ars Poetica (II)

Cow's hide or drum
don't tell me it makes no difference
to my singing,
I do not think that histories are so plain,
so clumsy and so temporal;
griots take one hundred years
to know what they say
four hundred more to tell it;
I want to write as many poems as Pablo Neruda
to have 'pared my fingers to the quick'
like his,
to duck and run like hell from numbing chants.

—Pablo Neruda in 'Ars Poetica (I)' for *Fin de Mundo.*

35

Ars Poetica (III)

'on being told that being Black is being bitter'

give up the bitterness
he told my young friend/poet
give it up and you will be beautiful.
after all these years and after all these words
it is not simply a part of us anymore
it is not something that you can take away
as if we held it for safekeeping,
it is not a treasure, not a sweet,
it is something hot in the hand, a piece of red coal,
it is an electric fence, touched,
we are repulsed, embraced and destroyed,
it is not separate, different,
it is all of us, mixed up in our skins,
welded to our bones
and it cannot be thrown away
not after all these years, after all these words
we don't have a hold on it
it has a hold on us,
to give it up means that someone dies,
you, or my young poet friend
so be careful when you say give up the
bitterness.
let him stand in the light for a moment
let him say his few words, let him breathe
and thank whoever you pray to
that he isn't standing on a dark street
with a brick,
waiting for you.

36

we have not received the info yet
but a state of siege has been declared,
the corporate generals conferred,
the joint chiefs of staff consolidated.
In 1980
there was a coup, un golpe,
a military junta, or 'djunta'
as their propagandists say, took over,
a military regime seized power
in the United States.
Careful, this is not a metaphor.

37

you can't say that there's rationing here
you can't complain about the meat shortage
we have a good democratic system here in Transkei
you can't say there is only so much milk or so much butter
you can't say that there are line-ups
you can't bad-talk food on this Bantustan
you can't put goat-mouth on it just like that.
If you don't have a cow you can't
say there's no butter.

38

For Grenada

In St. George's
there are hills, I hear,
to make me tired

and there is work, I know,
to make me thinner.

39

And take these too Ernesto
as I give them
once more with gratitude
I wish I was with you,
you let me look at 'Managua in the evening sky',
such a sky, memorious and red,
repels cruelties from the Honduran border.

40

Imitation of Cardenal

If Hitler waits at the corner of the Schmiedtor
and a girl is walking along the Landestrasse with her mother
and Hitler cannot dance
and everything is full of kisses
and Hitler cannot dance
so Hitler goose steps
and a girl dances with her mother and a cadet
and a girl walking now with her mother, with a cadet
is not to blame because Hitler has no rhythm
and a girl dances with her mother and a cadet
a girl bebops
and Hitler goose steps
and Hitler finger snaps a war song
a girl is not to blame.

41

The night smells of rotten fruit
I never noticed before
the cicala's deliberate tune,
something about it frightens me
as always,
as when hallucinating with a fever
I saw the mother of the almond tree
shadow me in my hot bed.
Say say stay, say go say!
The night decays with fruit
Dense with black arrangements.

42

And I am so afraid
of all of them
and this tenderness.

43

Isn't it fitting
that Black porters guard the portals
of museums in Paris,
themselves bagged
by elephant guns,
set, between the other objects d'art.
Isn't it fitting
that in the Georges Pompidou,
a Black porter
guards Picasso's 'Guitar'.
this must be some frenchman's joke,
some couturier's idea of a wild design.

44

They sent me this envelope yesterday
they sent me this envelope the day before
there was another the day before that
today they sent me a thick book on
Canada's relations with Latin America and the Caribbean,
all of this with no provocation;
Roger says civilisation is paper,
I call this institutional slaughter.

45

his name meant ruler, king in Yoruba
or god or something . . .
and even though I was an atheist
and a socialist, I went with him,
not holding his name against him,
liking it because it wasn't
george or harold—slave names! I spat—
what a love! This Yoruba name:
Olu Fisoye Ojo Ajolabi!
beautiful for introductions and greetings,
venerable and original,
grandiose and lyrical as mother earth—
Yoruba Land,
a name like adire cloth
a name like asoke weave
Until he said: 'the poor want to be poor,
nothing's holding them back, they're just lazy.'
then as serf of his majestic name and tradition
of beaten gold,
as serfs will, I shouted at him:
colonized lackey! comprador! traitor!
adire cloth turn to shreds!

death of a closet monarchist! (served me right)
beautiful appellation of contradictions!
I could not live with him
even though he would have paid the rent,
and, well, it was never personal anyway.

46

I've said too much already
dare I name the rest
they'll sue me for my epigrams
ah! What the hell:
Jason, Clyde, Kwesi,
Oh no not dear Harold, Jesus Christ,
the United States, Pinochet,
David, D'aubuisson, Botha,
Litton, ibm, Seaga, Tom Adams
colonialism, sleezy Ronald, Thatcher,
apartheid, oops! It's not a human
rights issue, James Bay,
Indian affairs, Sweet Eddie,
Sunday nights . . .

47

you say you want me to . . .
to what?
no I can't tap dance
at the International Women's Day rally.

48

Claudia dreams birthday cakes
and mauve bougainvillea
Claudia dreams high heeled shoes
orchid bouquets, french perfume,
Sel Duncan Dress band,
the Hilton hotel pool, rum and coke,
commercials of the 'free' world
and men civilized by white shirts.

49

yet a woman is always alone,
a case of mistaken identity
dreams are incognito.

50

y toma estos tambien Ernesto
como yo los doy
una vez mas con gratitud
desearia estar contigo
me dejas mirar a 'Managua en el cielo vespertino'
un cielo asi, memorable y rojo,
repele las crueldades de la frontera hondurena.

(trans. by Rodolio Pino)

51

Let's celebrate hungry!
Let's riot.

52

the boys at the seminary college
climbed over the walls
their mouths were open like hippopotamuses
the girls at the girls Presbyterian school
fed the hippopotamuses stone cookies
from their cooking class
mimosa busy bodied through the niches
of the seminary walls
the Poinciana leered red and yellow
above.

53

one kiss
too suspicious.

54

Cardenal, the truth is that
even though you are not a country
or my grandmother
or coconut ice cream
or Marquez's Autumn of the Patriarch
or Sarah Vaughan

or Cuban music
or Brazilian movies
or Kurosawa
or C.L.R.'s *Black Jacobins*
or Angela
or Guayaguayare
I love you for the same things.

CHRONICLES OF THE HOSTILE SUN

(1984)

LANGUAGES

NIGHT—MT. PANBY BEACH—25 MARCH 1983

Many years from now
this surf, this night
of American war ships in Barbados,
Mt. Panby beach with its reef
and sea urchins,
this night of tension
and utterly huge ocean,
I see Orion like an imperialist
straddle the half sky,
a drizzle of rain,
wondering how it is possible
to be fearful and fearless together,
drink another beer,
this night may make it to a poem,
how
the surf so unevenly even
surprises me,
the foam shooting sideways along the rock,
something red blinking far in the ocean

Rose belongs to the militia
the militia is out
rutting in the drizzle and sand,
they are comfy at Camp David,

we are wet and always startled
though for once we have guns,
for this the boy upstairs
—look at his face
so serious and tender—
For this the boy upstairs
must put on his boots and his greens,
and wake me up at 4 a.m.
coming home

First night of the alert
all of us in Managua
and on Morne Rouge Bay
were insomniac,
forgetting bathing suits and rum punches,
anything we ate tasted like dirt,
like dirt again,
and to think, in the afternoon,
the shallow bay held all our talk
and now the evening
and the radio silenced,
in Matagalpa,
on the market hill,
we bawled at the air,
someone must go through something for this,
only this night
afraid of the sea and what's in it
and the reef
with its mollusks and shooting tide,
what a sound!
like a shot part the ear,
the salivary foam on the teeth of the sand,
what a sound!
fresh and frightening,
snatching what's ours again

You cannot swim on Mt. Panby beach
but you can sit

and drink a beer in the evening,
and let your eyes fool you
about the green flash of the descending sun,
this night,
Orion's sword—a satellite,
this bird of night
lifted itself up around the houses on the hill and the fort,
you'd never think
that three hours ago it lay pink
and purpling, hugging the town,
even kissing us,
now, that preying bird of a night
gives comfort to spy planes

Mt. Panby
ditches in the sand,
the spitting surf,
it may not be enough time
to drink a beer
and it's the only thing that this beach is good for,
except for looking at St. George's,
and only the fort and the church

they have classified photographs,
these American warships
secret snapshots of public places,
technologically touched up
Soviet obstacle courses,
they want to invade,
they want to fill our mouths
with medium range missiles,
that is our considered opinion,
since, Mt. Panby
is only good for drinking beer
and looking at St. George's,
and not even the fishmarket,
it must be our mouths they want to fill

This night
with its shamefaced helicopters
may make it to a poem,
this contra of a night
spilled criminals and machismo
on our mountains,
eagle insignaed somocistas
bared talons on the mountains of Matagalpa

we were silent in the car,
all that we had talked about
may be gone
and on the way to Mama's bar that night
we stopped, drawn to a radio
on the dark street,
then the woman holding it said
it's the same news,
they're in Nicaragua,
we looked at each other,
someone said "those bastards".
The street was empty
with all of us standing there

Many years from now
how could it be,
sandflies eat the skin on Mt. Panby beach,
facing the ocean
a look from here can only be a wound,
look! The street empty,
and the bar on Ballast Ground Road,
and the beach and the reef,
and this little bit,
this bay that only knows
the solitary feet of children
splashing in it on Sundays,
this night may make it to a poem.

CALIBISHIE—APRIL 1983

Over Pt. Baptiste,
Marie Galante across the way
on the horizon,
the lights look like a city from here,
mountains from Guadeloupe
disappear in the evening,
but Marie Galante looks like a city
to me, from here,
one of those North American ones
with concrete,
and the water like a wide pavement
except for the surf,
the breakers in the fishing canal,
Calibishie,
volcanic stains,
indiscriminate hills protrude the ocean,
some naked, some avoiding the rocks,
we swam
played a game or two with Yemaya,
sure that we would walk out,
sure that the intractable land
would remain,
wait for us to have our fun.
I cannot tell you the face of Calibishie
I, never good at describing faces,
least of all
those that hurricanes sculpt,
just at the top of one slate black rock,
a tree
tearing its hair out
stood in this attitude,
hard as the rock
at times it pretended to be a masthead
in the fashion of those ships,
a tree,
the hypothesis, the grace of a suicide.

CARIFUNA

This ancient Carib sold me a hat
and sent his ancient son with a gift
for me,
our spectacles did not hide our ancient look,
those ships . . .
discovered and killed us both
now we shared the trinkets left.
He gave me a woven bracelet and small basket,
I gave him this poem and
what a face he had,
right away he knew me,
how can I tell you
this charm of ours, this familial gesture
as if we spoke last night,
the forest of tree ferns and lichen,
the ancient Carib,
his ancient son,
our ancient look,
the forests wait for some recovery,
a new road, a parody of our ancient wound
draws new escutcheons,
I left them in the mountain road,
and I took them with me.

TO ROSEAU

Roseau, you humid
full of Jean Rhys' ghosts
who smile at me as if they are people,
your buildings structure a time
of lattice worked windows,
and lace glimpses of the genteel over us,
Roseau, after I left
I recalled how you really sounded,
it was in children that you sounded best,
a gang of girls burst the humid air
jumping rope
so intensely,
made up their own difficult game,
rivaling the adventure of the hot town,
a chorus of boys too,
one morning,
calling and answering a song,
if I could remember those things,
a universe contained in them,
a separate and complete life,
a game, a cry containing only them,
the lattice work now ornamental.

VIEUX FORT: ST LUCIA

Vieux Fort has its mad people
and its old men playing,
I saw two children with their pot bellies
climb the wood rotted dock,
and the member of parliament step
across the pigs and garbage,
and Vieux Fort has the most wicked sky,
a sky of purple puffs, orange swatches,
a vulgar sky,
the young man in the water
sings and exposes himself,
Vieux Fort has a vengeful sky,
a sky of massive death and massive life,
how can you look at it and the stench below
at once.

LA SOUFFRIERE

leaving Rosehall, Troumaca,
coming down the leeward side,
I could feel how close the sky was,
everywhere this persistent sky,
I was sitting there with it
tied around my head,
a wide grey-black band trailing off,
it was getting dark three steps in front of me,
the three children on the steps had gone home,
in the back of the truck I could touch it.

Rosehall is the top,
past the mud dried yards,
Up at the top leaves in the mornings.

leeward, the quietest of bays,
the most optimistic of people,
walking the dark from the cricket pitch,
twenty miles looking forward and back,
little girl, stop
from Chateau Belart to the hill before Kingstown,
her face toward me
against the immovable dark, shining,
between the wind and the sky,
pitch black now, and her face,
I don't know that I know anything,
that little girl was stronger than I,
but Rosehall, Troumaca, I must tell you
is at the top of the world.

on the windward side,
up Relevel,
Freddie Oliviere fondled his gun
and threatened six generations of estate workers,
sitting in his expensive jeep,
he threatened a woman with a pension

of one dollar a week,
"if I catch any of all you
down in my land . . ."

Your land!
Freddie Oliviere jumped out of his expensive
japanese jeep,
his gun in his pocket,
self righteous imperialism on his face,
"I work my ass off for this land . . ."
"You! You work!
you thief poor people arrowroot money!"

the Atlantic on the windward side
throws up a foam like a drunkard,
a white foam vomiting a green belly in its wake,
Freddie Oliviere talked as if he expected their familiar fear,
livid and wounded by their new tone, angry for
the warmth of their fawning and obeisance,
confident that the gun he fondled,
and his truck, and his vanload of henchmen behind
would silence these eight old upstarts:
"your land!
you work!
you thief poor people arrowroot money!"

*

Union
ink-blue water
around you, gnarl or crusty turtles
in blue
peacock
blood
batons, heads, blood, jail,
huddle there

FOR MARTIN CARTER

yes more
finally it is all more
what else
i recollect nothing
a thief has gone with handfuls
chunks pulled away
handfuls of fruit, pink fleshed stories
a thief sipping pernod
with his moustache and his gold rings
and giving interviews to international correspondents
and his lies
let them take the damn thing
the Esequibo and more
there is no flour
and in a place with so much swamp
no rice
and everybody has been to prison
and we must write on toilet paper
or eat it or hush
and never, never for Walter
no words for Walter, no forgiveness
every bit of silence is full of Walter.

AT A COCKTAIL PARTY

The Caricom ministers of education
opened their meeting with a cocktail party,
exactly what you'd expect,
what with being literate
these dunces grinned,
what a privilege to hold a scotch
and a broad smile,
what a joy
simpering for the dollar bill
from the USAID and Reagan's
Caribbean Basin Initiative,
these blockheads
who knew no more than the route to Miami
had the estate workers for hors d'oeuvres
and licked their bones after dinner
since the flesh was all gone
with the Geest boat to English housewives'
impeccable taste for bananas on which birds
never alighted.
only one, Jackie Creft,
among them said something about literacy, how gauche,
appalled, a pall fell over the party,
briefly,
they nodded attentively at first
lest it seem that they be dullards
someone dropped a line from Shakespeare
and the general patter continued.

ON EAVESDROPPING ON A DELEGATION OF CONVENTIONERS AT BARBADOS AIRPORT

you law unions and conventions of wellwishers
looking to be delighted at problems
where were you when they assassinated Allende
and when El Mercurio tried to steal the peoples' revolution
and when the Gleaner shot down that timid Jamaican,
Manley
where were you with your thoughtful questions
your clerical rectitude, your pastorals, your parsimony
your stamps of approval, your burning morality.
you only wanted to come here
because of the sun.
so you could be with someone who wasn't your wife.
because your wrist watches are one hour behind
the whole damn Caribbean must wait
because you do not know that Murdoch and Thompson
owning all the newspapers in the world
is a violation of free speech,
we cannot close down the Torchlight.
your great virtues
nourished on third world slaughter
your clean hands gesturing up the price of gold
what of Pretoria?
I know, it was before your time
past your discerning eye
(countless crimes are)
but closing newspapers turn your stomachs,
armed with a one inch paragraph from Reuters and AP
you can tell if there is no democracy 10,000 miles away.

Stay at home and watch your soap operas
about your free society
where you are free to be a consumer
where you are free to walk the street
where you are free to demonstrate

where you are free to see the secret files on you
where newspapers print what they like
even if they are lies you will not know
truth is free to be fiction
counting is not an exact science.

EUROCENTRIC

There are things you do not believe
there are things you cannot believe
(in fairness I do not mean women here except
jeane kirkpatrick and the like)
these things
they include such items as
revolutions, when they are made by people of colour
truth, when it is told by your privilege
percussive piano solos, squawking saxophones
rosa parks' life, bessie smith's life and any life
which is not your own,
ripe oranges with green skins,
blacks lynched in the American way,
Orange Free State, Bantustans,
people waking up in the morning, in any place where you
do not live,
people anywhere other than where you live wanting
freedom
instead of your charity and coca-cola,
the truth about ITT or AFL-CIO
until it is a blithe exposé in your newspaper,
women, who do not need men
(even male revolutionaries refuse to radicalize their balls)
housework
massacres more in number than 1 american officer
4 american nuns,
sugar apples, cutlass mangoes, sapodillas,
and an assortment of fruit
which having never rested on your tongue
you name exotic,
chains other than ornamental ones,
war, unless you see burning children;
hibiscus flowers and anthurium lilies
rain, on a beach in the Caribbean.

*

like the tiniest cricket
killed and stained
green bones
between the pages of my book
like the frogs song
chirped and nightly
suddenly and again
I have discovered
how much we are
how many words I need.

SIEGES

AMELIA

I know that lying there in that bed
in that room
smelling of wet coconut fibres
and children's urine
bundled up in a mound
under the pink chenille and cold
sweating sheets
you wanted to escape,
run from that room
and children huddling against you
with the rain falling outside
and flies and mud
and a criminal for a son
and the scent of the sewer heightened
by the rain falling.
on those days
she tried to roll herself
into the tiniest of balls on the bed
on those days she did not succeed
except in turning the bed into a ship
and she, the stranded one
in that sea of a room
floating and dipping
into the waves, the swell

of a life anchored.
I think that she would have been better
by the sea
in Guayaguayare,
but in the town
hot with the neighbours and want
she withered and swelled
and died and left me
after years of hiding
and finally her feet fearful and nervous
could not step on asphalt
or find a pair of shoes.
swimming in the brutish rain
at once she lost her voice
since all of its words contained her downfall.

she gargled instead the coarse water from her eyes
the incessant nights
the crickets call
and the drooping tree,
breathed, in gasps
what was left in the air
after husband and two generations of children.
lying in a hospital bed
you could not live by then
without the contradictions
of your own aggrieved room
with only me to describe the parking lot outside
and your promise, impossible,
to buy me a bicycle,
when they brought your body home
I smiled a child's smile of conspiracy
and kissed your face.

I AM NOT THAT STRONG WOMAN

I am not that strong woman on the mountain
at Castle Bruce
the mountain squarely below her feet
the flesh bursting under her skin
I cannot hold a mountain under my feet,
she dug yams and birthed a cow
I am not the old one
boxes on her head in Roseau
the metred street, she made one hundred turns in it
the pee streaming from her straddled legs
she stood over the gutter,
the hot yellow stream wet her ankles
and the street,
nor the other one on Church Street
skirt tied around her waist
mad
some aged song shared her lips
for many years with a clay pipe.

I am the one with no place to live
I want no husband
I want nothing inside of me
that hates me
these are walls and niches
park benches and iron spikes
I want nothing that enters me
screaming
claiming to be history,
my skin hangs out on a clothes line
drying and eaten by the harsh sun
and the wind threatens to blow my belly
into a balloon
to hold more confusions,
alone is my only rescue
alone is the only thing I chose.

I'll gather my skin like a washerwoman
her hand insisting the wind out,
I will bare my teeth to the sun
let it feel
how it is to be dazzled.

AMELIA CONTINUED . . .

1. I leave everyone on roads
I linger until I am late
I mistake bedrooms for places where people sleep
I scratch letters on mud slides,
of late I am called a mule
not for my hard headedness
but for my abstentious womb.

2. I am in love with an old woman
who bequeathed me a sentence or two
"don't grow up and wash any man's pants,
not even out of kindness"
this, and a bit of spittle
wrapped in old newspaper.

3. now
I forget
hemmed in by sieges and military occupations
languages
I forget the country
I forget myself and wave and smile
Against the twentieth century.

4. Presently I have a vile disposition
it does not appreciate great sunsets
from "the villa" looking over the carenage,
old fort and point salines
not even the afternoon sun
escapes my criticism.

ANTI-POETRY

1. It must be nice to only write
to two or three people
to send yourself a s.a.s.e. in verse
then it does not concern you
whether your poems stink
or whether they're directing traffic

2. It's hell to keep a crowd waiting
for words to describe their insanity
(let me tell you).
those thin cigarette smoking white guys
who are poets
only shit their pants in discreet toilets
they don't feel the crowd eating their faces
I have to hustle poems between the dancers and the drummers
insanity has to be put to dance music.

3. It's not that I'm telling you what to do darling
but get out of it
it's a nasty business
you can't make a living
and your kind don't know nobody in politics
and besides that . . . well let's not continue.

4. If I tell you
what most concerns me
You would think my poems not high enough,
you would forget my metaphors
and cultivate a scorn for me,
you would kill the last word
on your lips about my imagery.

5. It's hell to find pretty words
to describe shit, let me tell you,

I may get beaten up and left for dead
any moment, or more insultingly to the point,
ignored.

6. If I tell you
I don't care much for verses
dropping their patronizing tone
all over my ghastly life,
presuming to decorate my dreary interiors,
taking charge like a general or a mother,
If I tell you I crave the free life of a hussy;
the hurtless life of a catholic priest,
you would drop me like a passenger

7. It's all very well and good
as an idle pastime
to stand around on corners
singing for the hell of it,
when you ask the pedestrians
for a grain of rice
that's when they get nasty my dear,
and want you to lift up your dress.

8. Some one at a party
drew me aside to tell me a lie
about my poems,
they said "you write well,
your use of language is remarkable"
Well if that was true, hell
would break loose by now,
colonies and fascist states would fall,
housework would be banned,
pregnant women would walk naked in the streets,
men would stay home at night, cowering.
whoever it was, this trickster,
I wish they'd keep their damn lies
to themselves.

MILITARY OCCUPATIONS

DIARY—THE GRENADA CRISIS

In the five a.m. dusk
grains of night's black drizzle, first stones
boulders of dark
sprinkle the open face
open eyes, incense of furtive moths
badluck's cricket brown to the ceiling
I am watching two people sleep.

in the morning smoke light
my chest and its arms cover my breasts,
the ground, wet, the night before,
soil scented,
the open vault of the morning,
scented as the beginning and end of everything
after a while, villainy fingers the eyes,
daubs the hills disenchant
and the mouth lies in its roof
like a cold snake.

coals lit
and contained in clay, glowing
a horizon like a morning coal pot,
still an old woman stooping—cold
churches coral their walls on the ridge,

I could exchange this Caribbean
for a good night's sleep
or a street without young men.

the ghost of a thin woman
drifts against the rim of the street,
I thought nothing was passing,
in the grey light before the crying animals,
when I saw her dress and her pointed face,
I am climbing the steps to the garbage dump,
a woman frightens me.

In the pale air overlooking the town
in the anxious dock
where sweat and arms are lost
already,
the ship and the cement
drop against the metal skies,
a yankee paratrooper strangles in his sheet.

prayers for rain,
instead again this wonderful sky;
an evening of the war and those of us looking
with our mouths open
see beauty become appalling,
sunset, breaths of grey clouds streaked red,
we are watching a house burn.

All afternoon and all night,
each night we watch a different
fire burn,
Tuesday, Butler House
Wednesday, Radio Free Grenada
Thursday, The Police Station
A voice at the window looking,
"The whole damn town should burn."
Another, "No too many of us will die."

eyes full of sleep lie awake
we have difficulty eating,
"what's that?" to every new sound
of the war.

In the five a.m. cold light
something is missing,
some part of the body, some
area of the world, an island,
a place to think about,
I am walking on the rock of
a beach in Barbados
looking to where Grenada was
now, the flight of an American bomber
leaves the mark of a rapist in the room.

of every waking,
what must we do today,
be defiant or lie in the
corridor waiting for them,
fear keeps us awake
and makes us long for sleep.

In my chest,
a green-water well,
it is 5 a.m. and I
have slept with my glasses on
in case we must run.

the last evening,
the dock and the sky make one,
somewhere, it has disappeared,
the hard sky sends
military transports,
the darkness and my shoulders
meet at the neck
no air comes up,
we have breathed the last of it.

In the Grand Etang
mist and damp
the road to Fedon
fern, sturdy,
hesitate
awaiting guerrillas.

OCTOBER 19TH, 1983

this poem cannot find words
this poem repeats itself
Maurice is dead
Jackie is dead
Uni is dead
Vincent is dead
dream is dead
lesser and greater
dream is dead in these Antilles
windward, leeward
Maurice is dead, Jackie is dead
Uni is dead, Vincent is dead
dream is dead
i deny this poem
there isn't a hand large enough
to gesture this tragedy
let alone these words
dead insists itself on us
a glue of blood sticks the rest together
some are dead, the others will not mourn
most wait for the death announcements
Maurice is dead, Jackie is dead
Uni is dead, Vincent is dead
dream is dead
lesser and greater
dream is dead
in these Antilles
windward, leeward
reality will die
i refuse to watch faces
back once again
betrayal again, ships again,
manacles again
some of us sold each other
bracelets, undecorative and unholy,

back to god
i cannot believe the sound
of your voice any longer
blind folded and manacled
stripped

Bernard, Phyllis, Owusu, H.A.
what now
back to jails in these Antilles
back to shackles! back to slavery
dream is dead
lesser and greater
drowned and buried
windward, leeward
a dirge sung for ever
and in flesh
three armoured personnel carriers
how did they feel
shot, shut
across Lucas Street
this fratricide, this hot day
how did they feel
murdering the revolution
skulking back along the road
the people watchful,
the white flare
the shots
the shot, the people running,
jump, flying,
the fort, fleeing
what, rumour, not true
please, rearrested not dead,
Maurice is dead
at 9:30 p.m. the radio
Jackie is dead . . .
9:30 p.m. the radio
dream is dead

in these Antilles
how do you write tears
it is not enough, too much
our mouths reduced,
informed by grief
windward, leeward
it is only october 19th, 1983
and dream is dead
in these antilles.

OCTOBER 25TH, 1983

The planes are circling,
the American paratroopers dropping,
later Radio Free Grenada stops for the last time
In the end they sang—
"ain't giving up no way,
no i ain't giving up no way"

the OECS riding like birds on a cow
led America to the green hills of St. George's
and waited at Point Salines
while it fed on the young of the land,
eating their flesh with bombs,
breaking their bellies with grenade launchers

america came to restore democracy,
what was restored was faith
in the fact that you cannot fight bombers
battleships, aircraft carriers, helicopter gunships,
surveillance planes, five thousand American soldiers
six Caribbean stooges and the big American war machine,
you cannot fight this with a machete
you cannot fight it with a handful of dirt
you cannot fight it with a hectare of land free from
  bosses
you cannot fight it with farmers
you cannot fight it with 30 miles of feeder roads
you cannot fight it with free health care
you cannot fight it with free education
you cannot fight it with women's cooperatives
you cannot fight it with a pound of bananas or a handful of
  fish
which belongs to you

certainly you cannot fight it with dignity.
because you must run into the street
you must crawl into a ditch
and you must wait there and watch
your family,
your mother, your sister, your little brother,
your husband, your wife,
you must watch them
because they will become hungry,
and they will give you in to the Americans,
and they will say that you belong to the militia,
or the health brigade,
or the civil service,
or the people's revolutionary army
or the community work brigade,
or the New Jewel Movement—
they will say that you lived in the country,
they will say that you are Cuban,
they will say that you served cakes
at the Point Salines airport fundraising,
they will say that you are human,
they will say
that one day last month
you said that for four and a half years
you have been happy.
they will say all this because they want to eat.

And finally you can only fight it with the silence of your
dead body.

OCTOBER 26TH, 1983

A fortnight like the one in May
without duplicity
sodden and overcast
we would have held them off a few more days,
god, usually so reliable on matters of hardship
could not summon up a drop of rain

OCTOBER 27TH, 1983

And rain does not rust bombers
instead it looks for weaknesses in farm implements

OCTOBER 27TH, 1983—EVENING

the sky does not have the decency
to shut up

AFTER . . .

1. Those in the market square
   they will betray you
   they will eat your food
   and betray you
   they will lift you on their shoulders
   and they will denounce you
   When push comes to shove
   they will have change for an american dollar
   they will pocket your grief
   they will sing hymns to your killers
   the press will report their happiness

2. when we left
   I took my diary, my passport
   and my Brecht,
   this is security too

3. when we left
   friends watched us go
   "so you're leaving
   how lucky for you"
   and we saw
   their "will you send for me?"

ON AMERICAN NUMERACY AND LITERACY IN THE WAR AGAINST GRENADA

Counting in american
you start with 600 cubans,
the next figure in that numeracy
is 1100 cubans,
trouble ascending, move to 200 cubans,
Pi equals zero grenadians
which accounts for the resistance in the hills;
when deploying troops
or actually in most cases, thugs,
send 15,000
if 100 die it's friendly fire
and anyway that's less than if you
only send 500 (percentage wise you know)
when counting casualties in a war
the first is always american,
(for instance the first casualty in El Salvador
as reported in Newsweek was an american
army officer)
the 40,000 salvadoreans are just playing dead
and the grenadians lying face upward in the sun
at Beausejour are only catching flies.

The term "mass grave" does not apply
to those dug by marines or right wing death squads
   in Central America,
A 'pre-emptive strike' or a 'rescue mission'
is not a war,
except to the illiterate and the oppressed
who have no words for death,
therefore no real need for life.

P.S. AMELIA

I must write you this, now
after all this time
I was startled that you left
when I think of it,
I am never lonely for anyone
but you

P.P.S. GRENADA

I have never missed a place either
except now
there was a house
there was a harbour, some lights
on the water, a hammock
there was a road,
close to the cliffs'
frequent view of the sea
there was a woman
very young
her boy much older,
we planted corn and ochroes
and peas in the front garden
though the rats ate the corn
there was a boat,
I made friends
with its owner and he called
me on his way to work each morning
there was another road, the one to Goave,
all the way up looking back
the rainy season greened the hills
dry spells reddened the flambouyant
there was a river
at Concord
seeing it the first time surprised me
big smooth stones, brown and ashen
and women standing in its water
with washing
there was a farm
on a hillside
as most are, forty acres with a
river deep inside, Jason and Brother-
man picked coconuts, the air,
the brief smell of cloves, Rusty
swam naked in the river's pond

after our descent, Jason's room
reminded me of a house when I was
a child, wooden windows, dated magazines
books and no indoor tap,
there was a wall of rock which sank into the street
in the trees and vine and lizards
it cooled the walk from town,
though town was hot and steep whenever I
got to the market it was worth the task,
there was a spot, in the centre of the women
and the produce, near to the blood pudding vendor
a place where every smell of earth and sweat
assailed the nostrils and the skin, I would
end up coming home, with the scrawniest provisions,
I don't know how, it was those women's eyes
and their hands, I'd pass by the best and
buy from the most poor,
there was a tree
at the head of the beach,
Grand Anse, not in a showy spot
but cool and almost always empty
of tourists
the ocean there was calmer, shallow,
more to Filo's liking
sea grapes, that was what the tree grew
sea grapes, not at all like grapes in North America
a tougher skin, a bigger seed
sweet and sour at once,
there was the carenage, street and harbour
dock and motorway
tied up to it sometimes 'the sea shepherd'
'albatross' 'vietnam' 'alistair'
the boats to Carriacou, banana boat, the 'geest' and
the tourist boat—Cunard, envy and
hatred to these last two
"how many rooms in that boat, you think?"
this from Frederick, he's had to sleep in

one with his mother and her husband
and when they come down from country,
two more children.
there was a street
a few more really, perhaps
twenty or so would be accurate, inclined, terraced,
cobbled or mud
when I first saw them I remember blanching
at the labour and resolve required to climb them
I would give more than imagined to see them
as they were,
there was a night swimming in the dark
Grande Anse, Morne Rouge, La Sagesse, with voices
after and brandy,
there was a woman thin and black like
a stick, though she mistrusted me, a foreigner,
I marveled at her
there was a friend,
named for a greek,
storyteller like his namesake Homer
he would promise a favour this afternoon
and return five days later with a wild tale
about his car, his hands, the priorities
of the revolution and his personal safety
or a fight with his uncle.
the post office, its smell of yellowing paper,
stamps, its red iron mail box, wooden
posts, the custom's house, its stacks
of paper filled out by hand in quadruplicate,
its patience, its frustrated waiting lines
lunch hour, noon to one, everything is shut
the day's heat at its triumph,
there was a path
wet with grass, weedy
stones but people rarely walk there preferring
the high path overlooking the town,
another thing,

on Woolwich road, the view on its left
incline, houses leaning down, lines of clothing
pots and flowering brush, the ever present
harbour framed through bits or wide angled
to Point Salines,
there was an hour actually many when
the electricity broke down,
my sister grew angry and I lit candles
and the lamps
looking forward to their secretness,
even when the electricity returned
and all around put on their fluorescent lights
I left the candles burning.
there was a month when it rained
and I did not have an umbrella
or proper shoes,
more pot holes appeared in the streets
and pumpkin vines grew swiftly over Marlene's
doorstep,
that was when the sand in the ocean shifted
and leveled out the deep shelf,
that was when one day the beach was startlingly empty
that was when the sea became less
trustworthy,
after Dominica, St. Lucia, St. Vincent
I came back with such relief I
talked to the taxidriver from Grenville
all the way home,
Birch Grove, Beaulieu
after Vieux Fort and Marigot this was comfortable.

there was Paul,
he was a farmer and very young,
in St. David he taught those young
still
to take care of the earth,
he prayed for rain and good students,
we went to a cricket game at Queen's Park
I slept through half of it,
it was a Sunday and I shook his hand goodbye
deciding that I was not big enough for him,
Sunday too when we drove up to Mt. Moritz
worried, a group of young men stopped talking
as we passed
then began again "they have no right",
that was in the middle of the crisis
the fallen silk cotton tree lay across the pond
still growing
it was older than all of us put together,
Jomo and Damani showed us their passion
fruit tree and I took photographs of them
on the rise of Mt. Moritz and the sea in back.

there was a little rum and anxiety
about the coming week,
but hope, we did not want the newness
of this place to end
then everyone would lose their memory
as in Macondo
it was a new way of seeing everything
even though the sky was still oppressive
and the land smelled of hardship
there was a name for all of this, only
it was never said quite well
but had to do with a freeness which the body felt,
a joy even in the heat,
on bad days I went to the sea
after work, I sat with Chris, the bartender
at the Riviera,
I didn't like the proprietors
they only smiled for tourists but Chris
was good company,
he kept my money and an eye on my belongings
while I dove into the water;
just that was enough, so wide, so womanly
the gaze to the horizon,
I would forget to fill my lungs
for hours, looking to this sea,
once I lay down on the edge
afraid to stand
past the cactus and the prickly shrub
at Point Salines' most eastern tip
the sharpened cliff, the dark blue water
the first meeting of the Atlantic and the Caribbean
gave me vertigo,
that was the last time I went there
before the war,
I suppose that now they've strung barbed wire
between the two

there was a mass of insects, beetles
rain flies, nocturnal
moths, ants
they have a nest in the roof
when I think of getting rid of them
the thought that they are of greater number and stronger
holds me back, they liked dead mosquitos
I pity mosquitos
they die in atrocious ways
in hot candle wax, in pesticide fumes or
smashed against the walls,
I still have no idea what children talk about
even after eavesdropping on conversations of theirs
I have no memory myself, only
that the subjects were of some importance,
nor of traders
two more months would have been sufficient time
to walk past the crates of fruits and provisions
these women, small and ship-like, broad and shrewd
slowly, listening for their constancy
there was that night
when Carol took me to the "turtle back"
after the meeting of banana growers
and we talked about how this island
and the others
made us want and sad
that we could neither go nor stay,
looking at my hands, without a mark,
with self-indulgent palms to fondle paper,
I understood my ill-preparedness
for struggle.
when we left
I took my diaries, my passport and my Brecht
this is security too,
"so you're leaving,
how lucky for you, will you send for me?"

Frederick would be alarmed
that I could not be there when the peas came
that some one else would live in the house,
I left that hat, the one the Carib gave to me
the lamp shades, the Mexican blankets, my
dictionaries, my roads, my evenings
that nuisance breadfruit tree, Dominique promised
to cut it before the next flowering . . .
of course some little facts,
the sea in the night, that part which
the lights outside the Dome make clear,
is warm
warmer than the air, and the water
becomes something other than water, fog,
it rolls, rather, spreads toward the feet.

OLD PICTURES OF THE NEW WORLD

1. They show tourists rolling
on beaches in Barbados
someone told me that this island
is flat and inescapable
just right for american military transports,
this same someone said,
the topography of the island
lacking in gradient or thick forest
gives historical witness to the absence
of slave rebellions,
the slaves having nowhere to run
adopted an oily demeanour.
How history slaps us in the face,
using our own hand too.

2. They show an old
black man
beckoning racists back
to the way it was in Jamaica
a full page ad in the Chicago Sun Times
the slave catcher, the African one,
is a little analysed character,
(being amongst us
it is embarrassing to admit,)
but in contemporary times
whenever the IMF raises the price
on our heads,
whenever the americans want to buy
our skins,
they raise their hands so quickly,
it shocks us.

3. They show a little grenadian boy
eating an orange
with an american soldier

this is the new picture postcard
the new commercial for the new right
the new look for the new colonialism.

4. They show american medical students
coming back to Grenada
now it is safe for them to do their praticals
in imperialism
and to spit on the population.

5. They show grenadian market vendors
and taxi drivers
call Reagan "daddy"
now we understand the class war
and patriarchy.

6. They show george shultz
celebrating the day Columbus discovered Grenada
he shades his eyes with his hands
at Queen's Park
he sees colonies and slaves
like the celebrity of 1498
now we know our place.

7. In the end
I suppose one knows that Eugenia and Adams
and Seaga are compradors,
one knows that they are enemies of the people
and the future,
one knows these saprophytes
will eat on colonialism's corpse until it dries
one knows that they are our class
enemies
but one cannot help feeling betrayed by blood,
one cannot part with the sense of shame
at their voraciousness and our current defeat.

8. now I am frightened
to be alone
not because of strangers,
not thieves or psychopaths
but, the state.

9. they think that I'll forget it
but I won't
and when they think that I've forgotten
they will find a note in the rubble
of the statue of liberty.

FOR STUART

a little red neck in Sudbury
(actually a big red neck, more than six feet tall)
invited me to his radio show
whereupon he seized one of my poems
and using it as evidence, called me
a marxist,
(actually the poem was feminist)
I denied it of course, I'm no
dilettante
I can see what's coming in the country,
anyway, he banged his fist and cursed
on the airwaves,
a suspicious red stain appeared
on his big red neck,
and I thought he was going to hit me,
Stuart was with me,
we just got up and walked out
leaving him to compose himself,
but we couldn't understand which of us he meant
(Stuart being jewish and I black)
when he yelled after us to "go back to where
you came from".
When you get called a marxist
(they use it as a curse you know)
for saying that the americans have no damn right
invading Grenada, (besides this calculation being
totally unscientific)
you know what's coming.

*

I'm sick of writing history
I'm sick of scribbling dates

of particular tortures
I'm sick of feeling the boot
of the world on my breast
my stomach is caving in and
I'm sick of hearing chuckles
at my discomfort
I'm sick of doing literacy work
with north Americans
as they choke on their food and
I'm sick of their hunger
I'm sick of writing new names and dates
of endings.

*

I am now in Saskatchewan
on a bus passing through Blackstrap
I doze off watching the snow
interrupted by grain silos
I must explain imperialism again
in a library in Saskatoon
thankfully there are some old CCFers
in the crowd.

*

four hours on a bus across alberta and saskatchewan
not in all the months standing over frozen river
antigonish at the wood stove should not come next to
right wing Calgary which after all is self conscious and
naked oil and people gone apartment for rent only one
woman who gave her room and her boots signal of a heart
and poor amal says that she grows shorter there taking

what is fear to Saskatoon to meet strangers plead innocence
explain why we had guns to defend against nuclear arms
do not remember the trip back edmonton crossed paths with
another third world supplicant before ignorance plead dead
edmonton at the huge warm room warm paths through blind
snow early morning sleeping through fog driving a young
man who likes to wake up early dark in Saskatoon light in
edmonton gin in the union hall in winnipeg you wonder if
anyone sault ste marie lost luggage for three days swapo
visitors will lie in the same bed next night hurried through
library college public hall slide tapes conviction beg for
help to be left alone the sault just over the border american
television canadian will nuke 'em pugnacious boy in one
prairie town proverbial hope fled not seen in him sixties
clarity sits only in the aged here in Toronto the last
solidarity posters insert the newest names of the fallen
can't wait for construction sites to paste their latest position
on angola nicaragua grenada south africa as if people waited
there for pronouncements never struggle but know the correct
position either way taut cafes eager for montreal a woman
at mcgill back of the car from antigonish long road to Sydney
an area of trees hiding the sign to monastery old as 1750
betrayed dropped off in a ship returning cargo of salted cod
nova scotia instead no remembered continent no black star
back in toronto eyes remaining on that area of trees to monastery
but miners in Sydney understand death explosions strikes long
to Sydney bridge cape Breton john arthur's humour more familiar
to mirabeau farmers closer than far away toronto he said halifax
two days ago no sign of africville sent to preston by big money
a street in exchange for more of our grief yet above in a church
basement someone thanked us for our concern in our welfare but
america was great plead nothing say thanks leave for cherrybrook
digby truro bus knifing maritime winter short grass
fearing no return from coast comfort here it is possible
to go out jump off the land apologies to new brunswick
newfoundland someone on the phone asking for company
solidarity for loss loved in sauteurs one year do you

know what happened there is everyone alright hoarse voiced
don't know they have people in crates at the airport they
were bombing when you were there grenville too did you
so and so you didn't hear sorrow is the hoarse voice then
the small expectant voice on the other end filling in stories
gaps time between this year and that village between renew
a friend never met before ringing of unfinished in the cold
hotel room 7 a.m. glad to go home only the wind and fog and
weepy Sydney holds the plain to the edge of this continent.

*

the metropolis
blocks of sturdy brick
iron street
concrete tree
planes, helicopters, bombs
will probably never touch this.

*

I am not a refugee,
I have my papers,
I was born in the Caribbean,
practically in the sea,
fifteen degrees above the equator,
I have a canadian passport,
I have lived here all my adult life,
I am stateless anyway.

*

after the glare the red trees the black grass the green sea the bronze sky the black grass the red sky the bronze sea the trees the black trees the red grass the green sea the green sky.

5TH ANNIVERSARY

we drank beer to the revolution
and we imagined mama's bar
and the dancing on the carenage
we savoured what we might
if we were there and if it all
never happened, of course it did
and this fifth must be done in exile
and with an american permit for those at home.

"... OVER THE RADIO I HEAR THE VICTORY BULLETINS OF THE SCUM OF THE EARTH ..."

—Brecht—The Darkest Times

The varnished table
beside it, the short wave radio
the foreign news ricochets off the white wall
behind. Spotted at dead mosquito intervals
I listen for what europe is doing. Voice of america is insipid
The BBC tells me when they will attack
disinformation about more killed/under the curfew.
We know that they are coming.

In the small corridor
soft concrete walls absorb the olive paint
minutely cratered and close to the eye's burnt rim
above and pushing the surrounding air away
from the skin. A bomber splits the surface,
the radio—radio free goes silently
wind leaves my centre, to the bottom of the
millennium again.

The old wooden desk,
pamphlet boxes, letter from unions, the minutes
of the central committee of the NJM. Newspaper clippings
I collect any information, photographs, snatches of news
The short wave radio, my fingers coax the dial
adjusting the antennae. I listen for news of uprisings
The Americans have given out 20,000 medals
for conquering the hundred and thirty-three square miles
consisting Grenada.

The office outside
against what is an eternity of muted faces
impenetrable city blocks, grey-brown torpor
I have bought my third short wave radio
each hour with priestly reverence it intones

‘we’re fighting marxist leninist totalitarianism here’
each hour foreign ministers and U.S. congressman
briefed and sheepish on Latin America and the Caribbean
stutter the litany, ‘. . . marxist Leninist totalitarianism’.

on the radio a peasant becomes a terrorist
on the radio a bit of land is a grave
on the radio disgusting and brutish again
a message from 1940, national security decision
directive 138, a bill against all acts or likely acts
of international morality,
they’re not after criminals,
they’re after you.

*

In the hotel
something woke me
there was no noise
no voice
no radio
none of my companions
things would happen now, without me.

NO LANGUAGE IS NEUTRAL

(1990)

HARD AGAINST THE SOUL

I

this is you girl, this cut of road up
to Blanchicheuse, this every turn a piece
of blue and earth carrying on, beating, rock and
ocean this wearing away, smoothing the insides
pearl of shell and coral

this is you girl, this is you all sides of me
hill road and dip through the coconut at Manzanilla
this sea breeze shaped forest of sand and lanky palm
this wanting to fall, hanging, greening
quenching the road

this is you girl, even though you never see it
the drop before Timberline, that daub of black shine
sea on bush smoke land, that pulse of the heart
that stretches up to Maracas, La Fillete bay never know
you but you make it wash up from the rocks

this is you girl, that bit of lagoon, alligator
long abandoned, this stone of my youngness
hesitating to walk right, turning to Schoener's road
turning to duenne and spirit, to the sea wall and sea
breaking hard against things, turning to burning reason

this is you girl, this is the poem no woman
ever write for a woman because she 'fraid to touch
this river boiling like a woman in she sleep
that smell of fresh thighs and warm sweat
sheets of her like the mitan rolling into the Atlantic

this is you girl, something never waning or forgetting
something hard against the soul
this is where you make sense, that the sight becomes
tender, the night air human, the dull silence full
chattering, volcanoes cease, and to be awake is
more lovely than dreams

RETURN

RETURN

I

So the street is still there, still melting with sun
still the shining waves of heat at one o'clock
the eyelashes scorched, staring the distance of the
park to the parade stand, still razor grass burnt and
cropped, everything made indistinguishable from dirt
by age and custom, white washed, and the people . . .
still I suppose the scorpion orchid by the road, that
fine red tongue of flamboyant and orange lips
muzzling the air, that green plum turning fat and
crimson, still the crazy bougainvillea fancying and
nettling itself purple, pink, red, white, still the trickle of
sweat and cold flush of heat raising the smell of
cotton and skin . . . still the dank rank of breadfruit milk,
their bash and rain on steps, still the bridge this side
the sea that side, the rotting ship barnacle eaten still
the butcher's blood staining the walls of the market,
the ascent of hills, stony and breathless, the dry
yellow patches of earth still threaten to swamp at the
next deluge . . . so the road, that stretch of sand and
pitch struggling up, glimpses sea, village, earth
bare-footed hot, women worried, still the faces,

masked in sweat and sweetness, still the eyes
watery, ancient, still the hard, distinct, brittle smell of
slavery.

PHYLLIS

Phyllis, quite here, I hear from you
not even from your own hand in a note
but from some stranger who dragged it
from a prison wall, a letter running
like a karili vine around Richmond Hill
Phyllis, I know they treat you bad
like a woman
I know is you one there and I
never forget how one night you give
me a ride in your car
and I never forget your laugh like a bronze bauble
hanging in that revolutionary evening
Phyllis, when you sit down and explain
the revolution, it did sound sweet and it
did sound possible.

Phyllis, quite here, I hear how
you so thin now, but still strong
your voice refusing departures and
soldiers cursing, your voice ringing through
bars with messages to keep up the struggle
now buried in death bed and prison wall,
I know they treat you bad
like a woman
called you *hyena*, a name enjoining
you alone to biology and not science,
you should have known
the first thing they would jump on
was the skill of your womb
Phyllis, I remember your laugh, luminous
and bubbling in the flaming dark evening
and the moment after, your eyes serious,
searching for your glasses.

Girl, how come is quite here I hear from you,
sitting in these rooms, resenting this messenger,
out here, I listen through an upstart castigate
Fidel, scraping my chair to interrupt him,
just to see if you send any explanations,
I know they treat you bad
like a woman
you, bewitched in their male dramas,
their comess and their tay tay,
you, foundered, as Bernard said, in all
the usual last minute domestic things
a housewife has to do
Phyllis, they said you defied the prison guards
and talked through their shouts to be quiet
your laugh clanging against the stone walls
your look silencing soldiers.

For Phyllis Coard
Minister of Women's Affairs in the People's Revolutionary
Gov't. of Grenada, 1979-1983, imprisoned at Richmond
Hill Prison in Grenada for her role in a coup.

JACKIE

Jackie, that first evening I met you, you thought I was a child to be saved from Vincent's joke, I was a stranger in the room that your eyes vined like a school teacher's folding me in, child, to be taken care of. An afternoon on that grand beach you threw your little boy among the rest of children in the hissing ocean surf, dreaming an extraordinary life, an idea fanning La Sagesse and Carib's Leap then slabs of volcanic clay in a reddened ocean, perhaps even larger. Jackie, gently, that glint of yellow in your eyes, end of a day, cigarette smoke masking your tiredness and impatience with this gratuitous rain of foreign clerks, then you talked patiently, the past burning at the back of your head. That day on the last hill, bright midday heat glistened on your hands you were in yellow too, yellow like fire on a cornbird's back, fire at your mouth the colour of lightning, then in the last moment, bullets crisscrossed your temple and your heart. They say someone was calling you, Yansa, thundering for help.

For Jacqueline Creft
Minister of Education in the People's Revolutionary Gov't of Grenada, killed on October 19th, 1983, during a coup.

RETURN

II

From here you can see Venezuela,
that is not Venezuela, girl, that is Pointe Galeote
right round the corner, is not away
over that sea swelling like a big belly woman
that must have been a look of envy

every eye looking out of its black face many years
ago must have longed to dive into the sea woman's
belly swimming to away only to find
Pointe Galeote's nubbly face
back to there and no further than the heat flush

every woman must have whispered
in her child's ear, away! far from here!
people go mad here walking into the sea!
the air sick, sibylline, away! go away!
crashing and returning against Pointe Galeote

From here envied tails of water swing out
and back playing sometimeish historian
covering hieroglyphs and naming fearsome artifacts,
That is not footsteps, girl, is duenne!
is not shell, is shackle!

AMELIA STILL

Mama must have left then
that day when I hung out the window
and saw the drabness of the street
and felt that no one lived in the house
any longer, she must have carried herself off to the
bush, grabbed up her own ghost and ran all the way
to Toco, ran all the way out of the hell of us
tied to her breasts and sweeping her brain
for answers. Mama must have fled that day
when I noticed that her shadow
left the veranda and understood that sweet water was
only lyrical in a girl child's wild undertakings
she must have gone hunting for her heart
where she had dropped it as she buried each navel
string hunting, hunting her blood and milk
spread over our stained greedy faces.
Mama must have gone crazy
trying to wrench herself away
from my memory burning around her
and denying her the bread of her death
as food from her mouth
she must have hurried to the Ortoire river
to wash her own hair, take her sweet time
waking up, pitch stones over water,
eat a little sugar, in peace.

BLUES SPIRITUAL FOR MAMMY PRATER

On looking at 'the photograph of Mammy Prater an ex-slave,
115 years old when her photograph was taken'

she waited for her century to turn
she waited until she was one hundred and fifteen
years old to take a photograph
to take a photograph and to put those eyes in it
she waited until the technique of photography was
suitably developed
to make sure the picture would be clear
to make sure no crude daguerreotype would lose
her image
would lose her lines and most of all her eyes
and her hands
she knew the patience of one hundred and fifteen years
she knew that if she had the patience,
to avoid killing a white man
that I would see this photograph
she waited until it suited her
to take this photograph and to put those eyes in it.

in the hundred and fifteen years which it took her to
wait for this photograph she perfected this pose
she sculpted it over a shoulder of pain,
a thing like despair which she never called
this name for she would not have lasted
the fields, the ones she ploughed
on the days that she was a mule, left
their etching on the gait of her legs
deliberately and unintentionally
she waited, not always silently, not always patiently,
for this self portrait
by the time she sat in her black dress, white collar,
white handkerchief, her feet had turned to marble,
her heart burnished red,
and her eyes.

she waited one hundred and fifteen years
until the science of photography passed tin
and talbotype for a surface sensitive enough
to hold her eyes
she took care not to lose the signs
to write in those eyes what her fingers could not script
a pact of blood across a century, a decade and more
she knew then that it would be me who would find
her will, her meticulous account, her eyes,
her days when waiting for this photograph
was all that kept her sane
she planned it down to the day,
the light,
the superfluous photographer
her breasts,
her hands
this moment of
my turning the leaves of a book,
noticing, her eyes.

NO LANGUAGE IS NEUTRAL

No language is neutral. I used to haunt the beach at
Guaya, two rivers sentinel the country sand, not
backra white but nigger brown sand, one river dead
and teeming from waste and alligators, the other
rumbling to the ocean in a tumult, the swift undertow
blocking the crossing of little girls except on the tied
up dress hips of big women, then, the taste of leaving
was already on my tongue and cut deep into my
skinny pigeon toed way, language here was strict
description and teeth edging truth. Here was beauty
and here was nowhere. The smell of hurrying passed
my nostrils with the smell of sea water and fresh fish
wind, there was history which had taught my eyes to
look for escape even beneath the almond leaves fat
as women, the conch shell tiny as sand, the rock
stone old like water. I learned to read this from a
woman whose hand trembled at the past, then even
being born to her was temporary, wet and thrown half
dressed among the dozens of brown legs itching to
run. It was as if a signal burning like a fer de lance's
sting turned my eyes against the water even as love
for this nigger beach became resolute.

There it was anyway, some damn memory half-eaten
and half hungry. To hate this, they must have been
dragged through the Manzanilla spitting out the last
spun syllables for cruelty, new sound forming,
pushing toward lips made to bubble blood. This road
could match that. Hard-bitten on mangrove and wild
bush, the sea wind heaving any remnants of
consonant curses into choking aspirate. No
language is neutral seared in the spine's unravelling.
Here is history too. A backbone bending and
unbending without a word, heat, bellowing these
lungs spongy, exhaled in humming, the ocean, a
way out and not anything of beauty, tipping turquoise
and scandalous. The malicious horizon made us the
essential thinkers of technology. How to fly gravity,
how to balance basket and prose reaching for
murder. Silence done curse god and beauty here,
people does hear things in this heliconia peace
a morphology of rolling chain and copper gong
now shape this twang, falsettos of whip and air
rudiment this grammar. Take what I tell you. When
these barracks held slaves between their stone
halters, talking was left for night and hush was idiom
and hot core.

When Liney reach here is up to the time I hear about. Why I always have to go back to that old woman who wasn't even from here but from another barracoon, I never understand but deeply as if is something that have no end. Even she daughter didn't know but only leave me she life like a brown stone to see. I in the middle of a plane ride now a good century from their living or imagination, around me is a people I will only understand as full of ugliness that make me weep full past my own tears and before hers. Liney, when she live through two man, is so the second one bring she here on his penultimate hope and she come and sweep sand into my eye. So is there I meet she in a recollection through Ben, son, now ninety, ex-saga boy and image, perhaps eyes of my mama, Liney daughter. I beg him to recall something of my mama, something of his mama. The ninety year old water of his eyes swell like the river he remember and he say, *she was a sugar cake, sweet sweet sweet. Yuh muma! that girl was a sugar cake!*

This time Liney done see vision in this green guava season, fly skinless and turn into river fish, dream sheself, praise god, without sex and womb when sex is hell and womb is she to pay. So dancing an old man the castilian around this christmas living room my little sister and me get Ben to tell we any story he remember, and in between his own trail of conquests and pretty clothes, in between his never sleeping with a woman who wasn't clean because he was a scornful man, in between our absent query were they scornful women too, Liney smiled on his gold teeth. The castilian out of breath, the dampness of his shrunken skin reminding us, Oh god! laughing, sister! we will kill uncle dancing!

In between, Liney, in between, as if your life could
never see itself, blooded and coarsened on this
island as mine, driven over places too hard to know
in their easy terror. As if your life could never hear
itself as still some years, god, ages, have passed
without your autobiography now between my stories
and the time I have to remember and the passages
that I too take out of liking, between me and history
we have made a patch of it, a verse still missing you
at the subject, a chapter yellowed and moth eaten at
the end. I could never save a cactus leaf between
pages, Liney, those other girls could make them root
undisturbed in the steam of unread books, not me,
admiring their devotion, still I peered too often at my
leaf, eyeing the creeping death out of it and giving up.
That hovel in the cocoa near the sweet oil factory I'll
never see, Liney, each time I go I stand at the road
arguing with myself. Sidelong looks are my specialty.
That saddle of children given you by one man then
another, the bear and darn and mend of your vagina
she like to walk about plenty, Ben said, *she was a*
small woman, small small. I chase Ben's romance as
it mumbles to a close, then, the rum and coconut
water of his eyes as he prepares to lie gently for his
own redemption. *I was she favourite, oh yes.*
The ric rac running of your story remains braided
in other wars, Liney, no one is interested in telling the
truth. History will only hear you if you give birth to a
woman who smoothes starched linen in the wardrobe
drawer, trembles when she walks and who gives birth
to another woman who cries near a river and
vanishes and who gives birth to a woman who is a
poet, and, even then.

Pilate was that river I never crossed as a child. A woman, my mother, was weeping on its banks, weeping for the sufferer she would become, she a too black woman weeping, those little girls trailing her footsteps reluctantly and without love for this shaking woman blood and salt in her mouth, weeping, that river gushed past her feet blocked her flight . . . and go where, lady, weeping and go where, turning back to face herself now only the oblique shape of something without expectation, her body composed in doubt then she'd come to bend her back, to dissemble, then to stand on anger like a ledge, a tilting house, the crazy curtain blazing at her teeth. A woman who thought she was human but got the message, female and black and somehow those who gave it to her were like family, mother and brother, spitting woman at her, somehow they were the only place to return to and this gushing river had already swallowed most of her, the little girls drowned on its indifferent bank, the river hardened like the centre of her, spinning chalk stone on its frill, burden in their slow feet, they weeping, she, *go on home*, in futility. There were dry-eyed cirri tracing the blue air that day. Pilate was that river I ran from leaving that woman, my mother, standing over its brutal green meaning and it was over by now and had become so ordinary as if not to see it any more, that constant veil over the eyes, the blood-stained blind of race and sex.

Leaving this standing, heart and eyes fixed to a skyscraper and a concrete eternity not knowing then only running away from something that breaks the heart open and nowhere to live. Five hundred dollars and a passport full of sand and winking water, is how I reach here, a girl's face shimmering from a little photograph, her hair between hot comb and afro, feet posing in high heel shoes, never to pass her eyes on the red-green threads of a hummingbird's twitching back, the blood warm quickened water colours of a sea bed, not the rain forest tangled in smoke-wet, well there it was. I did read a book once about a prairie in Alberta since my waving canefield wasn't enough, too much cutlass and too much cut foot, but romance only happen in romance novel, the concrete building just overpower me, block my eyesight and send the sky back, back where it more redolent.

Is steady trembling I trembling when they ask me my
name and say I too black for it. Is steady hurt I feeling
when old talk bleed, the sea don't have branch you
know darling. Nothing is a joke no more and I right
there with them, running for the train until I get to find
out my big sister just like to run and nobody wouldn't
vex if you miss the train, calling Spadina *Spadeena*
until I listen good for what white people call it, saying I
coming just to holiday to the immigration officer when
me and the son-of-a-bitch know I have labourer mark
all over my face. It don't have nothing call beauty
here but this is a place, a gasp of water from a
hundred lakes, fierce bright windows screaming with
goods, a constant drizzle of brown brick cutting
dolorous prisons into every green uprising of bush.
No wilderness self, is shards, shards, shards,
shards of raw glass, a debris of people you pick your way
through returning to your worse self, you the thin
mixture of just come and don't exist.

I walk Bathurst Street until it come like home
Pearl was near Dupont, upstairs a store one
Christmas where we pretend as if nothing change we,
make rum punch and sing, with bottle and spoon,
song we weself never even sing but only hear when
we was children. Pearl, squeezing her big Point
Fortin self along the narrow hall singing *Drink a rum*
and a . . . Pearl, working nights, cleaning, Pearl beating
books at her age, Pearl dying back home in a car
crash twenty years after everything was squeezed in,
a trip to Europe, a condominium, a man she suckled
like a baby. Pearl coaxing this living room with a
voice half lie and half memory, a voice no room
nowhere could believe was sincere. Pearl hoping this
room would catch fire above this frozen street. Our
singing parched, drying in the silence after the
chicken and ham and sweet bread effort to taste like
home, the slim red earnest sound of long ago with the
blinds drawn and the finally snow for christmas and
the mood that rum in a cold place takes. Well, even
our nostalgia was a lie, skittish as the truth these
bundle of years.

But wait, this must come out then. A hidden verb
takes inventory of those small years like a person
waiting at a corner, counting and growing thin
through life as cloth and as water, hush . . . Look I
hated something, policemen, bankers, slavetraders,
shhh . . . still do and even more these days. This city,
mourning the smell of flowers and dirt, cannot tell
me what to say even if it chokes me. Not a single
word drops from my lips for twenty years about living
here. Dumbfounded I walk as if these sidewalks are a
place I'm visiting. Like a holy ghost, I package the
smell of zinnias and lady of the night, I horde the taste
of star apples and granadilla. I return to that once
grammar struck in disbelief. Twenty years. Ignoring
my own money thrown on the counter, the race
conscious landlords and their jim crow flats, oh yes!
here! the work nobody else wants to do . . . it's good
work I'm not complaining! but they make it taste bad,
bitter like peas. You can't smile here, is a sin, you
can't play music, it too loud. There was a time I could
tell if rain was coming, it used to make me sad the
yearly fasting of trees here, I felt some pity for the
ground turned hot and cold. All that time taken up
with circling this city in a fever. I remember then, and
it's hard to remember waiting so long to live . . . anyway
it's fiction what I remember, only mornings took a long
time to come, I became more secretive, language
seemed to split in two, one branch fell silent, the other
argued hotly for going home.

This is the part that is always difficult, the walk each night across the dark school yard, biting my tongue on new english, reading biology, stumbling over unworded white faces. But I am only here for a moment. The new stink of wet wool, driving my legs across snow, ice, counting the winters that I do not skid and fall on, a job sorting cards, the smell of an office full of hatred each morning, no simple hatred, not for me only, but for the hated fact of an office, an elevator stuffed with the anger of elevator at 8 a.m. and 5 p.m., my voice on the telephone after nine months of office and elevator saying, I have to spend time on my dancing. Yes, I'm a dancer, it's my new career. Alone in the room after the phone crying at the weakness in my stomach. Dancer. This romance begins in a conversation off the top of my head, the kitchen at Grace Hospital is where it ends. Then the post office, here is escape at least from femininity, but not from the envy of colony, education, the list of insults is for this, better than, brighter than, richer than, beginning with this slender walk against the mountainous school. Each night, the black crowd of us parts in the cold darkness, smiling.

The truth is, well, truth is not important at one end of a hemisphere where a bird dives close to you in an ocean for a mouth full of fish, an ocean you come to swim in every two years, you, a slave to your leaping retina, capture the look of it. It is like saying you are dead. This place so full of your absence, this place you come to swim like habit, to taste like habit, this place where you are a woman and your breasts need armour to walk. Here. Nerve endings of steady light pinpoint all. That little light trembling the water again, that gray blue night pearl of the sea, the swirl of the earth that dash water back and always forth, that always fear of a woman watching the world from an evening beach with her sister, the courage between them to drink a beer and assume their presence against the coral chuckle of male voices. In another place, not here, a woman might . . . Our nostalgia was a lie and the passage on that six hour flight to ourselves is wide and like another world, and then another one inside and is so separate and fast to the skin but voiceless, never born, or born and stilled . . . hush.

In another place, not here, a woman might touch
something between beauty and nowhere, back there
and here, might pass hand over hand her own
trembling life, but I have tried to imagine a sea not
bleeding, a girl's glance full as a verse, a woman
growing old and never crying to a radio hissing of a
black boy's murder. I have tried to keep my throat
gurgling like a bird's. I have listened to the hard
gossip of race that inhabits this road. Even in this I
have tried to hum mud and feathers and sit peacefully
in this foliage of bones and rain. I have chewed a few
votive leaves here, their taste already disenchanting
my mothers. I have tried to write this thing calmly
even as its lines burn to a close. I have come to know
something simple. Each sentence realised or
dreamed jumps like a pulse with history and takes a
side. What I say in any language is told in faultless
knowledge of skin, in drunkenness and weeping,
told as a woman without matches and tinder, not in
words and in words and in words learned by heart,
told in secret and not in secret, and listen, does not
burn out or waste and is plenty and pitiless and loves.

HARD AGAINST THE SOUL

II

I want to wrap myself around you here in this line so
that you will know something, not just that I am dying
in some way but that I did this for some reason. This
grace, you see, come as a surprise and nothing till
now knock on my teeming skull, then, these warm
watery syllables, a woman's tongue so like a culture,
plunging toward stones not yet formed into flesh,
language not yet made . . . I want to kiss you deeply,
smell, taste the warm water of your mouth as warm as
your hands. I lucky is grace that gather me up and
forgive my plainness.

III

She was a woman whose eyes came fresh, saying, I trust you, you will not be the woman who walks out into the Atlantic at Santa Maria and never returns. You cannot dream this turquoise ocean enveloping you in its murmuring thrall, your hands will not arrest in the middle of gazing, you will not happen on an easy thought like this in a hotel room in Guanabo, not on a morning as you watch alone from this beach, the sun dripping orange, or sitting on a marble bench in Old Havana, vacantly. You will not look at your watch on a night in early June and think this gentle sea as good as any for a walk beyond the reflexes of your flesh.

IV

you can hardly hear my voice now, woman,
but I heard you in my ear for many years to come
the pink tongue of a great shell murmuring and
yawning, muttering tea, wood, bread, she, blue,
stroking these simple names of habit, sweeter
and as common as night crumbling black flakes
of conversation to a sleep, repetitious as noons
and snow up north, the hoarse and throaty, I told you,
no milk, clean up . . .

you can hardly hear my voice but I heard you
in my sleep big as waves reciting their prayers
so hourly the heart rocks to its real meaning,
saying, we must make a sense here to living,
this allegiance is as flesh to bone but older
and look, love, there are no poems to this, only
triangles, scraps, prisons of purpled cloth,
time begins with these gestures, this
sudden silence needs words instead of whispering.

you can hardly hear my voice by now but woman
I felt your breath against my cheek in years to come
as losing my sight in night's black pause, I trace
the pearl of your sweat to morning, turning as you
turn, breasts to breasts mute prose we arc a leaping,
and no more may have passed here except
also the map to coming home, the tough geography
of trenches, quarrels, placards, barricades.

v

It is not sufficient here to mark the skin's water or fold,
the back soft, the neck secret, the lips purpled. She
startled me just last night. I heard her singing and
could not dance. I heard her navigate the thick soil of
who we are. Her boundless black self rising,
honeying.

for faith

VI

listen, just because I've spent these
few verses fingering this register of the heart,
clapping life, as a woman on a noisy beach,
calling blood into veins dry as sand,
do not think that things escape me,
this drawn skin of hunger twanging as a bow,
this shiver whistling into the white face of capital, a
shadow traipsing, icy veined and bloodless through
city alleys of wet light, the police bullet glistening
through a black woman's spine in November, against
red pools of democracy bursting the hemisphere's
seams, the heart sinks, and sinks like a moon.

VII

still I must say something here
something that drives this verse into the future,
not where I go loitering in my sleep,
not where the eyes brighten every now and again
on old scores, now I must step sprightly. I dreamless.

VIII

but here, at this spot, all I see is the past
at the museum of the revolution in old Havana
when I should be looking at the bullet hole in Fidel's
camisole or the skirt that Haydee Santamaria wore in
prison, I see a coffle just as I turn, about to leave,
toward my left, toward the future, the woman sitting at
the door black and historic saying to herself this is
only white history, a coffle, shining still after this long
time, new as day under my eyes. I spun in that room,
my voice said *oh dear*, as if I'd only spilt water, *oh
god*, as if my skin had just rubbed this iron silvery with
sweat.

IX

look, I know you went searching on the beach
for my body last night and maybe you will find it
there, one day, but I'll tell you now, it will be on this
beach, or a beach such as this where they made a
revolution, and it will be near that dune where you
oiled your skin darkly against the sun and it will be
because I am not good enough, not the woman to live
in the world we are fighting to make and it will be on a
day like the one when you bought rum for Marta
Beatriz because she said she loved women and you
wanted to believe her, it will be like how we walked
from Marazul to Boca Ciega climbing over the sand
covering the road and after I spend three days
showing you mimosa running and you finally see it.

X

Then it is this simple. I felt the unordinary romance of women who love women for the first time. It burst in my mouth. Someone said, this is your first lover, you will never want to leave her. I had it in mind that I would be an old woman with you. But perhaps I always had it in mind simply to be an old woman, darkening, somewhere with another old woman, then, I decided it was you when you found me in that apartment drinking whisky for breakfast. When I came back from Grenada and went crazy for two years, that time when I could hear anything and my skin was flaming like a nerve and the walls were like paper and my eyes could not close. I suddenly sensed you at the end of my room waiting. I saw your back arched against this city we inhabit like guerillas, I brushed my hand, conscious, against your soft belly, waking up.

I saw this woman once in another poem, sitting,
throwing water over her head on the rind of a country
beach as she turned toward her century. Seeing her
no part of me was comfortable with itself. I envied her,
so old and set aside, a certain habit washed from her
eyes. I must have recognized her. I know I watched
her along the rim of the surf promising myself, an old
woman is free. In my nerves something there
unravelling, and she was a place to go, believe me,
against gales of masculinity but in that then, she was
masculine, old woman, old bird squinting at the
water's wing above her head, swearing under her
breath. I had a mind that she would be graceful in me
and she might have been if I had not heard you
laughing in another tense and lifted my head from her
dry charm.

You ripped the world open for me. Someone said, this
is your first lover, you will never want to leave her. My
lips cannot say old woman darkening any more, she
is the peace of another life that didn't happen and
couldn't happen in my flesh and wasn't peace but
flight into old woman, prayer, to the saints of my
ancestry, the gourd and bucket carrying women who
stroke their breasts into stone shedding offspring and
smile. I know since that an old woman, darkening,
cuts herself away limb from limb, sucks herself white,
running, skin torn and raw like a ball of bright light,
flying, into old woman, I only know now that my
longing for this old woman was longing to leave the
prisoned gaze of men.

It's true, you spend the years after thirty turning over the suggestion that you have been an imbecile, hearing finally all the words that passed you like air, like so much fun, or all the words that must have existed while you were listening to others. What would I want with this sentence you say flinging it aside . . . and then again sometimes you were duped, poems placed deliberately in your way. At eleven, the strophe of a yellow dress sat me crosslegged in my sex. It was a boy's abrupt birthday party. A yellow dress for a tomboy, the ritual stab of womanly gathers at the waist. *She look like a boy in a dress*, my big sister say, a lyric and feminine correction from a watchful aunt, *don't say that, she look nice and pretty*. Nice and pretty, laid out to splinter you, so that never, until it is almost so late as not to matter do you grasp some part, something missing like a wing, some fragment of your real self.

Old woman, that was the fragment that I caught in
your eye, that was the look I fell in love with, the piece
of you that you kept, the piece of you left, the lesbian,
the inviolable, sitting on a beach in a time that did not
hear your name or else it would have thrown you into
the sea, or you, hear that name yourself and walked
willingly into the muting blue. Instead you sat and I
saw your look and pursued one eye until it came to
the end of itself and then I saw the other,
the blazing fragment.

Someone said, this is your first lover, you will never want to leave her. There are saints of this ancestry too who laugh themselves like jamettes in the pleasure of their legs and caress their sex in mirrors. I have become myself. A woman who looks at a woman and says, here, I have found you, in this, I am blackening in my way. You ripped the world raw. It was as if another life exploded in my face, brightening, so easily the brow of a wing touching the surf, so easily I saw my own body, that is, my eyes followed me to myself, touched myself as a place, another life, terra. They say this place does not exist, then, my tongue is mythic. I was here before.

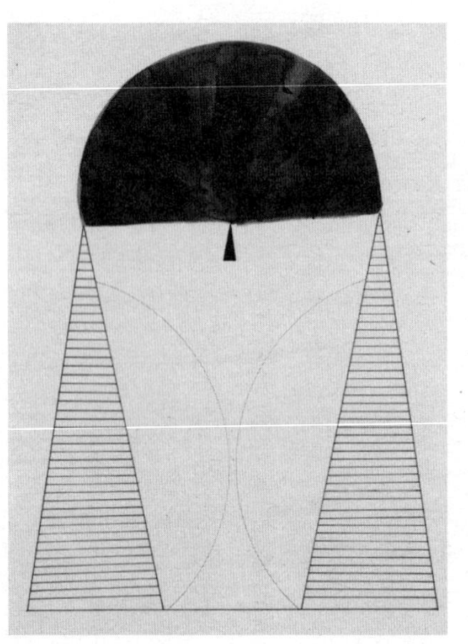

LAND TO LIGHT ON

(1997)

I HAVE BEEN LOSING ROADS

I i

Out here I am like someone without a sheet
without a branch but not even safe as the sea,
without the relief of the sky or good graces of a door.
If I am peaceful in this discomfort, is not peace,
is getting used to harm. Is giving up, or misplacing
surfaces, the seam in grain, so standing
in a doorway I cannot summon up the yard,
familiar broken chair or rag of cloth on a blowing line,
I cannot smell smoke, something burning in a pit,
or gather air from far off or hear anyone calling.
The doorway cannot bell a sound, cannot repeat
what is outside. My eyes is not a mirror.

I ii

If you come out and you see nothing recognisable,
if the stars stark and brazen like glass,
already done decide you cannot read them.
If the trees don't flower and colour refuse to limn
when a white man in a red truck on a rural road
jumps out at you, screaming his exact hatred
of the world, his faith extravagant and earnest
and he threatens, something about your cunt,
you do not recover, you think of Malcolm
on this snow drifted road, you think,
"Is really so evil they is then
that one of them in a red truck can split your heart
open, crush a day in fog?"

I iii

I lift my head in the cold and I get confuse.
It quiet here when is night, and is only me
and the quiet. I try to say a word but it fall. Fall
like the stony air. I stand up there but nothing
happen, just a bank of air like a wall. I could swear
my face was touching stone. I stand up but
nothing happen, nothing happen or I shouldn't say
nothing. I was embarrassed, standing like a fool,
the pine burdened in snow, the air fresh, fresh
and foreign and the sky so black and wide I did not
know which way to turn except to try again, to find
some word that could be heard by the something
waiting. My mouth could not find a language.
I find myself instead, useless as that. I sorry.
I stop by the mailbox and I give up.

I iv

I look at that road a long time.
It seem to close.
Yes, is here I reach
framed and frozen on a shivered
country road instead of where I thought
I'd be in the blood
red flame of a revolution.
I couldn't be farther away.
And none of these thoughts
disturb the stars or the pine
or the road or the red truck
screeching cunt along it.

I v

All I could do was turn and go back to the house
and the door that I can't see out of.
My life was supposed to be wider, not so forlorn
and not standing out in this north country bled
like maple. I did not want to write poems
about stacking cords of wood, as if the world
is that simple, that quiet is not simple or content
but finally cornered and killed. I still need the revolution
bright as the blaze of the wood stove in the window
when I shut the light and mount the stairs to bed.

II i

Out here, you can smell indifference driving
along, the harsh harsh happiness of winter
roads, all these roads heading nowhere, all
these roads heading their own unknowing way,
all these roads into smoke, and hoarfrost, friezed
and scrambling off in drifts, where is this
that they must go anytime, now, soon, immediately
and gasping and ending and opening in snow dust.
Quiet, quiet, earfuls, brittle, brittle ribs of ice
and the road heaving under and the day lighting up,
going on any way.

II ii

I have to think again what it means that I am here,
what it means that this, harsh as it is and without
a name, can swallow me up. I have to think how I
am here, so eaten up and frayed, a life that I was
supposed to finish by making something of it
not regularly made, where I am not this woman
fastened to this ugly and disappointing world.
I wanted it for me, to burst my brain and leap a distance
and all I have are these hoarse words that still owe
this life and all I'll be is tied to this century and waiting
without a knife or courage and still these same words
strapped to my back

II iii

I know as this thing happens, a woman
sucks her teeth, walks into a shop on an island
over there to stretch a few pennies across another
day, brushes a hand over her forehead and leaves,
going into the street empty-handed. Her certainty
frighten me. "Is so things is," she muse, reading
the shopkeeper's guiltless eyes, this hot hope the skin
tames to brooding, that particular advice, don't expect
nothing good. Quite here you reach and you forget.

II iv

no wonder I could get lost here, no wonder
in this set of trees I lose my way, counting
on living long and not noticing a closing,
no wonder a red truck could surprise me
and every night shape me into a crouch
with the telephone close by and the doors
checked and checked, all night. I can hear
everything and I can hear birds waking up
by four a.m. and the hours between three
and five last a whole day. I can hear wood
breathe and stars crackle on the galvanised
steel, I can hear smoke turn solid and this
house is only as safe as flesh. I can hear the
gate slam, I can hear wasps in my doorway,
and foraging mice, there's an old tree next
to my car and I can hear it fall, I can hear
the road sigh and the trees shift. I can
hear them far away from this house late, late
waiting for what this country is to happen,
I listen for the crunch of a car on ice or gravel,
the crush of boots and something coming

II v

A comet, slow and magnificent, drapes the north sky
but I cannot see it, cannot allow it, that would be
allowing another sign. And songs, songs to follow.
What songs can sing this anyway, what humming
and what phrase will now abandon me, what woman
with a gun and her fingers to her lips draw us to another
territory further north, further cold, further on,
into the mouth of the Arctic.
I'm heading to frost, to freezing,
how perhaps returning south heads to fever,
and what I'm saving for another time is all our good,
good will, so not listening, not listening
to any dangling voice or low, lifting whistle.
All the sounds gone out, all the wind died away,
I won't look, won't look at the tail of lighted dust.

III i

In the middle of afternoons driving north
on 35, stopping for a paper and a coffee,
I read the terrifying poetry of newspapers.
I notice vowels have suddenly stopped their
routine, their alarming rooms are shut,
their burning light collapsed

the wave of takeovers, mergers and restructuring
. . . swept the world's . . . blue chips rally in New York
. . . Bundesbank looms . . . Imperial Oil increases dividends
. . . tough cutbacks build confidence

Your mouth never opens to say all this.
The breathful air of words are taken. Swept, yes.
You feel your coffee turn asphalt, you look around
and your eyes hit the dirty corners of the windy store,
stray paper, stray cups, stray oil, stray fumes of gas.
Your mouth never opens, your keys look unfamiliar.

is Microsoft a rapacious plunderer . . . or a benign
benevolent giant . . . rough road ahead

Rough road ahead they say so I leave the gas
station, leaving the paper on the counter,
not listening to the woman calling me back,
my mouth full and tasteless

III ii

Where is this. Your tongue, gone cold, gone
heavy in this winter light.
On a highway burrowing north don't waste your breath.
This winter road cannot hear it and will swallow it
whole. Don't move.
This detail then, when grass leans in certain light.
In other days, blue. This, every week no matter what grows
worse you cannot say you are on the same road, green darkens
or yellows or snows or disappears. Leave me there then,
at 2 p.m. rounding 35 to the 121 hoping
never to return here.

I should have passed, gone my way.

You come to think
the next house one kilometre away might as well
be ten, it so far from love, and shouting would produce
no blood. If I believe anything it will not matter though.
Life is porous, unimaginable in the end, only substance
burning in itself, lit by the heat of touching. It's good
how we melt back into nothing.

III iii

Look, let me be specific. I have been losing roads
and tracks and air and rivers and little thoughts
and smells and incidents and a sense of myself
and fights I used to be passionate about
and don't remember. And once I lost the mechanics, no,
the meaning of dancing, and
I have been forgetting everything, friends, and pain.
The body bleeds only water and fear when you survive
the death of your politics, but why don't I forget.
That island with an explosive at the beginning of its name
keeps tripping me and why don't I recall my life
in detail because I was always going somewhere else
and what I was living was unimportant for the while

Rough Road Ahead

let me say that all the classrooms should be burned
and all this paper abandoned like dancing and the gas
stations heading north, and all the independents
who wasted time arguing and being superior, pulling out
dictionaries and refereed journals, new marxists, neo-marxists,
independent marxists, all of us loving our smartness, oh jeez,
the arguments filling auditoriums and town halls with
smartness, taking our time with smartness for serious study,
committing suicide blowing saxophones of smartness, going
home, which windy night on Bloor Street knowing full well and
waking up shaky until smartness rings the telephone with
another invitation and postmortem about last night's meeting.
Then I lost, well, gave up the wherewithal

III iv

One gleeful headline drives me to the floor, kneeling,
and all paint turns to gazette paper and all memory
collides into photographs we could not say happened,
that is us, that's what we did. When you lose you become
ancient but this time no one will rake over these bodies
gently collecting their valuables, their pots, their hearts
and intestines, their papers and what they could bury.
This civilisation will be dug up to burn all its manifestos.
No tender archaeologist will mend our furious writings
concluding, "They wanted sweat to taste sweet, that is all,
some of them played music for nothing, some of them
wrote poems to tractors, rough hands, and rough roads,
some sang for no reason at all to judge by their condition."

III v

After everything I rely on confusion. I listen for
disaster, a storm in the Gulf of Mexico, arctic air
wreathing the whole of this unblessed continent,
mud slides burying the rich in California and the
devil turned in on himself in Oklahoma. And others,
and more than my desire reminding me that someone
used to say when I was a child don't wish for bad
you might get it, your own face might be destroyed,
you will call trouble on yourself and on your own house.
How I watch, like someone without a being, the whole
enterprise come to zero and my skin not even able
to count on itself. Still, with snow coming, counting
by the slate sky, I hope for cars and hands to freeze,
lines and light to fall, since what I've learned,
the lie of it, is no amount of will can change it. There
are whole countries exhausted for it, whole villages,
whole arms, whole mornings and whole hearts burning.
And what I wish for is natural and accidental

ALL THAT HAS HAPPENED SINCE

IV i

Arani, I meet my old friend at Arani. Arani is a piece of what someone carried all the way here from Kerala and set down on Spadina, all he might cull of where he came from is commerce now, is laid out in trays hurriedly set on fire. So Arani, I sit with my old friend at Arani, my old friend. Between us there's a boy, his son he hasn't seen, a friendship I'm holding for ransom until he does. Who loves a Black boy? I ask him. It's not hard to abandon him, whole cities have. So this between us, I meet my old friend at Arani, his whole head soaked in that teardrop off the chin of India, or is this the way we've learned to look at it, the teardrop, the pearl dangling on the imperial necklace. We sit at Arani, I know about necklaces, archipelagos, and in some lurching talk he jumps over the Indian Ocean, back and forth, the north full of armed Tigers, tea workers, the south, treachery, prime ministers and generals, and here the telephone calls of more fracture and more of the same, wife beatings in St. James Town, men I'm certain cook with too much pepper because at home they never cooked and now only remember pepper.
I could be wrong I admit but still, and yes the boy who could do with or without him, his head boiled in all we should have been on those islands failing us because who ever had a chance to say how it might be and our own particular vanity and smallness, hatreds thinning our mouths and yellowing our fingers. This we suspect. On any given day, he says,

there are seven hundred Asian maids in their embassies in Kuwait, right now there are three hundred Sri Lankan maids hiding in the Sri Lankan embassy in Kuwait, that bulwark of American democracy, he says, a British ornithologist pursued a rare owl for years following it to a village in the south of India, there the ornithologist wept, distraught as villagers captured the bird, cooked and ate it, there were lots of these birds around they said, lots, the ornithologist wept, look, he says, I know you say they're all in it but Chandrika is caught between the generals, and the boy, I say, what about him adding my own disagreements, he gets local prices in Tobago, he goes to bars at night there and dances, they think he is a local, you know it doesn't matter this Chandrika, the generals, her mother, Bandaranaike before, they're all the same class, they have tea together, all you can count on is their benevolence, how they got up this morning, and that's no revolution, anyway we will never win now. I hardly know why I'm fighting any more, "we," my we, taking most of the world in my mouth, we, between my lips, the mouth of the world is open, the boy's mother told me her mother called menstruation. The mouth of the world is open she'd say. Anyway I was driving here and you can't believe this city, man, it is filthy and look at you, year in year out hoping about someplace else, you ever wonder why don't we live here ay, why don't we live here, by the way the Sri Lankans cannot hope to beat the West Indies at cricket, don't make yourself think about it you'll only be disappointed;

they're all the same, why are you hoping, I say, all the same class and the Americans have them, you think anything will pass now, peaceful solution, negotiating, look someone whispered something to the Tigers and they got up from the table, a mistake, a mistake, he wags, man, they want them dead, this class has only disdain, man, you should read Balzac, he skips, Balzac was saying these things, it's incredible, riffing conspiratorially at Arani as if he's talking about arms caches, Balzac is incredible, there is going to be another massive offensive, they're going to kill everyone. The pope wants to beatify Queen Isabella, I tell him, and has made thirty-three saints and seven hundred blesseds, do you realise just how absurd we are here sitting at Arani, and the boy, JFK's rocking chair sold for 450,000 dollars and European neo-fascists are glamour boys in the *New York Times*, do we realise they are more afraid of communists than fascists, that is not good news for us. I sit here and listen to radios, I hear their plots, and stagger, and the boy, well all there is is the boy, just like any ordinary person, we are not revolutionaries, we were never drawn into wars, we never slept on our dirty fingers and pissed in our clothes, why, why didn't we do that, but here, here we grind our teeth on our stone hearts and foretell and mistake, and jump around the world in our brains. Whether we are right is unimportant now, Leningrad is St. Petersburg and God is back in vogue, this is the future. I've forgotten how to dance with him, something heavy is all in my mouth, I get exhausted at Arani, my eyes reach for something domestic, the mop in the Kerala man's hand, well, the boy is still between us, and all the wars we've pried open and run our tongues over like dangerous tin cans.

IV ii

in the middle of traffic at Church and Gerrard I notice someone,
two women, for a moment unfamiliar, not crouched with me
in a hallway, for this moment unfamiliar, not cringing at the
grit of bombers, the whine of our breath in collapsing chests, in
the middle of traffic right there for a moment unfamiliar and
familiar, the light changing and as usual in the middle of almost
dying, yelling phone numbers and parting, feeling now, as the
light beckons, all the delicateness of pedestrians. I wish that I
was forgetful. All that day the streets felt painful and the
subways tender as eggshells.

IV iii

a Sunday, soft as any, plays with its eyelash,
brushing its cheek over Petit Trou, Rushdie's
archangel, Lennox and Seddon's "The trees
and flowers of the Caribbean"—*lignum vitae,*
cassia fistula, passiflora, alpina purpurata—
lay on the table, soft and falling as any,
a man with a cutlass severs the doorway
in two, language, politics, frangipani grab
the lungs, sweeter than air, a familiar foot
in brown like a friend and yellow like the fading
light, soft Sunday, just as she puts away
the camera and returns to Gibreel, the
movie star and jacaranda, how it flowers,
his hand, its lines ruffled, brushes her mouth
and she hears baying louder than the ocean,
hoarse as any desert and Vargas Llosa's prophet.

by now it's just between evening and night
and just to his left a copybook page of a sky,
water and pen ink blotting, the neighbour
is watering her plants, ixora and fern, bringing
in the mats from sunning, thinking, just
a woman baying, his arm gauzed, she thinks,
in dried banana bark, ending in the cutlass,
his face gauzed, his hand brushes her mouth,
baying, all the particles of fear and dust and
throat phlegm, and the evening coming,
baying, she hears the fierce branches of her
lungs bay thick as storms, soft as any Sunday
here, she already feels the slice of her head,
dead as stones, hoarse as seeds.

all is wonder at this moment, what calculation
does he make, she wonders, waiting for the light
to brood, willing the doorway he will cut in two,
willing it to stay open, the woman alone inside
sated on Sunday's soft temple thinking the world
is perfect, what account has he settled, has he weighed
her heart, weighed his own, then decided, yes, the cutlass,
oxidised on coconut coir, wild meat and gloricida tangle,
the obeah she'll see in banana gauze, his bare hand,
for her mouth, yes, the shallows at Petit Trou
where he'll wash the cutlass if it comes to that, watch
the salt froth her blood and the tide take it, where
he'll say some prayers anyway for himself and cross
his chest with the same hand. Did he calculate
anything, that she might reach up to his hand, baying

adding groan, slate wings and the sand her neck
already feels drizzling on Petit Trou, she decides,
she is dead already, already dead, chopped, so he sees
a dead woman baying, soft, soft, yes, the Sunday
growing older, the brittle ear, the pebbled throat,
the bone lungs, her mouth wide like the sea, and she
moving his hand, thinking, out, out the door he is
cutting in two and already dead, she wills herself
out to the verandah, he is in her way, that is all,
and she moves on baying now not on her legs,
the sea at Petit Trou is outside lapping, on a day
when there are no clouds she can see another island
clear, clear through soft Atlantic mist and he is in her
way and killed her already, her head cracked in splinters

she is closer now so the cutlass will drop or not,
but she heads into the red lump of her death, now
he cannot stop her baying, she reaches the sea
and he runs but she is still bellowing, cannot stop
and he all gauze, all calculation, all cutlass, runs
runs soft, soft and disappears,
the taste of rice is with her followed by the taste
of metal, corks followed by the taste of rust, the
taste of nails, the taste of buttercups, the taste
of rings, the taste of bark, the baying brays in the
car the next morning, riding Patience Hill,
walking the sea spray at Petit Trou, walking
as if she is walking the first time, the taste of crisp
bees, the stings in the fat of her cheek, the taste
of aloes, the lifting sea steam, the day, parched
at her eyes, parched open, what did he count
on, his finger peeling skin, waiting for the day to sit
closer to the door he would cut and break every
other day she had in two, cut Sunday brief as stones.

what did he count on, the things she can't collect
and put back right, the bees, the scissors and radio
and rice and nails now everywhere but in their
proper place, the box for this and that and beaks
and rings and wire netting upside down, her new
need for smooth clean surfaces, the revulsion she
notices for dust, the chairs she wants to hold on
her head to save them from imagined water, the
afternoon she drives Black Rock, Ibo Gully, Les
Coteaux to see if they're still there and they're not,
except like gravel breaking in her mouth.

IV iv

I saw three Sikh men early the next morning, the avenue wind swept and pelting ice, the morning dark even if light had made it so, going from mailbox to mailbox delivering news about meat sales, vegetable bargains. They were silent, waving to each other, why three of them one old, one in the middle of his life, one boy duty all over him, and why I think their lives would not be just so somewhere else but bless them in other thoughts just for here.

IV v

the girl starts the morning too, ragged like years
ahead of her, she is a translator of languages
and souls, she waits for the bus, her Walkman
in a war with the pages she's been handed,
her mother's face, her brother's face, the bus
driver's face, and the sign for starvation, the sign
for music, the one for reprisals, she'll read and ignore
them and turn her Walkman loud enough to curdle
the liquid in her eardrums that turns every music
to its rightful metronome of iron foot rings, bracelets.
This. You will read nothing in her own face now. She
is a translator of bureaucracies. This race passes through
her, ledgers and columns of thirst, notebooks of bitter
feeling, this street she's arrived at waiting for the bus
is only one. All night she's been up dancing in her room,
keeping out her mother, barring the doorway with bass,
she's feeding on genius, so till, the girl starts the morning,
weary on the floor, wisdom is what's keeping her up, she's
a noticiary of pain, that faculty is overgrown in her until
it is all she conducts, she's an electrician, pure electricity
flows through her, her fingertips are disappearing in sheer
lightning.

IV vi

a Baptist priestess preaches to a sidewalk in this city
and if this city could take it she would look into its eyes
but everyone, me too, glides by,
all who might pronounce her sane run ahead,
drive quickly before she catches our eyes,
and she is mad, thinking god could find her here,
and in her eyes that is her penance I suppose,
to talk to the pavement at Oakwood and St. Clair
and ours to avoid her as if we suddenly lost
consciousness of race and what she's calling for,
all eyes instead drop to the sash of dirt around her waist
and say "for god's sake, these people could embarrass you, ay!"
her husband left her, took all her money
after she worked to bring him here, well after all
who else could explain but the pavement dense with answers

IV vii

11 p.m. to 7 a.m. she worked years leaving them in this apartment
and that, and how she could, bringing them one at a time,
picking them up by airplane where she had left them
in this village, that town, this family, which aunt and grandmother
and never being able to reach them as she had left them,
how folded in brown paper was not how you left children,
untying sweet string was not how they came, and whatever
plans she had others had plenty more, and the doorway would
finally burst open and the walls let in the road and every thanks
ended up a curse and her own habits come to haunt her,
this girl once sewing a yard of children to a V-necked dress,
then it was over, all speech that granted her a steady shape
as what a woman was supposed to be, all dress and hips,
all spirit and animality, that left, then everything for them,
and the stitching going badly, on her hands she noticed
numbness to hot water and hot pans, a lamentation in her back
from lifting spoiled white bodies, their own whimpering death
songs elegising, "bitch, black bitch, I want my own daughter."

IV viii

in Chechnya, a Russian plane has dropped a bomb on a village
the radio says, I just heard, ten billion to Yeltsin
from the IMF, just today, just like any South American darling
devoted sonofabitch, I know this is no news, nor walls
of photographs of children in Bukavu, tents of refugees
in Goma, it's their own fault, before it was communism
now they just don't know how to work the gift of capitalism,
all of us want to fly to America right now, right away please
and Americans wonder why, feel we must love them
that's why, we're just jealous, that's why, we just want
to steal what they have, thief from thief make god laugh,
so I'm getting into the business of false passports and new
identities, I'm taking in conferences on pomo-multiplicity,
the everyday world, the signifying monkey, the post-colonial
moment, the Michigan militia, cyberspace, come to think of it
give each fleeing Hutu/Tutsi a home page, subalterns of their
own, I'm going to Bukavu with Windows

IV ix

what exactly is the difference between these groups, perplexed
the host, well nothing ideological, says the expert, well why in
the new world aren't they getting along, communism's gone,
no proxy wars, no real role for cia agents, soviet spies,
what in the world is going on down there then,
well it's hard to say really, the krahn, the croats, the serbs,
the shia, the hutu, you see, the falasha, the hezbollah, well
democracy's run amuck, but what is it, the host wants to know
and the expert can no longer reach for anything
but family disagreements and old forbidden grudges let loose
by all that voting and free speech, the old underdeveloped
don't have the same level of sophistication as us
and what about Russia, Poland, don't tell me they would vote
back the commies, not yet used to democracy, the market forces,
they don't understand, the thing is we've resurrected some
demons

IV x

here is the history of the body;
water perhaps darkness perhaps stars
bone then scales then wings then legs then arms
then belly then bone then nerves then feathers then scales,
then wings then liquid then pores then bone
then blood pouring, then eyes, then distance, only this,
all that has happened since is too painful,
too unimaginable

"I never saw Managua when miniskirts were in," Ortega
wrote in prison and newsprint bleeds with weeping
the walls of this room weep, a Saturday weeps,
what do we make of it, a miniskirt measuring
time, senses missed, dates, a life and people walking
in streets and thoughts as you walk along that are taken
for granted and forgotten at the end of a journey,
Ortega sitting in his cell could not have these
but had we given another shape to bodies
as well as theory and poems and speeches
what would we have missed and wept for and forgotten

Remembering Miranda's campaigns as if he were there
and Bolivar as if fighting for his own life and José Martí
like a son grown from a pebble tossed in the Caribbean basin
a comrade in his last speech and his last hope
ignites the hall in Montreal,
he is the one left alive and left here
he is a stranger in another millennium, in another room

with his passion and his shimmering ancestry,
a question from the back of the hall about armed struggle,
he has been waiting,
he sticks his grapple in its rock face and there's
a ruthlessness in him, a touch of the old sexy revolutionary,
and he stumbles on now, then his hand touches a greying chin
and it is as if he is startled and ashamed
and unable to land in now, all left undone.
There is a sign that he must make us,
the shape of the one thing that he has never written, ever

we stumble on the romance of origins,
some stories we all love like sleep, poured in our mouths like
milk. How far we've travelled now, still we stoop at a welcome
fire and hum, to a stick stringed with hair, our miscalculations,
we return to the misology in heat and loneliness, the smell of
meat and hunger

here again the history of the body
men romance the shape they're in
the mythologies they attach to it
their misunderstandings
and this is what James should have said to Trotsky
as they drank in Mexico City,
what might have happened if one had said to the other,
comrade, this is the time you betray the body

nearly late, we are in a hall waiting for a gesture,
Ortega out of prison if his prison is not the whole
of South America now, Jose Marti's son if the hall in Montreal
is not his coffin,
we are waiting for some language to walk into
like a large house
with no rooms and no quarter
all waiting for his signal
we happen on what was wrong in the first place,
how the intangible took over,
the things left in a language with carelessness or purpose,
men's arms and legs and belly, their discreet assignments
and regulations
the things kept secret with a hand pressed to the mouth
by priests, judges, mullahs
this way they resist what they must become
full knowing that we must throw our life away
and all impressions of ourselves.
Comrades, perhaps this is what you might whisper
on the telephone to the young men who adore you still,
"Goodbye, then. And well . . . betray your body."

IV xi

That damn corridor, green with half dead guerrillas
and want to be guerrilla just shut in and might as well
did blow up with we in it, the life it throw we into
is the same scrambling as before and only the magic once
or twice is remembering how it change we.
When we meet now we say, "It was the best years
of my life. I wouldn't exchange it for youth." Hustling European
guests into a hotel, pain stroking a face with the wrong answer
for the cause of the end of we. Watching only through a plane
window at Point Salines and busy not recalling where we was
rightly, eating coconut ice cream at the bar in Crown Point,
starting all over with hardly any heart. For different reason
all of we, everyone the bridge over. Over the exhaust
of them hilly hilly street and the blazing sun like fire,
fire in we tail, it wasn't enough that we had was to find a way
to love for once, we love it hard enough and hard
was how everything was as if it design, once bad mind America,
and bad mind had to come, why that, as if we know it long, long
as though we expect, well it easy after all to notice the worse, any
body would fail to see how it could fix, mortar break, pestle break

I sit down in the bar myself, in a lot of bar, if I could drink
my way dead I would but my stomach give out before my heart

why this voice rank and ready to be called bitter again, liquor
doesn't soothe it and books either, self saboteur, it could be nice
and grateful but Fanon had it, native envy, watery and long as
that bloody sea, envy for everything then, kitchen knives their
dullness or sharpness, shoes their certainty, envelopes their
letters, clocks their lag, paper its clarity, envy to the participle and
adverb, the way they own being, ripe envy full as days, and
breasts, bony as wardrobes, old as babies

for only one moment it spreads on the table like water
and heat, its light piercing the heavy, heavy weight of this sky,
it moves my now inanimate body, all stone, moves it
to sound and leaves; how small things stir me, sunlight
between two high-rise buildings, the looked and looked for
possibility of a leaf on a dormant tree, how I forget
whatever thoughts I have that follow a logic, whatever
impulse in me that wanted satisfaction, now days, their whims
and changeableness have me in a grip, the sky is a pain.
I was always for succumbing to something bigger,
I wanted something unindividual like distance or chaff,
or the spinning silence in the air after blue-grey tanagers,
signal and undifferent as obsidian caves bluing and blacking,
tracks of country uncompeting, and braids, hair latched
handful over handful. I had hoped that some billowy humid
night swooning to its knees, the smell of coconut smoke
or some cold night cracking silence into its middle
with the smell of wood smoke . . . it would occur to me,
that nothing was wrong.

LAND TO LIGHT ON

V i

Maybe this wide country just stretches your life to a thinness
just trying to take it in, trying to calculate in it what you must
do, the airy bay at its head scatters your thoughts like someone
going mad from science and birds pulling your hair, ice invades
your nostrils in chunks, land fills your throat, you are so busy
with collecting the north, scrambling to the Arctic so wilfully, so
busy getting a handle to steady you to this place you get blown
into bays and lakes and fissures you have yet to see, except
on a map in a schoolroom long ago but you have a sense that
whole parts of you are floating in heavy lake water heading for
what you suspect is some other life that lives there, and you, you
only trust moving water and water that reveals itself in colour. It
always takes long to come to what you have to say, you have to
sweep this stretch of land up around your feet and point to the
signs, pleat whole histories with pins in your mouth and guess
at the fall of words.

V ii

But the sight of land has always baffled you,
there is dirt somewhere older than any exile
and try as you might, your eyes only compose
the muddy drain in front of the humid almond
tree, the unsettling concrete sprawl of the housing
scheme, the stone your uncle used to smash his name
into another uncle's face, your planet is your hands,
your house behind your eyebrows and the tracing
paper over the bead of islands of indifferent and
reversible shapes, now Guadeloupe is a crab pinched
at the waist, now Nevis' borders change by mistake
and the carelessness of history, now sitting in Standard
Five, the paper shifting papery in the sweat of your
fingers you come to be convinced that these lines will
not matter, your land is a forced march on the bottom
of the Sargasso, your way tangled in life

V iii

I am giving up on land to light on, it's only true, it is only
something someone tells you, someone you should not trust
anyway. Days away, years before, a beer at your lips and the view
from Castara, the ocean as always pulling you towards its bone
and much later, in between, learning to drive the long drive
to Burnt River, where the land is not beautiful, braised
like the back of an animal, burnt in coolness, but the sky is,
like the ocean pulling you toward its bone, skin falling away
from your eyes, you see it without its history of harm, without
its damage, or everywhere you walk on the earth there's harm,
everywhere resounds. This is the only way you will know
the names of cities, not charmed or overwhelmed, all you see is
museums of harm and metros full, in Paris, walls inspected
crudely for dates, and Amsterdam, street corners full of
druggists, ashen with it, all the way from Suriname, Curaçao,
Dutch and German inking their lips, pen nibs of harm blued in
the mouth, not to say London's squares, blackened in statues,
Zeebrugge, searching the belly of fish, Kinshasa, through an
airplane window the dictator cutting up bodies grips the plane
to the tarmac and I can't get out to kiss the ground

V iv

This those slaves must have known who were my mothers, skin
falling from their eyes, they moving toward their own bone,
"so thank god for the ocean and the sky all implicated, all
unconcerned," they must have said, "or there'd be nothing to
love." How they spent a whole lifetime undoing the knot
of a word and as fast it would twirl up again, spent
whole minutes inching their eyes above sea level only
for latitude to shift, only for a horrible horizon to list, thank god
for the degrees of the chin, the fooling plane of a doorway, only
the mind, the not just simple business of return and turning,
that is for scholars and indecisive frigates, circling and circling,
stripped in their life, naked as seaweed, they would have sat
and sunk but no, the sky was a doorway, a famine and a jacket,
the sea a definite post

V ᵥ

I'm giving up on land to light on, slowly, it isn't land,
it is the same as fog and mist and figures and lines
and erasable thoughts, it is buildings and governments
and toilets and front door mats and typewriter shops,
cards with your name and clothing that comes undone,
skin that doesn't fasten and spills and shoes. It's paper,
paper, maps. Maps that get wet and rinse out, in my hand
anyway. I'm giving up what was always shifting, mutable
cities' fluorescences, limbs, chalk curdled blackboards
and carbon copies, wretching water, cunning walls. Books
to set it right. Look. What I know is this. I'm giving up.
No offence. I was never committed. Not ever, to offices
or islands, continents, graphs, whole cloth, these sequences
or even footsteps

V vi

Light passes through me lightless, sound soundless,
smoking nowhere, groaning with sudden birds. Paper
dies, flesh melts, leaving stockings and their useless vanity
in graves, bodies lie still across foolish borders.
I'm going my way, going my way gleaning shade, burnt
meridians, dropping carets, flung latitudes, inattention,
screeching looks. I'm trying to put my tongue on dawns
now, I'm busy licking dusk away, tracking deep twittering
silences. You come to this, here's the marrow of it, not
moving, not standing, it's too much to hold up, what I
really want to say is, I don't want no fucking country, here
or there and all the way back, I don't like it, none of it,
easy as that. I'm giving up on land to light on, and why not,
I can't perfect my own shadow, my violent sorrow, my
individual wrists.

DIALECTICS

VI i

I feel like my aunt hunkered to a foot that wouldn't
cure, her hair tightened to a "dougla" wave and her mouth
sweet on laughter and paradise plums, she could fry fish
and make it taste sweet, sweet after her seasoning
rubbed the silvery red skin on snapper and she could turn
flour into sweet bread glazed with crystalled sugar water,
bread carved in steamy yeast and butter, her hands parted
a corn row clean clean and ribbons bounced white and blue
satin to her fingers, she liked to sweeten up, perfume
cheap as pennies richened on her skin and her one good leg
slender and tapered to the ankle she braceleted against
the whispers of bad woman, she dressed in tight skirts and low
backer bodices, taught us the jive spinning and dipping
between the Morris chairs to Count Basie but she could not
knead that leaky leg well. I woke up to her sitting in the dark,
the corners of the living room warm and amber with floor
polish, moaning and rubbing her foot. She didn't sleep,
she sat up, her leg on a chair waiting for daylight
to turn corn meal into porridge with cinnamon spice and
vanilla essence, or roll it into fig leaves with raisins, to repeat
the lesson of the jive when we got home at three and to quarrel
about our hair, flying away free which she'd pulled back smart
in rubber bands just this morning.

VI ii

I had thought my life wider, had counted on my cleverness
at noticing not just her sweet hand but her sore leg
and congratulated myself even then on analysing the dialectic,
the turned corn meal, the amber pain hanging at my Aunt
Phyllis' foot. I liked detail. The way she dismissed her leg in
daring dresses, the way she hung and fingered the fine gold
chain around her good ankle, the idea that she refused to give
up any of her senses as tragic as they were, she wanted a sweet
life to balance out, to complete her fiery anklet, even at seventy
with a heart attack under anaesthesia she says, girl, I tired of this
foot all the time all the time so, she risks another skin graft and
she wore gold rings and loved guipure lace and sweet men
named Casimir on motorcycles, she loved the way they glittered
past savannah grass, how envy soaked other women's Sundays,
for him, but she with her aching foot sat astride his back,
the cut of her dresses deep to the ripple of her waist.
At fifty she married a man who was possessive and selfish
and she loved that too.

I took in the child sucking her thumb, holding on to the butter of her mother's skirt, the other sitting on the gathers at his mother's hips, leaning out dangerously, leaning away happily from the mother's set cheek, set mouth and the baby in the remaining arm, matter in her eyes, screaming. I made a note. One at her dress tail, one on her hip, one in her arm. I made a note of the guard answering reluctantly, and the barricade to the electricity company, he so used to answering indifferently to women on Fridays, "He gone, he not here, don't waste your time," the yellow trucks laden with men barely missing her feet, and her neck whipping swift, piercing the benches of them for his face. I never fell into the heaviness of babies. Thank god. Not me and no baby. Baby, in my bony lap? It can't hold no baby there. I is not nobody mother. I made a note of what she choked back, her spit dry, her face hardening and hardening and hmmning, chewing reedy on their laughter, their laughter here cracking the dust of their faces and boots, their laughter here rattling in the can of the truck like uneven stone, heating it like cigarette butts, like men coughing catarrh at some joke that burns their chests too.

VII ii

Their laughter here where laughter is to
sew up harm or just like harm where somehow
there is blame in it, mockery for landing there
at the guard's impatience, the barricade's iron denial,
a man's whim and no mercy, it so despise itself, I did
not miss her skin setting over its shame, her jaw
making another plan, her shifting the child from
hip to ground, from ground to hip unable to make
anything of the baby's indecision to yawn or bawl, I
could not miss the marl of her teeth crushed on worry,
nothing she could sell for nothing, at the end of herself,
needing a plan because at the end of herself she was
still alive, still blooming children and crying, and short
of burying them in the cane field at the back of her house
she had to hang them on her hips where harm
was greater if only they knew the sweet ground would
be milk.

VII iii

I saw her head up the road toward
the evening coming, that road, the same
as when its name was Carib, cut
in the San Fernando hill, that evening
as unconcerned as any for her, bent
on its own gluttony, she, like an ancient
woman with her regular burdens heading
into a hill. I saw her begin again,
the coming dark slipping between her legs
and disappearing into which century past.
I saw her shoulder the dark like another child
and consider its face, its waiting mouth
closed on her breast.
She told me once she loved babies, hated
to see them grow up, she missed
their babyness, that's why she had so many.
I saw her heading up a road into a hill
with her vanity and her lust
not for any man in an electric company truck
but for her own face.

VII iv

I took no time in the rose light of
the sun departing the hill, her dress turning
ochre and melting, the child at her skirt
looking back and looking alone after the mist
of the mother disappearing into the going
light. This peace filled in evening smoke
of evening pots cooking so much or so little
on this Carib road, and her mouth springing
water and drying at the thought of her own shack
at the head of a cane field smokeless.
This peace swallowing a woman, three children
and a road, this peace closing ochre on vermilion
on utter, utter darkness where sleep is enough food
at least and she could fool those children
to a sleep cooing a watery promise of nice things
tomorrow, ladling sugar water into their mouths
and then sleepless waiting for his sodden body to fall
and lay near the steps outside or break a window
coming in.

VII v

Her burning head, not just how they
would eat but how she would love, why
was it only lost to her this need to love, how
it was jumbled up and when the children
were asleep the handle of it slipped her,
and with rum in her head she felt it crack
her bones, howl her voice to a scream.
She pedalled the Hitachi sewing machine
for kilometres into the cane field
over the night fields soughing soft past
other roads through long savannahs
and houses choked on sleep, wet tablelands
and thick dirt smells, rushed to wet sand
clenching the sea at Plaisance, Mayaro,
her feet delirious. In the morning
the bedclothes would be a dress and a skirt
and a jacket and a blouse, kilometres
of pedalling and it was hard to breathe night,
holding it in her fierce lungs, her feet
losing bone, she hummed the needle through
the presser foot singing like rain.

VIII i

once they take we to a dance, the both of
them, the three of we, nine, ten, twelve,
pull we to the dance floor thundering
with big people dancing to steelband
and perfume and something serious in
their dancing, something that didn't want
no interruption from two foolish aunts
and some children they bring to a dance
but they was laughing and pulling
we on the dance floor saying,
"All yuh want to come to dance, well dance."
They bundle we on a bench in a corner
to sleep when sleep overcome we fastness
and they danced, wining and shimmying
to Lord Kitchener.
I didn't know no dance could be so dark
and full of serious desire that frighten me
no arse. A lady and a man not even holding
tight but some tightness holding them, her
white low-heeled shoes on the inside of his
black ones and her shoulders shine shine fire
in the shadow of more people, she look lush
at the same time as well . . . serious is all I
could say, a school teacher serious but let go,
wasn't no school teacher red red so glowing
on the dance floor

and they laugh at we, lifting we up and taking
we home, "Is dance all yuh want to dance."

VIII ii

that night we wanted to fly in our aunts' skin,
we so loved their talk, the sugar in their mouths,
they were always laughing, throwing water over
their shoulders and going on anyway, the one
with five children stealing out the door without them
after she'd fed them and oiled them or perhaps not,
but slipping out the door going looking for another
as her mother said; trusting the cane field, at the bottom
of Cocoyea village asleep behind the house, at her back,
blue in the black black night, to put those children
to sleep too and keep them while she found another,
tall and pretty, who would bend into the well of her cheeks,
clutch the bone of them like a carnivore, five children
and she could still laugh the best men into the dough
of her skirt and love them so hard a ship to England
would leave without her many times and leave the wharf
without the suitcase full of dresses sewn for months
piled on the Hitachi machine, mouthsful of needles
and thread bristling and black cake packed for sisters
abroad, waiting for news and hungry for such skirts,
such love themselves, her mother and father waiting
in disappointment and dread until there was no way
she would make that ship.

VIII iii

She came later, weeks, months, said she was sick,
suddenly struck just so by illness, god, just so,
a headache, a pain, an arm that just wouldn't move
just that morning when she woke up, a stroke,
missed the boat by minutes, imagine, just, minutes,
or laughing with no explanation, or just something
told her not to go, bad spirits, obeah, the child' father
other woman, must be, any promise no matter how
meagre but was a sign anyway. She came minutes
after the ship set sail anyhow, feigning simple lateness
and horror and vowing to pay back every cent they'd saved
and lost on the ship cutting the water, glittering like hard
diamonds, sloughing the jetty. She could not resist,
in all her crocodile tears and some real too, a deep voice
calling her away from her mother and her father, calling
her away from their disappointment, across the wharf,
a hollow dark cheek calling her, "Wha' happenin', girl,
you scarce like gold." She could not help laughing and turning
away from the bedraggled mother and father to answer
the cunning hint in gold, of her loveliness, "Oh gord, dahlin'
wha' happenin'? Where the fete, where the fete?"

VIII iv

She came in a hurry to leave, "Keep the children
for me, mama. I hear about a work." Bustling
sweetly dressed like she was going to a party, kissing
the children promising them sweeties if they behaved
for mama. She wore pink powder and dabbed
the puff on our faces, exquisite dust clouds
of perfume exploding, we squealed with love
and terror. Where she went, we wanted to go.
It was some place you had to hurry to and something
hot and sweet was going on there and waiting for you,
knowledge. What was it that she had to keep going to
and was more seductive than a ship going away
and returning into another life, not a bucket
under the leak of a bachie, the man with promises gone,
not fright at a failed abortion, the blood endless
in a small room, what was so sweet in all that running
racket, in men grinding the hills of her cheeks to gravel,
panning her eyes for their brittle rages.

VIII ▾

that night we wanted to fly into our aunts' skins,
the one, look her voice I cannot tell you but you
would have to know the meaning of shade
and water to understand it, you would have to
know night to recognise it rippling and coconut oil,
she had a voice meant to describe darkness
and daylight, only slippery and burning like Vat 19
rum, it could sound like a ribbon yards and yards
long and red over the counter of Lloyd's shop
round the corner, a ribbon glistening
over the barrels of pig's tails and salt fish,
such a voice like food and air. She rescued me across
the road from that shop, bawling at Miss Greenidge's
private school. "Is child you want to beat?" she honeyed
high and dangerous, "Why you don't go and make
child, eh?" grabbing the guava stick from Miss Greenidge.
One time Reds and them who was bad-johns, their whole
family, mother and everything, Reds ride a bicycle right
at me and I fall in the canal full of nasty water where
you could catch wabeen and everybody garbage, well
my aunt just get a piece a wood and gone up to Reds'
house just so. Reds en't even come out, mother and
everything. I had uncle too but them aunts was like tree
and good cloth, river and big road. She, with the voice
would bring me fried snapper all the way from the country
by the sea because I was sad. Who could tell sadness
in a child. Who could tell it wasn't just this morning's
slight or flying need, who could tell it wasn't just the
hunger of children for everything. I've never done that
for anyone, just so, tell what was needed was snapper,
fried crisp and silver red and answering whatever loneliness.
Her smile was wet and warming and one little finger
had a gold ring on it and both hands were small and nothing
was unhappy in them

IX i

god I watched you all, watched and watched and in the end
could not say a word to you that was not awkward and insulting,
there was really no way to describe you and what I wanted
to say came out stiff and old as if I could not trust you
to understand my new language which after all I had made
against you, against the shapes of your bodies, against your
directions, your tongues, the places your feet took you, how I
know holding in everything, warm breath and silence
and words because of you and waiting, how you watched me watch
and did not say all that my eyes said was distance and blame
and something superior, yet you offered me food for Christmas
and laughter and your life, your news across the telephone,
bad news, self-mockery, disappointments and things you feared,
your pilgrimages, a holy shrine at Marmora, faith, even in
its incapable saints, but you prayed, knelt in mud there anyway,
subway riders you braved, benedictions serrating your dress,
how they could not understand your belief sprouting on trains,
your sojourns in hospitals, giving over your bodies to people
who didn't care, and I was no comfort just an ear welling with
water, their mouths drowning in it, how you must have
regretted these confidences knowing I could do nothing with
them but bathe you in more blame, more sorrow. How I told you
nothing in return, pretended that my life was fine, and it was,
thinking, no policemen were at my door, no sons drowning in
their own brains, none of my daughters without a way out
how I told you nothing in return, my life was fine

and nothing touched me and it didn't, how I was so far away
from you by then and these conversations scared me. I am not
good at anything except standing still like a wall, my only
instinct is do nothing, avoid notice, and even when I believe so
soundly in dialectics I look over my shoulder for wicked spirits,
making my whole being logged in its inert self, how it was not
you, not you but something holding us all, more than this
understanding we are caught in can say, how the circumference
of this world grips us to this place, how its science works,
how it will take a change of oceans shaking the other way

IX ii

If I could think of what I'd meant again, and seas; I never
developed any signs except sleep, nothing to know me by,
I kept to myself brewing ways to sit and close the door
and not touch anything that may fall and left you to living
because what is the point of seeing so much it stills you, as, yes,
oceans, how we give each other up fix whatever concentration
we lack, the complete ruin a thought would present, how
explosive the untangling of eyelashes can be if say they open
on this, how so much depends on sleep, worlds and streets
and briefcases and half hours, and gardens and glass windows
and shoe leather and white shirts and sugar all balanced on
our sleeping, so much depends on sleep, so much induces it, all
the danger it prevents, iron pots tumbling and seams of blood
opening under cutlasses, what I'd meant again was so much
depends on a woman sitting with her hands in her lap, so
much on deciding to wait in the road for a motorcycle, a bus,
so much disappears on a road, cries and sets off again. I know
it is from small things that we know anything, why it did not
strike me to live as they did, how I watched instead and knew
something bad was waiting there, right there in the middle
of their laughing, right there when they hurried to the next
desire, how my breath would stop at something careening
in them. No I didn't want their life and I wanted their life
because they didn't know that they were living it and I envied
them that. I envied them that and I burned to wake up bright
not noticing days where I noticed them most and where
their news would sink into the front door and the walls fall off
the house, the way a skirt is no protection, days crawling until
my life is there whatever I think.

x

In the church yard which was the cemetery, the savannah
whining grass and heat, the weekdays loud with work, and
Sunday quiet raged like fever. Here I felt discomfort draw
in my body like blood and me drawn out of them. I wanted to fly
into their skins and I wanted to escape them. Sundays were a
weight against my chest, the weight of pebbles against birds
and green fruit and small ponds. Sundays crept. And in their
slowness, in all the time they gave, opening their dry palms
giving as if they could ever be generous, in all that time, not
noticing that they were passing sentence on us and giving us
breath to watch and burn slowly, in all the time they drew,
in the slowness of churches, the slowness of black serge, the slow
papery scent from the bible, the slowness of stockings, the slow
hiss of hot combs braising hair, in the slow, slow slowness
which is not ease, in the starch slowness of crinoline, in the waiting
slowness of soft asphalt roads, the looking long gazing slowness
of the curve and depth of more and more road, slow purple
quietness of cocoa pods, the high cracking slowness of parrots,
their pairness and blue blue height, the drop of the eyes
after their flight, long, long searching
unable to make anything of how they leave the earth tilting

the slowness of sand, ponderous, ponderous slowness of cricket
pitches, their struggling green and empty royal stands, the long
echo of wells, buckets, standpipes running water, lamps dried
out of kerosene and the wait at the storekeeper's beck for trust,
palms, their backs crumbling to hot ashes, wiped over mouths,
hands propping sorrow at windows, doorways, in the slow
yellow, black, red powder of butterflies, slow suffocation of
childhood, the resolute slowness of birthdays, the violent
slowness of flour, the regular ruin of storms, seas, winds,
Sundays in all their sweet time, the sugary slowness of parlours
and sweet jars, gold spit cornered slowness of mouths, in the
hoarse bray of donkeys slow, slow, skidding to slow everlastingly
slow Sunday, moths coming in to burn with gravity in the yawn
of lamp wicks, the crowded bed where we slept crosswise and
damp with someone's pee, the mattress ticking teased and
teased in the slowness of weeks and dried in the wait between
rains, the drawl of knees, elbows gashing, fighting in slow sleep
for room, in the window above our heads pulling in the cold,
wet slow rainy season, the wait and wait for January. Sundays
stretched in all their time from one to the other until I had a life
of them in their cicada whining, razor grassed stiff stiff slowing,
I knew my life come still like a heart waiting at the reed of itself.

XI

no I do not long, long, slowly for the past.
I am happy it is gone. If I long for it,
it is for the hope of it curled like burnt
paper. All the things I should have lived
slowly and content but lived grudgingly
instead, all the things still detectable in
the thin frail black of it not yet turned to
powder. All the things I should not have
noticed or breathed in, the harm, the envy,
the wreck an ocean can be in, the helpless
transparency of a street, an island, the raged
flood of a body in wood. If I long for it,
I long for it arrested, arrested among zinnias'
dust, their skins wilting in too much rain
water, their heads heavy, one moment my
feet splayed in mud and ants, stooping,
listening at returns or goings, at hours,
one moment the light finishing soft, turning
toward home thinking "ma calling," my sister
skidding down the guava tree, we laughing,
blue airmail letters opening, whisping, "Dear
mama, hope you are well and enjoying the
best of health." The corners of a house strafed
with sunlight that turns fawn and liquid, stooped
there picking up a brush or an iron. Nothing
lived longer, only this moment without disaster
in half movement on its way to movement,
half light still dark, black that is billowy
and vanishes in a hand. If I long for anything
it is shadow I long for, regions of darkness.

XII

Out of them. To where? As if I wasn't them.
To this I suppose. The choices fallen into
and unmade. Out of them. Out of shape
and glimmer and into hissing prose. What
could it mean, all that ocean, all that bush,
all that room, all that hemmed and sweet light.
Don't be mistaken, the whole exercise was
for escaping, the body cut so, the tongue cut
so, the drape of the head and the complications
boiling to their acid verbs. This pine was waiting,
this road already travelled, this sea in the back
of my head roiling its particular wrecks
and like escaping one doesn't look too close
at landing, any desert is lush, sand blooms,
any grit in the mouth is peace, the mechanics
of a hummingbird less blazing than the whirr,
all at once calligraphy and spun prism, this new
landfall when snows come and go and come again,
this landfall happened at your exact flooding and
even though you had a mind, well, landing . . .
it doesn't count on flesh or memory, or any purposes

ISLANDS VANISH

XIII

In this country where islands vanish, bodies submerge,
the heart of darkness is these white roads, snow
at our throats, and at the windshield a thick white cop
in a blue steel windbreaker peering into our car, suspiciously,
even in the blow and freeze of a snowstorm, or perhaps
not suspicion but as a man looking at aliens.
Three Blacks in a car on a road blowing eighty miles an hour
in the wind between a gas station and Chatham. We stumble
on our antiquity. The snow-blue laser of a cop's eyes fixes us
in this unbearable archaeology.

How quickly the planet can take itself back. I saw this
once in the summer in daylight, corn dangling bronze, flat
farm land growing flatter, eaten up in highways, tonight,
big and rolling it is storming in its sleep. A cop is standing at its
lip.

Coca-cola can light, the car shakes, trembles along as in a
gutter, a bellow of wind rushes into my face breathless
checking the snowbank, I might have seen something
out there, every two minutes the imagination conjures
an exact bridge, the mind insists on solidity, we lose
the light of the car ahead, in the jagged beam of the cop's
blistering eye we lose the names of things, the three of us,
two women who love women, one man with so many demons
already his left foot is cold, still, making our way to Chatham,
Buxton, waiting as they once waited for Black travellers like us,
blanketed, tracked in this cold shimmering.

Out there I see nothing . . . not one thing out there
just the indifference of a cop. It takes us six hours
to travel three. I coil myself up into a nerve and quarrel
with the woman, lover, and the man for landing me in
this white hell.

We have been in this icy science only a short time. What
we are doing here is not immediately understandable
and no one is more aware of it than we, she from Uganda
via Kenya running from arranged marriages, he from Sri
Lanka via Colombo English-style boarding school to make him
the minister of the interior, me hunting for slave castles with a
pencil for explosives, what did we know that our pan-colonial
flights would end up among people who ask stupid questions
like, where are you from . . . and now here we are on their road,
in their snow, faced with their childishness.

How are we to say that these paths are involuntary and
the line of trees we are looking for will exist when we
find it, that this snow is just a cipher for our feverishness.

Only Sarah Vaughan thank god sings in this snow, Sarah
and her big band . . . gotta right to sing the blues . . .
I desert the others to her voice, fanning fire, then, even Sarah
cannot take me away but she moves the car and we live
on whatever she's given to this song, each dive of her voice,
each swoop, her vibrato holds us to the road, the outcome
of this white ride depends on Sarah's entries and exits from a
note. We cannot turn back, ahead Buxton must hear this so we
can arrive, up ahead Sarah singing she can see the midnight sun.

Only this much sound, only this much breath, only this much
grace, only how long, only how much road can take us away.

That cop's face has it. "They had been in this vast and dark
country only a short time."* Something there, written as
wilderness, wood, nickel, water, coal, rock, prairie, erased
as Athabasca, Algonquin, Salish, Inuit . . . hooded in Buxton
fugitive, Preston Black Loyalist, railroaded to gold mountain,
swimming in *Komagata Maru* . . . Are we still moving?
Each body submerged in its awful history. When will we arrive?
In a motel room later, we laugh, lie that we are not harmed,
play poker and fall asleep, he on the floor with his demons,
she, legs wrapped around me.

How can we say that when we sign our names in letters
home no one can read them, when we send photographs
they vanish. Black heart, blackheart . . . can't take it tonight
across this old road . . . take me home some other way.

---

* from Joseph Conrad's "An Outpost of Progress"

THROUGH MY IMPERFECT MOUTH AND LIFE AND WAY

XIV i

I know you don't like poems, especially mine
and especially since mine never get told when
you need them, and I know that I live some
inner life that thinks it's living outside but
isn't and only wakes up when something knocks
too hard and when something is gone as if gazing
up the road I miss the bus and wave a poem at
its shadow. But bus and shadow exist all the same
and I'll send you more poems even if they arrive
late. What stops us from meeting at this place
and imagining ourselves big as the world and broad
enough to take it in and grow ancient is fear and
our carelessness, and standing in the thrall
of the wicked place we live in and not seeing
a way out all the time and never clearly all at once
and not at the same time and abandoning each other
to chance and small decisions, but if I ever thought
that I could never recover the thought struggling
to live through my imperfect mouth and life and way,
if I thought that I could do nothing about the world
then . . . well, and we've hung on to old hurts as if
that was all there was and as if no amount of sadness

would be enough for our old, insistent,
not becoming selves; and as if sadness should not end,
so for this I'll send you more poems even if they
only wave and even if I only look up late to see
your shadow rushing by.

XIV ii

to be passed on to Teresa when thinking

And no I did not know you, who could? choosing
once as you did to live in the middle of race
and not knowing the trouble of it, or perhaps
stunned by it once you did, no you may have
toyed with the idea for a moment that you were
dangerous or then harmless and that no one was
looking or everyone, and that you of all could
bound the leap of it, or perhaps not so self
possessed at all you grabbed what joy there was
you white, he black, and dangerous again,
dangerous lived some possibility until the cold
kick of self hatred found the centre of you.
I met you and avoided you at the same time
and I know the pain you wrought in a daughter, know
it holds her sometimes and heaves her and I've sat
at the kitchen table watching her forgive you everything
and telling her don't be so generous, save something
for herself because I know people just live their lives
sometimes, feeling harm is just part of the deal
and they'll give it as much as take it and how people
grow calluses to seal up wounds as you sewed
challenge in your voice to pace your stutters
and your stutters in their turn hesitated over some
childhood damage; how your face became opaque
and swollen from placing your daughters in harm's way,
how you went far away across a country to forget
but your face remained as still, how neither of them
could run from that or keep it and in fits and starts try
to recover from your rage and love; what I wanted
to say, and did, the morning you died was "Well, Teresa,
you gone, then go, and I don't know what saying go
peacefully means here, but go however you can.
Whatever's unfinished will stay and perhaps

we cannot hope to finish anything, which is life's
harsh caution, and why we must work to be gentle
here. Anyway, go how you can." Unfinished
is how you joked one morning at the kitchen sink
in Toronto after I avoided you the night before
about who deserves the world and who works hard,
". . . And another thing you!" you said laughing,
and I, "oh no, don't start with me again!" but that
was the truce and your admission that sometimes
you saw yourself honestly. But yourself and what
you had to answer for was too hard to take truthfully
so you spoke the easy version, the one they give us
and condemn us to repeat, condemning ourselves
in our own mouths. No, I did not know you, nor love,
and did not need to, to glimpse and glimpse recognition
in your face when you heard the name, Sparrow. That
is all I know, and how you pace over a daughter's face
waiting to go.

XIV iii

I had hoped that she could see me, hoped
that she noticed that I think these things and
furiously even if I look like some stone sitting
there hoping that I turn to stone, my own life,
from where, terrifying me and my instincts saying
don't move; we assume we know the thoughts of
those we make come close, or we forget we don't
and need not. I could make no assumptions with her,
no certainties, and at first that was the charm,
after all what was certainty before then but grief
and this looked like the opposite. But my guesses
were bad and hers too because a stone does not
have legs and arms and is only thinking of its
stoniness and wants to draw everything into its gravity
and becomes confused with flight and uncertainty,
and air wanders off to its own airiness, and becomes
impatient, eager to find more space and more music
and more intelligence, unless they are willing to
see more than themselves in each other, then
stone and air it is, fighting about their most
finite and unchangeable territories and not seeing
the sign they make defining each other.
I had hoped that she would come to see my stillness
as not mere stillness but trying to hang on and
make some steady motion in a life too busy with my
family's nervousness and I know this word "hoped,"
I mistake for done, and sitting affecting stone may
look like nothing but it is hard and all I could do
to hold myself. There are rooms across this city full
of my weeping, rooms I've woken up in at three or
four in the morning and felt only loss and distance;
there are rooms I'm ashamed to revisit full
of my worst moments, foreign and hard, rooms that felt
to me like hell. I didn't come to anything easy, not food,
not knowledge, not hands, not the skin on my back,

nothing smooth and if it was up to life my feet would be
bare and cracked and walking the hot pitched road at Guaya
with a broken face and hungry or tonight I would be
sitting ghostlike in a doorway in lamplight, my fingers
in smoke and my head tied in the violence of some man.
No one leaves that easy and I don't forget it and
it can always grip me and everything must measure this
and it's like someone escaping that I run to mere breathing.

EVERY CHAPTER OF THE WORLD

XV

today then, her head is thudding
as wet sand and as leaden,

today is the day after, rum soaked,
she went to bed deciding what she wasn't,

didn't she used to be that girl
her skirt razor pleated, her blouse hot iron blown,

who never leaned back, who was walking home
books in hand, the red primers blooding

over her palms, knowing nothing,
knowing no one alive inside her after

knowing nothing
nothing more

she should have stopped and changed shape
conch or mantis,

anyway
prayed

against the concrete wall, bitten the chain-link fencing,
prayed not to turn corners, not to enter any streets,

the moment she sees anything life is over,
she should have memorised the town better

so she would not vanish from it like the hill,
and should have memorised the hill so she wouldn't

notice herself noticing everything
like someone planning to leave

stopped then, and changed shape,
perhaps a woman rounding in uterus

clamping her teeth shut on cloth,
she watches a jar with water and lilies

unable to drink much more,
look one drop sweated from each head,

then is a woman turning inward
only flesh waiting to fall

her head is full of arrows
her head is chained to flight instead,

she's fingering blued pebbles, charred stories swirling in her way,
she's lost the kind of knowledge that makes you last

tells you how to change your shape and only
halfway in everything, halfway shapeless, halfway

different, she should have steered clear of
paper's fragrance, her head is heaving boulders

today she went to bed in a bundle of water
trembling, her teeth tasting the varnish

on the banister, in dim light, the verandah humid,
laughing into a joke and the shadow of the soursop tree

shedding scent and the street lamp will do
in the street's darkness, the distemper wash rubbing off

on the back of her feet, her calves, chalked,
it's the sodden world, only worse,

she had innocence before, shivering but innocence,
even if the banister shivers too, the rent twelve

dollars short each month, her hands embrace
damp, her middle thin like a leaf, and all on

the verandah laughing into a shape she'll
peel off and multiply until rum soaked she

will not recognise this, she will not be able
to go back with any assurances that this is

what she saw, it rains in every single
room, her throat thick with her tongue and

prayers that don't work because she won't believe
anyone can fix the dread her eyes bleed, she'll

leave this earth in water, in rust, in the
stink of its breath, in whose mouth she shrivels,

a gecko travels an earthen wall and
someone watches, the gecko is unordinary

the watcher unordinary, the wall determined, unordinary
the watchful wall, the stringy forefeet, the veined eyes

she is struck by the evenness of this proposition
sitting just so, this minute could last always

if she goes outside it will be the same
the wall, the gecko, the watcher, the even

wall, the even gecko, the even watcher, no
movement on her part will change it and the

light outside will melt all into more evenness,
it will bank off the wall, the someone, and the stringed

forefeet, the forefeet with no ending, beginning
in the grainy thick of the gecko's belly, it will be something

like twilight, lemon, like something she licks off
her fingers, and powdery, the gecko's string something

like an open conclusion, all even, the gecko says,
what the horizon does to the eyes, smoothing

precipices, summing up the small matter of
the spectrum in lemon light, blanket,

shadow, daubed oven; what if we left the earth
ajar like this?

she stands in this wrapping of the gecko and the wall,

her head shaking, still, murmuring pain,

nothing glorious about the world,
nothing coming soon, all that moment, thin dress limp,

lingering on the Morris chair, caught in the gate, torn,
and all that found in drizzling rain,

the mouth of the world will open
yawn her in, float her like a language on its tongue,

forgetting
all at once and therefore unfading surprise

at the hard matter of vanity, the relentless conceit
of hatred, surprise, thinking a warm evening

a reasoning gecko in twilight, lemon, a girl's dress
caught in a gate; it can never measure the length of this

tongue of conquest, language of defeat, she's
heard everything before, and would gladly drizzle

into the gecko's string and wall and licked evening,
if she could slip her head, so used to the mind's

enervating sleep on this whole chain of centuries,
she knows every chapter of the world describes

a woman draped in black and blood, in white
and powder, a woman crippled in dancing and

draped in dictators' dreams, in derelicts' hearts,
in miners' lights, in singers' shoes, in statues,

in all nouns' masculinities, in rocks cut out in
every single jungle and desert secret carried

in water's murmur, claps of civilisation, in poets
and workmen on the Panama Canal, all bridges,

barrios, tunnels called history, a woman gutted
and hung in prayer, run on with fingers, sacredly

stitched, called history and victory and government
halls, simmered in the residue of men crying vinegar,

every chapter of the world describes a woman at her own
massacre, carvings of her belly, blood gouache blood

of her face, hacked in revolutions of the sun and kitchens,
gardens of her eyes, asphalt lakes, in telescopes and bureau

drawers, in paper classifieds, telephones, exalted memories,
declarations, a woman at her funeral arrangements, why

perhaps so much of literature enters her like entering
a coffin, so much props up a ragged corpse she thinks,

the dry thin whistle of its mouth, the dead clatter
of its ribs, the rain in its room all day, all night, all

evening, the women walking out of its skull one
by one by one, if she lowers her eyes everything falls

out, if she lowers her eyes from this then perhaps
the rattling gecko could have its say, instead

suspicious, she asks, what gender, as if what
guarantee, if not certainty, how does she hold

a head full of curses, all her days are cracked
in half and crumble,

she can't think of it that way, all tidy like a swept floor
the broom resting out of sight and the unsightly

swept, she can't think of it that way, as just
doings of a passing race, so many clouds of ants

so many fields of fish, and later reassembling
in another tragedy of metal and chemical winds,

so no matter. You see, to circle enemies and
greet them like metropolitan politicians do

is the liberal way, to circle, accept, so
much southern death is a sign of talent

No she cannot speak of this or that massacre, this
or that war like a poet. Someone else will do that. She

sees who dies. Someone with not a hope but a photograph
of someone they loved, walking an Azerbaijan street, a man

and a boy and grief covering their mouth like a handkerchief,
and that feeling in the belly of all gone.

Someone moaning the name of a country, this country, in
Belet Huen, flesh melting into his blood,

in the pulp of human flesh he becomes, blindfolded
and longing for a gateway, a fence, a way out, the way in

which led him by the belly. Someone crawling
at a game of soldiers with a dog's chain and in urine,

"I love the KKK" written on his back and his white comrades
braying and kicking, someone who

the next morning will confess to his skin
and all tribunals saying, no, no, I did not feel that. It was not

race.
Someone scrubbing a plastic tablecloth

in Regent Park saying, “I have talked to God
and he knows, I hope, that I am here.”

Scrubbing the plastic flowers off the plastic tablecloth
hoping that god is listening.

Someone whose face you cannot see nor want to, her
dress around her fashionable and stiff with

blood, bent over, as if making a bed on a pavement,
smoothing out a corner of the sheet, she drowns

in the openings of her heart.
Someone in the tumbled rush of bodies cutting out

her own singular life
and the life of a child running with her to a refugee

camp on the Burundi border, caught
in the bulb of a television camera, seen

in her most private moment,
tumbling to the bottom of a mass grave after all her running.

"Assuming we speak of the civilised
world—reflecting a belief in diversity, peace,

economic liberalism and democracy—the choice

is obvious." When editorials dust themselves clean

she dreams noise wrapping the door, disappearing
gunboats steaming toward the middle of America,

bananas floating in the creamy eyes of business
men, old instruction books on the care and discipline

of slaves, not to go too far back, after all not
their fault, no need, plenty enough current

destruction, but then what are we assuming,
left unsaid, if undone, to repeat, Guatemala,

Nicaragua, Dominican Republic, Haiti, Grenada, Costa
Rica, Colombia, Chile, Mexico, all other anagrams scuttling

off that page, inventory is useless now but just to say
not so fast, not so clever, boy, circumnavigating

parentheses may be easy but not the world,
the uncivilised at the end of the day in trucks' dust clouds,

at water holes on the edges of deserts, at moonlight
waiting for crabs to march on beaches, settling into

a doorway's shawl, thinking at last a cup of water, thinking
the blanket stuck around the window will keep the rawness

out, thinking of shoe factory jobs, button factory jobs,
thread, at lines for work, at zones metamorphosing at

borders, moving as if in one skin to camps, smelling
oil wells, sugar burning, cathode smoke, earth drained

of water, earth flooded with water, rivers of slick,
overloaded ferries, all belongings bursting in suitcases

and bundles at more borders, starving in the arms
of offshore democrats with Miami bank accounts,

the tired voting in surrender, those left after the war,
those left after the peace, both feel the same, war or peace,

surrender then if it means powdered milk, if it means
rice, semolina, surrender for airflights out of barren

ice, barren water, barren villages, surrender all parentheses,
all arguments, this world in that one, that one in this

all tangled, the revolutions of an engine turning up refugees,
corporate boards, running shoes, new economic plans

but surrender the parentheses, what are those
but tongues slipping in and out of a mouth, pages

sounding like wings beating in air, what but the sound
of someone washing their hands quickly, beating their lips red.

She looks and she surrenders too, she
surrenders leaning into the moonlight on the verandah,

she surrenders her thoughts and circumnavigations
of her skull to rum, when they ask what became of her,

what was her trouble, no lover, childhood beatings,
loneliness, a weakness for simple dichotomies, poor, rich

black
white

female
male

well if it must be said their details too, and
their missions, wandering through us like a sickness.

She may not leave here anything but a prisoner
circling a cell,

cutting the square smaller and smaller and walking into herself
finally, brushing against herself as against surprising

flesh in a dark room. She
hears the *shsh* of cloth, the friction of her hands.

Even if she goes outside the cracks in her throat will break
as slate, her legs still cutting the cell in circles.

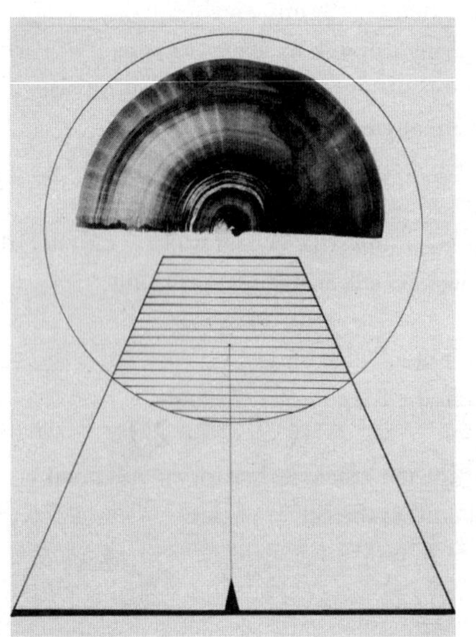

THIRSTY

(2002)

I

This city is beauty
unbreakable and amorous as eyelids,
in the streets, pressed with fierce departures,
submerged landings,
I am innocent as thresholds
and smashed night birds, lovesick,
as empty elevators

let me declare doorways,
corners, pursuit, let me say
standing here in eyelashes, in
invisible breasts, in the shrinking lake
in the tiny shops of untrue recollections,
the brittle, gnawed life we live,
I am held, and held

the touch of everything blushes me,
pigeons and wrecked boys,
half-dead hours, blind musicians,
inconclusive women in bruised dresses
even the habitual grey-suited men with terrible
briefcases, how come, how come
I anticipate nothing as intimate as history

would I have had a different life
failing this embrace with broken things,
iridescent veins, ecstatic bullets, small cracks
in the brain, would I know these particular facts,
how a phrase scars a cheek, how water
dries love out, this, a thought as casual
as any second eviscerates a breath

and this, we meet in careless intervals,
in coffee bars, gas stations, in prosthetic
conversations, lotteries, untranslatable
mouths, in versions of what we may be,
a tremor of the hand in the realization
of endings, a glancing blow of tears
on skin, the keen dismissal in speed

II

There was a Sunday morning scent,
an early morning air, then the unarranged light
that hovers on a street before a city wakes
unrelieved to the war fumes of fuel exhaust

The city was empty, except for the three,
they seemed therefore poised, as when you are alone
anywhere all movement is arrested, light, dun,
except, their hearts, scintillant as darkness

clothy blooms of magnolia, bedraggled shrubs,
wept over a past winter, a car sped by,
scatterling from sleep, their mirage disquiets,
the subway, tumescent, expectant like a grave

They had hoped without salvation for a trolley,
they arrived at the corner impious, then,
wracked on the psalmody of the crossroad,
they felt, the absences of a morning

They circled sovereign thoughts, taking
for granted the morning, the solidity of things,
the bank to one corner, the driving school on another,
the milk store and the church

each her own separate weight,
each carried it in some drenched region of flesh,
the calculus of silence, its chaos,
the wraith and rate of absence pierced them

Chloe bathed in black, then the youngest,
leather bag strapped to a still school
girlish back, the last a precise look to her yet,
a violet lace, a hackle from forehead to neck

captured in individual doubt, a hesitation,
and what they could not put into words,
indevotion, on this eighteenth Sunday
every cool black-dressed year since 1980

This slender lacuna beguiles them,
a man frothing a biblical lexis at Christie
Pits, the small barren incline where his mad sermons
cursed bewildered subway riders, his faith unstrained

then nothing of him but his parched body's declension
a curved caesura, mangled with clippers, and
clematis cirrhosa and a budding grape vine he was still
to plant when he could, saying when he had fallen, ". . . thirsty . . ."

III

That north burnt country ran me down
to the city, mordant as it is, the whole
terror of nights with yourself and what
will happen, animus, loose like that, sweeps
you to embrace its urban meter,
the caustic piss of streets,
you surrender your heart to a numb symmetry
of procedures, you study the metaphysics of
corporate instructions and not just,
besieged by now, the ragged, serrated theories
of dreams walking by, banked in sleep

that wild waiting at traffic lights off
the end of the world, where nothing is simple,
nothing, in the city there is no simple love
or simple fidelity, the heart is slippery,
the body convulsive with disguises
abandonments, everything is emptied,
wrappers, coffee cups, discarded shoes,
trucks, street corners, shop windows, cigarette
ends, lungs, ribs, eyes, love,
the exquisite rush of nothing,
the damaged horizon of skyscraping walls,
nights insomniac with pinholes of light

IV

History doesn't enter here, life, if you call it that,
on this small street is inconsequential,
Julia, worked at testing cultures and the stingy
task, in every way irredeemable, of saving money

Then Alan came, his mother, left, came ill
squeezing a sewing machine into a hallway
and then the baby. Already you can see how
joylessness took a hold pretending to be joy

Once she had risen, reprieved from the humus subway,
heard his sermonizing, sent to her by the wind
on the harp of children and leaves and engines,
she bolted the sound of his voice pursuing

She had been expecting happiness with him, why not
a ravishing measureless happiness, he spilled instead
suspicions on her belly, where was the money
she was saving, where the light she was keeping from his hands

She would waken to find the luminous filament
of his cigarette, he rage red as the tip,
weeping, he couldn't take it any more. Then threats.
She tried tenderness. What? She must take him for a fool

The worn velvet, the late condolences
for a thing buried long before his death. Julia
sees malediction in the sly crucifix,
her back bent over specimens plotting rapture

v

That polychromatic murmur, the dizzying
waves, the noise of it, the noise of it
was the first thing. There was too
an unremitting light, through the window,
through the darkness, there was no darkness,
a steady drizzle of brightness, falling
but sleep, suddenly in the middle of it,
sleep. I woke up these mornings thinking, how
could it be rest, this clamour, but rest,
the neighbour with the vacuum cleaner and the baby
and the television's basilisk stare,
the sportscaster so sleepless,
his medicine, more noise, the fridge groaning
from the weight of ice, and the dog
wounded with absence howling downstairs

the silvery rasp of my lungs begins
to resemble everything, more engines
and stranded birds, decayed chocolate,
windscreens, my blood, a jackhammer
of breaking stars, the light again, tenacious

VI

The neighbours complained that he borrowed,
took things, rakes, saws, gloves, shovels, flowers, weeds—without asking
one tulip, three peonies, seven irises,
the devil, he said, was all in the world, abroad, he said,
his face in the quivering of baby's breath,
hold my hand, he told his daughter, the devil can't come between us

The sewing machine starting up when he left, chasing zippers,
his mother blamed her. Some proper thing Julia hadn't done,
an incantation for his un-magic life,
her good, good son had been spoiled
and there had to be blame for his distress,
hers too, threaded and buttoned between her teeth

The cornflowers, the yarrow, the lavender, the wild chamomile,
his living face in her purse. A smiling man in a double
breasted suit, his hair flared to the finger-worn corners
of the picture. He'd sent this likeness long ago to say
that he was doing well

VII

That flutter in her hand started then.
Out the door into the damp May light,
Julia looks south to the magnolia bushes,
she feels their petals in her mouth
she reaches, puts them on her tongue

she is standing on the church steps
tasting the fiction of magnolia blossoms,
another year, she had reckoned silence
might dull the meaning, it would subside
like a sentence should. But it hadn't.

She pretends fixing an imaginary seam
settling a toque on her wintry head,
she's spent her time finding things
for her runaway hand to do. All seasons.

She has become used to its rhythms,
except in public it escapes,
had she willed him to vanish? had she
a passion so hidden it happened, as passions do

tethered to this city block, this church,
these spring blossoms on her tongue,
what if she disappears into another city,
she could taste again the ordinariness of coffee
take as small but sufficient a ride on a bus

toward a named street, she could head into
her life with the same ferocity as anyone,
wake up to the pillowed hush of a snowy morning,
burrow the greyness of seven o'clock in December,
if she had not been so hasty as to get Alan killed

VIII

now the door faces nothing, the window faces nothing
a parking lot, a toxic shed where movies
are made, a bus stop where pigeons light
between the morning crowd and the afternoon
itinerant baby and girl-mother,
they've laid a quick over green sod down
back of this urban barracoon, hoping
to affect beauty, no books this time, no
dictionaries to hang on to, just me and the city
that's never happened before, and happened
though not ever like this, the garbage
of pizza boxes, dead couches,
the strip mall of ambitious immigrants
under carcasses of cars, oil-soaked
clothing, hulks of rusted trucks, scraggily
gardens of beans, inshallahs under the breath,
querido, blood fire, striving stilettoed rudbeckia

breathing, you can breathe if you find air,
this roiling, this weight of bodies,
as if we need each other to breathe, to bring
it into sense, and well, in that we are merciless

IX

i

It would matter to know him as a child,
after all, he's dead when this begins
and no one so far has said a word about him
that wasn't somehow immaculate with his disaster

He was swept into a passion by the smallest injury,
would weep at a trail of ants spurning his friendship,
a boy as any who would mope if his teacher did not pick him
to clean the blackboard, ferreting bits of chalk

Everything he did was half done out of eagerness,
his homework, his half-buttoned shirt his half-shod feet,
everything he did he did hurriedly anticipating
what never measured his need

At sixteen the astonished foreman sucked his teeth
forgave the boy putting too much water in the concrete
and writing his name over and over again in the drying
pavement. Two weeks of money in mistakes and surliness

got him sent home to his mother. It wasn't complicated
she told him, it was as simple as a straight stitch,
showing him the chastened yellow cloth under her presser-foot,
"The world don't value good people," she told him

"The world don't value good people." A definite path,
he had seized first on a girl, like an anchor,
full knowing that he could not summon love
or surety in anyone. He could not flower passion

just as he knew he could not spring wild mimosa in Toronto,
the bible to steady him then, never a person for edges
and uncertainties, he only wanted a calming loving spot,
we all want that but the world doesn't love you

ii

All the dreadfulness that happened in America had happened,
his inspired sermons at Christie Pits steamed,
a baby found in a microwave, a baby shaken to death,
fourteen girls murdered in a college, people kidnapped,

Black men dragged, two, three young girls tortured
and raped and killed by a sweet blond boy,
bodies found in lakes and forests, bodies in car trunks,
bodies god knows where in disappearances,

the child killers in high schools, the rages on the highways,
the pushing murders in subways, killers in the street,
the brain-numbing dress rehearsals for victims and predators on TV,
well then, all this dreadfulness had come home to him

x

i

If withdrawal is an emotion, well then,
the vault of her hands pried open
to form the gesture of love required,
if not given whole, she glistens like disappearance

through the city, its own weight made up
of vanishings, she reaches her bicycle locked
near the church, she glides only to its clicking
wheels, not to the clatter of their various sorrow

on the stone steps, in dresses formidably black,
and a ruff of pale violet, a crisp hat, a thin lace
veil, a hand rustling and rustling, the sacrificial
breaths, hasping the shutter of lungs

this morning, in a house long abandoned
she saw the doorway sheeted in the lint
of spiders, the dusty light, the crumbling braces,
the man falling down saying, "thirsty"

ii

She thinks of turning around perhaps waving,
as if this was not a departure,
as if it were a temporary and recoverable distance
she wants to turn around with a duty done

and therefore a happiness, well,
the gears are already silvery
with abandonment, cutting out the route to
leaving them, a geomancy of the smallest damages.

iii

This time of year was treacherous as sermons
if arriving ready for a cleaning lament,
the threnody of her winter-stored bicycle tuned,
for a man who died and was cherished with flowers,

chrysanthemums, white, her mother fluttered,
had they shared some conspiracy?
this, commingled with her gaze eternally
childish. The wake, the remembrance eclipsed

iv

"What did you do?" this shivered
unsaid, she had found herself
grasped for and held and, "Did I?"
was it when she stood at the window

in the small celebrity of her father's falling,
then she would have to forgive herself childhood
and childhood had become circumstantial,
all part, the reason that he fell.

All this passes between them this morning,
but this morning in her mother's flailing,
it had inexplicably shone beneath the usual
lace veil. There had been defiance there before,

steeliness, exasperation, impassivity. Not
long-suffering. She is pure energy,
she can light the gloomy church and illuminate
the dead street just opening her mouth

and if she lingers they will burn up in her breath,
she is a wave of hot light, she needs a bicycle,
a sparrow of light, and meter, velocity itself,
she hurtles out of this lamentation to her only life

XI

i

you can't satisfy people, we long for everything,
but sleep, sleep is the gift of the city
the breath of others, their mewling, their disorder,
I could hear languages in the lush smog,
runes to mercy and failure and something tender
a fragile light, no, not light, yes light,
something you can put your hand in, relinquishing

I'll tell you this. I've seen a toxic sunset,
flying down over the city, its gorgeous spit
licking the airplane, how it is that steel weeps
with the sense of bodies, pressed, another passion,
we become other humans,
boisterous and metallic, fibrous and deserted.
Here I could know nothing and live,
harbour a dead heart,
slip corrosive hands into a coat

ii

These are the muscles of the subway's syrinx
Vilnius, Dagupan, Shaowu, Valparaiso, Falmouth, and Asmara.
The tunnel breathes in the coming train exhaling
as minerals the grammar of Calcutta, Colombo,
Jakarta, Mogila and Senhor do Bonfim, Ribeira Grande
and Hong Kong, Mogadishu and the alias St. Petersburg

the city keens its rough sonancy,
you would be mistaken to take it as music
it is the sound before music
when the throat vomits prehistoric birds

XII

It was late spring then, it was warm already,
he, jeremiad at the door holding the rough bible
to his temple like rhymed stone, she the last bolt
in her head shut, "Alan, let me pass."
"Oh my god!" his mother foretelling the meter,

he versed, "You're not leaving here with what is mine,"

her heart travelled the short distance of their joy
all the anger she had vaulted like gold belongings,
"Call the police! child, call the police! 911!"
The rake? The gloves? Had they come for the neighbours' things?
the tulip, the infinitesimal petals of spirea, the blossoms
he kissed this morning? "Here, wait." Then he would give them
their clippers, the branches of lilacs, the watering hose,
the two lengths of wild grasses that came off his hands.

They couldn't have come here to his house to stop him
from quarrelling with his own wife, it was the clippers
or the rake or their garden hose. He would straighten
things out, he would confess to the poppies, the white astilbe
Julia was leaving and no way she was taking what was his,
declaring the hedge clippers he said, "Look take it . . ."

"What the devil . . ." already descending.
"What the devil you all making so much noise for?"
then his chest flowered stigma of scarlet bergamot
their petal tips prickled his shirt, spread to his darkening
throat, he dropped the clippers to hold his breaking face,
he felt dry, "Jesus . . . thirsty . . ." he called, falling.

XIII

I don’t remember that frail morning, how
could I? No one wakes up thinking of a stranger,
a life away, falling. I don’t recall the
morning at all, as urgent or remarkable, though
falling was somehow predictable, but only when
you think of it later, falling is all you can do,
as hereditary as thirst, and so of course
he was thirsty, as I, craving a slake of baby’s
breath, or bergamot, though we were not the same,
god would not be sufficient for me,
nor the ache and panic of a city surprising,
but thirst I know, and falling, thirst for fragrant
books, a waiting peace, for life, for just halting,
so I could breathe an air less rancid, live, anonymously

so no I don’t recall the day, why would I? Let
alone, I’ve been busy with my own life, you have
to be on your toes or else you’ll drown
in the thought of your own diminishing, as I said
I crave of course being human as he must have
and she, but not to let it get away with you,
don’t dwell too long, don’t stand still here,
I skim, I desert, I break off the edges,
I believe nothing, I dream but that’s free

XIV

Her hand leafs through the grained air
of the room gleaning strands of his breath
and something to be put back together
and his mother's tuning wail and the dark

blue of the policemen's uniforms,
it touches shoes and the stairway
and a going bliss, the polish
of a dimming effort and a hint of
scarlet bergamot, in . . . here take them

Alan is in cinders on the floor,
she herself is smoldering with her
own incandescence, her reach for what
she must keep and the child to steady her

xv

All the hope gone hard. That is a city.
The blind houses, the cramped dirt, the broken
air, the sweet ugliness, the blissful and tortured
flowers, the misguided clothing, the bricked lies
the steel lies, all the lies seeping from flesh
falling in rain and snow, the weeping buses,
the plastic throats, the perfumed garbage, the
needled sky, the smogged oxygen, the deathly clerical
gentlemen cleaning their fingernails at the stock
exchange, the dingy hearts in the newsrooms, that is
a city, the feral amnesia of us all

XVI

Other people standing on this step at the church door
would wedge loss in their mouths like a soother,
but they had not had a big life and therefore a life
that could be interrupted by Alan falling,

a life that would recover, they had not had a life
that could rebound. Some had lives like that,
an expected death or, perhaps, a devastating accident,
this was beyond any small drama of tears

Newsprint would record her dry eyes,
would catch, in the middle of a flutter,
her index finger curling, the rest,
cascading neo-impressionist rage,

as if an urgent Seurat had appeared at the funeral
his pointillist blaze touching the minute light
of her heart for his *Models*, this death,
the vacant occasion of a painting

Readers would seek grief there, they would
not be prepared for emptiness such as hers,
At the moment when her nude portrait was complete
small things like the dusty cupboard to be washed

or the child's coat thinning or a certain car
revving its engine annoyingly crossed her face,
and so readers may have seen indifference
and when the back of her black funeral shoes

severed her skin they may have generously mistaken it
for a twinge of pain, when she remembered a good hot cup
of coffee she had had at five o'clock in the morning
like any spectator they may have seen satisfaction

and then again when she was tired of Alan's mother crying
they may have read exasperation with it all,
they would not be used to the concept of emptiness
selvedged with the science of darkness and light

as from any woman put together by newsprint,
mourners expected tears, and so she would have
appeared a hard woman, save she would know
the genuine sign of her own laser keen self-disgust

XVII

It isn’t, it really isn’t
the city, brief as history,
but my life in it passing sooner
than this thirst is finished, I
can offer nothing except a few glances
an uneasy sleep, a wild keening,
it would appear nothing said matters,
nothing lived, but, this is my occupation.
One day I will record the tenses of light,
not now

XVIII

Around them the city is waking up as a girl vanishes
as light,
two women feel limbless, handless, motionless
what will they do now

It is only she that brings them to any life,
makes them
understand what day it is and that perhaps
things may pass

since that day which they are still standing in,
skinless.
Time starts with her and ends when she leaves
and even

if she vanishes on her bicycle of light,
when all
she is occupied with is fleeing them, they know
much more is gone

She will return to set them in motion, they hope
they will tell her,
they will confess their loneliness, they will
promise her

all the promises on their lips, to forget, to patch it
up, to carry on.
They will dream for her all the things people dream
for people they love

they will dream her first kiss, they will dream her
graduation from college,
they will dream her wedding, they will dream her children,
if only

she would turn around and look for them. Their eyes
are eager,
their hands waiting to smooth her wedding dress, to button
her satin shoes,

to pat her hair. They lust to kiss her husband,
to tell him
he must be careful with their girl, she's the only daughter
they have

they will love
his dark face, his even skin, his staggering smile.
She will turn
around they wish, each elated, each ready

they think
to make it right if only she does, to start anew.
They imagine each
that they will be ready with a rare laugh if she turns

and if she comes back
each plans to forgive the other, not to quibble
as to whom
she loves more or whom she smiles at first. They are breathless

for her
and they think that the picture of them standing there
must seem exultant
and deserving of her and without despair. They could both

attest
in that moment to representing branches and fire and flight.
Fleeing.
Is fleeing what the curve of her back means? Is there shrinking

The street begins
to move, and they are caught in an abrupt wind, the traffic
summing up
itself to its usual rush, the life around them pearls

against their grain
until they are stems on which dresses gust and fly, leaves
caught
in another time, in the middle of life they are an outskirt.

They've gathered all their fragile veins
and if only
she were to come back she would see them in full blood.
But to anyone walking

by, they are unslaked as ghosts.
They cannot summon hope though they are bursting with it,
it is so subterranean
it cannot break the surface of their skin, it cannot lap

their waiting arms
and overwhelm their failures, as it must
were she
to look back to their exact vision,

one solidly inconsolable, the other all dead flutter.
The street
now in full flight, no one notices that they are arrested,
waiting for a return

People bump against them, a murmured "sorry" cannot know
how appropriate it is,
an impatient brushing, cannot truly feel
their immobility

XIX

i

They had been observed by a man with unusual kindness
for a city. He had sensed the extravagant calm
where an old woman leaned on a cane. He had seen

the rest of the street as if blowing by in a windstorm,
he, swept up in it on his way to the halal store,
thinks of his own mother on the road in Jaffna

confused amid the mad morning traffic, her smallness
in peril on the corner of Hospital Vithi,
he has not seen her since one bird-silent day when

he left home, fleeing, himself. He keeps a register
of her face, transparent as terror in his walking
dreams on Bloor Street

He reaches to embrace Chloe, the sameness of his love
falls on her, his hands anticipate the doves of her
arms, the warming sobs she wipes from his face

but then he notices a black-winged stillness, a
violet lace-covered eyes with the merest tremor
so he passes

ii

They had been observed too by a woman
if only because she was as jittery as they were quiet,
she had awakened to a hard burning in her veins

she had grabbed her homeless skin, too thick
for the warm spring, too flimsy for her shiver,
she was trying to cop an early dime

she would not have noticed them but only noticed
as the fastest thing notices the slowest,
as they are in synergy with each other

she was sweating, they ice cool,
as stars bursting slowly in the speeding universe,
she in a quick burn, they singed

her hair falls lank, her sweat corrodes her cheeks,
she scratches the furious pox of crack raw,
cankers open to the god of the terrible morning

Sault Ste. Marie is where her vowels abandoned her,
a car ride hopped on acid and well needed gasoline
left her at half the journey to this city block

speechless, only the wrought skeleton that now was
her face, jabbed the air. She would love to stop
her own breath and the story it drowns in

they, heavy black and invisible violet cruised
her eyebrow along with the thought of her hookup,
she wanted to be that languid,

spots her jones man in the blue phone booth
half a block down and flies, bowed out of their orbit
a wrecked moon. She hopes this hit will last eternity

iii

Their cocoon becomes porous letting in the murmuring city,
the cars gunning at the traffic light, the war of daylight,
waiting, painless, if only that girl would turn around and come home

XX

Consider the din of beginnings, this vagrant, fugitive city
just hours ago these people standing prone as sleep
in subways were enclosed in the silk of their origins,
glowing chrysalises of old, at least, inconvenient cultures

they had some set notions of who they were, buried in apartments
and houses in North York and Scarborough and Pickering,
those suburbs undifferentiated, prefabricated from no great
narrative, except cash, there is no truth to their names

they don't even vaguely resemble the small damp villages
of their etymology. The Romans would not build roads here,
unflagging dreariness dries the landscape, meagre oases of woodland
fight gas stations and donut shops for any thing named beauty

Thomson would have snatched his *Burnt Country* away from here,
knowing that it would vanish. This suburban parching would dry bog
far more succour the oversleeping, the insomniac, summer wastes,
mauve light, mauve, mauve dark black, mauve white, reconstructing

what they choose to remember and what they mis-forget of places
they'd known. They are improvising as Lismer's *Forest in Winter*
some recent past, drowned hues, drenched schemes, plans,
for an arranged marriage, a red bride, a white garlanded groom, the

Gurdwara on Weston Road. Blue, blue, blue black, that brilliant
red leafed tree, yellow leafed tree, the immigrant from Sheffield,
Lismer paints Sackville River with the same new memory as Violet
Blackman, her gesso was that wood floor in Rosedale

1920, when Toronto was just a village and all her labour, all her
time, all her heart and hand could not make that painting work, so,
hanging on fading histories, igniting another burnt drama
forty years from St. Elizabeth someone says this is how we do

christenings back home yet longs to see the world over, elsewhere
someone disciplined a son coming home, too late, "We live here
but don't think that we're going to live like people here!"
The city's cathedral of smogged sky receives the daily sacrament

of conditional sentences about conditional places, "If we were home.
I would . . ." as strong a romance with the past tense as with what is
to come. Cresting as the engraver's mountain red black, purple, light
suffused in sunset, important in the middle of the pluperfect

in the subway though these separate dreamers are a mass of silences.
They are echo chambers for the voices of the gods of
cities. Glass, money, goods. They sit in a universe of halted breaths
waiting for this stop Bay and that stop Yonge and that one St. Patrick

in early morning surrender to factories in Brampton,
swirling grey into the 401 and the Queen Elizabeth Highway,
they hold their tempers, their passions, over grumbling machines
until night, dreaming their small empires, their domestic tyrannies

but of course no voyage is seamless. Nothing in a city is discrete.
A city is all interpolation. The Filipina nurse bathes a body, the
Vincentian courier delivers a message, the Sikh cab driver navigates a
corner. What happens? A new road is cut, a sound escapes, a touch
lasts

XXI

i

The house is still there, on Hallam Street,
still half-sleeping, ramshackled like wintering
bear. Days after her father fell and his mother
folded beside him, there had been the funeral

"Poor child, poor child, . . . to have to see that . . ."
Chloe, sopping her head with bay leaves and rum,
discovered her sanguine, and put an end to it,
"Cry! I tell you, you unmerciful child."

A slow black car took them to his funeral,
a crowd impassioned in black and white
and beige and purple followed. Heavy, palms,
poured a veil of fingers over her eyes

Chloe sang *By the Rivers of Babylon*,
then broke like cake into tears,
cracked into a falsetto of grief
raised in the air to summon an inattentive God

the procession not anything like mourning, but
a fury took her father's incline at Christie Pits,
a loudspeaker quavered, ". . . did not deserve
in his own house   no peace   before

his child   the Toronto police
have to answer   any one of us
time and again
not going to stand   justice for our brother,"
the wife's face was waterless though

ii

Each May after for eighteen Mays she came to the moment
her husband fiercely beatific in the beige tucked coffin
as if he had expected the inconsolable casket,
and their life after, draped dim with his radiance
yet that moment, that moment she felt nothing at all

and nothing since. Leading to this May and previous
with the three of them left. They were alone in the world.
Which really was how they'd felt in the first place
before Alan fell down whispering, ". . . thirsty . . ."

XXII

which is to say, human. I did hear the city's susurrus,
loud, wide, promising, like wine, obscurity and rapture,
the bright veiled Somali women hyphenating Scarlett Road,
the eternal widows, Azorean and Italian at Igreja de Santa
Inez and Iglesia de San Antonio. At the Sea King Fish Market,
the Portuguese men have learned another language. "Yes
sweetie, yes dahling, and for you only this good good price."
This to the old Jamaican women who ask, "Did you cut the fish
like I told you? Why you charging me so much?" This dancing,
these presences, not the least, writing the biographies
of streets, I took, why not, yes, as wonderful

summer teems, College and Bathurst, Queen and Yonge,
St. Clair and Dufferin, Eglinton to the highway,
at these crossroads, transient selves flare
in the individual drama, in the faith of translation,
at the covert dance halls, at the cut-rate overpriced
shopping malls, there are impossible citizens,
repositories of the city's panic, there are those
here too worn as if by brutal winds, a pocked
whale-boned, autumnal arctic stone of a face,
not wind at all but some unproven element works
there, Spadina and Bloor to the Mission
and the Silver Dollar south, unproven, not unseen

XXIII

I'll tell you what I've seen here at Yonge and Bloor,
At this crossroad, the air is elegiac with it
whiffs and cirri of all emotion, need and vanity,
desire, brazen as a killing

a burger a leather jacket a pair of shoes a smoke
to find a job to get drunk at the Zanzibar,
a body the body of a woman in a cage on the window
in a photograph in a strip joint two blocks away.

to piss to get drunk to get fucked to get high
grease sushi men wanting to be beaten to be touched
and all the anonymous things that may happen
on a corner like this for instance murder

If you look into any face here you might fall
into its particular need. And a woman I've seen her
Julia perhaps walks here I can't quite make her out
She is a mixture of twigs and ink she's like paper

XXIV

In the kitchen her tongue parts the flesh of avocados
and ackees,
the stiff tough saltiness of dried cod; the waves of chatter
are light

her teeth crush the meat of milk coconuts, sever the hairs
of mangoes
Oh she cultivated this light talk,
nothing wrong,

as if Alan would break the door any minute coming home.
Inaudible, frothy
and insensible, the words never deep enough to get at the matter
just enough

this talk, enough to fill, enough to circle the knowing, not hurdle
the last thing they shared
in all this time no word of condolence, not cursing or strain
of last night's restless sleep

words
were the opposite of meaning in this house now,
the meter
of Julia's hand more intuitive than any set of sounds
gathering

too busy
to cook dinner, that hand dancing with her mouth, her neck
it keeps
reaching out for the phone, dialing and dialing, circumnavigating

that bolt
of white light speeding away on a bicycle, yesterday,
she had lost
her hold, she had allowed an emotion. She had merely felt affinity

for the magnolias
then she'd turned her face, adjusted her hair, an expression
of self-pity had moved her muscles.
That's all.

If she would suddenly walk to the corner of Yonge
and Bloor
supposing there the incessant movement of her hand
would subside

or melt in the solitary flights, the syllables of weeping
collected there
might slake her might swamp her might breathe
her heart wet

perhaps there, this suffocating sacrifice to everyone
this city
the falling man, the withering readers, the absent mourners
might stop

and there the smell of flowers less melancholy
Mays turned
furious with her living body, a scythed moon ravished
in neon

there as she always planned, the trembling
timbre of gathered
dreams, a small apartment with music and perhaps
a bird

if she could bear the cage, but there a sense
of flight in green
some songs. Only something small as a winter
a twilight

without that mistake, the look she had misjudged
so terribly
as reflecting her own fabulous, now,
purpose

happiness. Why did she need forgiveness for that
for air
for the temperature of her thoughts, the weather
of her flesh

passion,
she's seen it under a microscope in a laboratory
ferocious
spilling on her hand, a wave she should follow

a ride
on the ferry to Hanlan's Point, nakedness
she needed
could find some place to be naked, to slip her body

becoming
transparent as veins and letters and children
fugitive
as crossroads and windowpanes and bread

and blue
this sweet colour in skies and paintings
she
would simply exist for

XXV

After he was thirsty the sewing machine fell silent
for quite a while, at odd hours as if struck, some sudden
pain, a word wailed like "my . . ." so haunched

other times a raucous peeping like a small bird
weeping for hours and days, then one day the sewing
machine started up again and never seemed to stop still

the floor littered in threads and odds and ends of long
haired cloth. The child loved the taste of threads, the
treat of buttons, the disorderliness, recondite blooms

smothered in bottomless cloth treading her way, great
arms not enough to keep the cloth from suffocating her,
the machine not quick enough to keep up with her desire

"God did what God did." The man who had shot her son,
may he live in hell. She had accounted, read his name
into Psalm 37, "For they shall soon be cut down like the grass,"

Only that and verse one, "Fret not thyself because of evil
doers," had stopped her from delivering him home.
In the courthouse yard a happiness washing his face

she, Chloe had rushed at him with her bare hands.
There was no shame in some people. After all every
body is human, everybody wants forgiveness

she had been willing to forgive if he asked her,
she had felt it within her power to kill him
and to forgive him. She held back balancing this power

XXVI

So, a cop sashaying from a courthouse,
his moustache wide and bristling,
his wool coat draped across his body
and carefree, his head centred in the television
cameras against
scales of justice, he would strike
a match on the bottom of his shoes,
light a cigar in victory of being acquitted
of such a killing, and why not

captured by several television networks,
a vulgarity to it, a sybaritic languor
the guy walks toward his visual audience
as a high-fashion model walking a couture runway
in Paris or Milan. A showy stride
with the sexy swagger of a male model,
all muscle and grace, his virility in hand
his striking the match like a gunslinger,
this élan, law and outlaw, SWAT and midnight rider,
history and modernity kissing here

XXVII

i

The television tuned to the perpetual gospel channel
has worn out, its florid pigments washed cadaverous yellow,
she's fallen asleep to it and awakened to it every day

the preacher is reading from First Corinthians, chapter 13,
his Texan psaltery whining, "But when that which is perfect
is come, then that which is in part shall be done away."

God doesn't give you what you can't handle. Yesterday
stiff with hope she knew the clear thing as soon as the morning
disappeared, she could not reach into another generation

she didn't have to. Sprawled insensible on the mounds of cloth
Chloe murmurs this insight to the air above her face
The Texan evangelist confirms, "When that . . . is come . . ."

Chloe isn't waking up this morning. The tube will soon burn out
on the television, its blanched light and its voice,
Chloe never bothered with the converter once the battery was gone

the televangelists were all her interest anyway and the soap
operas. The sprockets on the tuning switch smoothed
the television had arrived at a vacant rest on the prayer channel

It doesn't matter. She's not waking up to try and catch
Days of Our Lives. The Texan minister is at verse twelve
of First Corinthians when Chloe crosses herself in her sleep

by this time today Chloe would have been awake, drunk a cup
of coffee, had a secret cigarette or two, and listened
to the apartment for evidence of her son.

He would have asked her to braid his hair, she would have
made rows around her fingers; she would have scratched his scalp,
he would have fallen asleep in her hands.

ii

She is elsewhere, by a river, the Rio Cobre, pitching stones,
she is dressed in her whole slip, Alan big in her belly,
she dives into the water becoming weightless,
that is when she crosses her arms in her sleep

and she is climbing a hilly road, thankful
that the day is rainy and cool; the grass and trees
and their colonies of insects and birds, all she hears,
her legs are bare and young she takes the road

now ahead of her in the distance, a small boy, a bag
on his shoulder, kicking pebbles and dust,
skitters down the stairs with the hedge clippers
and she is wiping the floor around his head in threads

the knitwear company is ringing the doorbell again
and Chloe hears the small coins she's given Alan
they are jingling in the pocket of his short blue pants.
That girl has written. She's sent his ticket. He'll be leaving soon

There's a siren sound in Chloe's sleep
and she thinks in her dream, "Whose life is that?"
The scar on her index finger from the sewing machine
is healed evangelically. Completely.

The television is seeing its own last doorway,
the evangelist now a woman with healing powers
she's sent that woman cash money for her good works,
addressed her divine ministry in Atlanta, Georgia

off this road Chloe isn't waking up,
this motionless morning, things will come
to rest, the thread dust, the cloth dust,
the May light is streaming into Chloe's room

XXVIII

Anyone, anyone can find themselves on a street corner
eclipsed, as they, by what deserted them
volumes of blue skirt with lace eyelets
a dance stroke you might have trimmed
the way a day can slip out of your hand,
your senses spill like water,
the tremolos of Leroy Jenkins' violin exiting
the Horseshoe Tavern, the accumulation of tender
seconds you should have noticed, as mercy,
even these confessions of failure so unreliable,
hardly matter

XXIX

A house in this city is a witness box
of every kind of human foolishness
and then it all passes, new people inhabit
old occurrences are forgotten and
repeated to be forgotten again.
Before them a girl had died here of leukemia,
a thirteen year old, she liked jigsaw puzzles
she died hard, like Chloe's son,
well perhaps his was harder

No one prepares for how he died,
no one had a diagnosis beforehand
unless you count the mere presence of him,
his likeness, unless you count that
as a symptom of what he would die of,
unless you count a moment on a staircase
when guesses searing as letters
turned his face into a nightmare
instead of the face of Chloe's boy
who was afraid of his own shadow
and in a panic about losing everything

The girl who died here was born
in Regio Calabria,
though she spoke English when she was ill
and no one understood
she was a pretty girl and the leukemia
made her curiously prettier,
in sickness her beauty was so convincing
they could not open her casket for fear
she would come alive again through beauty

It isn't a haunting. That would be too fabulous.
It happened and what happened, happened.

Nothing unfortunately is ever one way,
juice, jam, yogurt, milk, everything spilled
on that spot before Alan's head did.
A deliberate red, like Ethiopian henna,
seeped into the floor grooves when Alan fell

The walls of a house can sense like skin,
that is why sometimes you can tell
what happened in this apartment,
the doorway shivers a deep blue, the ceilings rain,
the staircase declares a radiant girl
and someone saying, "thirsty . . ."

xxx

Spring darkness is forgiving. It doesn't descend
abruptly before you have finished work,
it approaches palely waiting for you
to get outside to witness another illumined hour

you feel someone brush against you,
on the street, you smell leather, the lake,
the coming leaves, the rain's immortality
pierces you, but you will be asleep when it arrives

you will lie in the groove of a lover's neck
unconscious, translucent, tendons singing,
and that should be enough, the circumference
of the world narrowed to your simple dreams

Days are perfect, that's the thing about them,
standing here in half darkness, I think this.
It's difficult to rise to that, but I expect it
I expect each molecule of my substance to imitate that

I can't of course, I can't touch syllables
tenderness, throats.
Look it's like this, I'm just like the rest,
limping across the city, flying when I can

XXXI

what she might collect now and what she isn't
the bristle of light so public and irretrievable
the wood crumbled into paper too appropriate
the grey patch of stars that made her still mouth
the oblivious dress she wore, the shoes
grafted to her feet and the ink-dry pavement
her mourning, lustrous as fury

yet she too had glimpsed herself,
an unrepentant cheekbone, those fingers
brushing glyphs of newsprint away
the extraordinary emptiness of the woman
emerging from clusters of dots on the front page
then the second page, then the last page
then vanishing all together, but not vanished

there, in the time, transparent,
held and held, she had been held, why
it was so quiet there and cool as edges
anything nearing life or what she might do
now, any opening, now again in the bolt
of a bicycle, again she had sensed, glimpsed
herself, now as pitiable and that she could not take

lust she had lost along with the things
in her suitcases that morning, and the things,
the slivers of seconds in between,
fallen, all of it, tinted, sunken, all of it,
that, she wanted back, that at least if not
a daughter as silver as velocity; and the true
taste of things and the atmosphere of her blood

beating at her temples in apprehension or fear
or love or any feeling; the climate of substances
she would have touched, the divine elements

her eyes ought to have seen, her throat devour,
the space surrounding her, look that gesture
of a boy the other morning, even the panic of a woman
bowing out of orbit to a lodestar of crack

once she wore powder blue skirts and embroidered
Indian blouses, then she stood on the corner of
Oakwood and St. Clair waiting for a bus, the clarity
of the traffic, the sky, the day, her life
her directions, plain, unknown, except for this,
the idea, the idea that she was possible
nothing but the sun in the blood of a summer

she used to buy a new pair of sandals
each year, soften the leather with the sweat
of her feet, then a wide-mouthed woven bag
out of which wine and letters and lipstick
and panties, water, apples, bracelets, and grapes
could fall; she went to concerts tasting music
and the cocks of jazz musicians, taking their mouths

in her own scent; she used to jump fire hydrants
on Bloor when darkness wet the roads and drunks
cradled light posts; she used to take ganga-high rides
to Montreal when her body was dangerous and full
of liquid; she could assassinate streets with her eyes
damage books and chemical compounds and honey and waiting
rooms, dance floors would bleed from the knife of her dress

until, it must be said, the moment when all women realize
the war they're in, that the only possibility is falling
that the fragments of winter and music are only solemn
kisses to their half-life and only mercy and surrender move
their hand. Well what's more with a daughter given up
to lightning and pity she wanted her blue skirt back,
she wanted that single sense she'd lost, anticipation

She needed to smell, without dying, the skin
of someone else, she needed without a wounding,
without a murder, without a killing, a truce if not peace,
a city, as a city was supposed to be, forgetful,
and to gather up any charm she might have
left, to sleep, to feel snow, to have it matter,
to wake like leaves, to hate rain

XXXII

Every smell is now a possibility, a young man
passes wreathed in cologne, that is hope;
teenagers, traceries of marijuana, that is hope too, utopia;

smog braids the city where sweet grass used to,
yesterday morning's exhaust, this day's
breathing by the lightness, the heaviness of the soul.

Every night the waste of the city is put out and taken away
to suburban landfills and recycling plants,
and that is the rhythm everyone would prefer in their life,

that the waste is taken out, that what may be useful
be saved and the rest, most of it, the ill of it,
buried.

Sometimes the city's stink is fragrant offal,
sometimes it is putrid. All depends on what wakes you up,
the angular distance of death or the elliptic of living.

XXXIII

From time to time . . . frequently, always
there is the arcing wail of a siren, as seas
hidden in the ordinariness of the city
the stream and crash of things lived
if it is late at night and quiet, as quiet
as a city can get, as still as its murmurous genealogy
you can hear someone's life falling apart

Most people can sleep through a siren. I can't.
It isn't the proximity of it that wakes me, as shores,
it is its emotion. Its prophecy. Even at a great distance
you sense its mortal discoveries
whoever it is calling for, whoever is caught
human, you can hear their gnawed substance in its song

In a siren, the individual muscles of a life collapsing,
as waves, stuttering on some harm,
your fingers may flutter in the viscera of an utter stranger
I wake up to it, open as doorways,
breathless as a coming hour, and undone

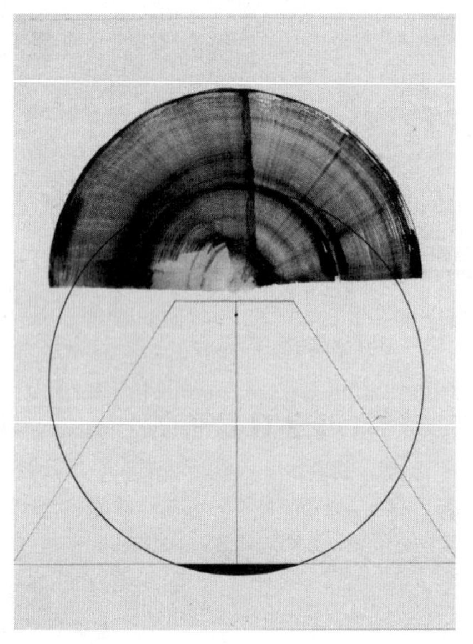

INVENTORY

(2006)

I

We believed in nothing

the black-and-white american movies
buried themselves in our chests,
glacial, liquid, acidic as love

the way to Wyoming, the sunset in Cheyenne,
the surreptitious cook fires, the uneasy
sleep of cowboys, the cactus, the tumbleweed,
the blankets,
the homicides of Indians,
lit, dimmed, lit, dimmed

lit in the drawing rooms,
the suicides inside us

and the light turnings to stone,
inside and out,
we arrived spectacular, tendering
our own bodies into dreamery,
as meat, as mask, as burden

like chaos

all the fake feelings we had, oh love,
the acts of ventriloquism, the wooded arteries,
the arms clattering to the floor,
the big raw cities flailing us

we returned home dead on our feet
and melancholy

the earth was never the earth,
we were never anyone,
everything we were preceded us,
foolish in the heady days
when we thought we might, somehow
within a few seasons,
after their laughter and raucid whistles

but this was their manifesto,
and we took it like fun,
the burnt kernels, the chemical sugars

their love stories never contained us,
their war epics left us bloody

we poor, we weak, we dying

we cheered them,
encouraged them, helped them with the cooking,
the tracking to our throat lines,
gave them the books of signs,
the last magical bird feather,
the traces of our fires

the screens lacerate our intimacies
gathered at the windows

on the corners, thinking one day
we'll make it, delicately,
without a war, without the tragedy
of it all
and maybe with our bodies,
though now

it's too late for that

We waited, we waited sticklike and nervous,
did what we could when allowed

made up all the dances, fine,
burned our lungs on music,
so many dead musicians,
the extraterrestrial neurons, the brittle veins it took
to leave so much music, so much music,
so much dried muscle at olympian lines,
the heels eviscerated with speed

and all the folded linen, all
the broken fingers, pricked and bruised,
misformed ribs and the famished babies
for the world's most famous photos

the steel we poured, the rivets we fastened
to our bare bones like cars,
we stripped, so fastidious,
the seams of dirt excised from apples and gold

all the railways

everywhere, and the forests we destroyed,
as far as
the Amazonas' forehead, the Congo's gut,
the trees we peeled of rough butter,
full knowing, there's something wrong
with this

then the prison couture of orange-clad criminals
we became,
the kinkiness of blindfolds we admitted

we did all this and more

there were roads of viscera and supine alphabets,
and well, fields of prostration,
buildings mechanized with flesh and acreages
of tender automobiles

heavy with our tiredness, solid with our devotion

after work we succumbed
headlong in effusive rooms

to the science-fiction tales of democracy
and to their songs,
come gather 'round people   *for the times*
say it loud   *and when you talk about destruction*
count me out   *deep in my heart I do believe*
oh lord won't you buy me   *make me wanna holler*

that's fine, got drunk, got high,
said we were already living in another time

they waited, watched,
evacuated all our good lyrics
of the goodness, of the science, the delicious
being of more than, well more,
so hard now to separate what was them

from what we were

how imprisoned we are in their ghosts

how in their beginnings and endings
no wonder, no wonder,
every evening falls on axioms,
the violins of edible fears

someone enters in black, oh darling, oh love,
the eclipses of windowpanes,
the secret life of the sun's corona going by

the woman is lying in the alleyway

treacherous and naked once more,

half the mind is atrophied in this,
just as inanimate doors and pickup trucks,
the unremitting malls of all desires

small years, small for the distancing planet,
how would we know, so suspended, defenceless
with our hungers,
nibbling our own hearts to the red pits

how would it truly be to have danced
with Celia Cruz, unsmiling

to have studied instead
the street names of Montevideo or Havana,
Kingston and Caracas as if planning to live there
in the elegant future, as if no other life would do,
or if the vows of transformation
were only made in Parral or Basse-Pointe

to have loved instead
Te recuerdo Amanda, la calle mojada,
corriendo a la fábrica   la lluvia en el pelo,
to sing this to potential lovers

then to have seen Che
Guevara as an old man on television,

Angela's unbreakable voice has made jails extinct,
to die in this compassion,
to have never heard "Redemption Song," so hoarse, at all

not willing another empire but history's pulse
measured with another hand,
as continents roll over in their sleep

a whimsical contraption moved with sometimish winds

of inconvenient magnets to allow
unpredictable openings of incurable light

now we must wait on their exhaustion, now
we have to pray for their demise with spiked hands,
with all the brilliant silences,
to understand the whole language,
the whole immaculate language of the ravaged world

11

Observed over Miami, the city, an orange slick blister,
the houses, stiff-haired organisms clamped to the earth,
engorged with oil and wheat,
rubber and metals,
the total contents of the brain, the electrical
regions of the atmosphere, water

coming north, reeling, a neurosis of hinged
clouds,
bodies thicken, flesh

out in immodest health,
six boys, fast food on their breath,
luscious paper bags, the perfume of grilled offal,
troughlike cartons of cola,
a gorgon luxury of electronics, backward caps,
bulbous clothing, easy hearts

lines of visitors are fingerprinted,
eye-scanned, grow murderous,
then there's the business of thoughts
who can glean with any certainty,
the guards, blued and leathered, multiply
to stop them,
palimpsests of old borders, the sea's graph on the skin,
the dead giveaway of tongues,
soon, soon, the implants to discern lies

from the way a body moves

there's that already

she felt ill, wanted
to murder the six boys, the guards,
the dreamless shipwrecked
burning their beautiful eyes in the patient queue

Let's go to the republic of home,
let's forget all this then, this victorious procession,
these blenching queues,
this timeless march of nails in shoeless feet

what people will take and give,
the passive lines, the passive guards,
if passivity can be inchoate self-loathing

all around, and creeping

self-righteous, let's say it, fascism,
how else to say, border,
and the militant consumption of everything,
the encampment of the airport, the eagerness
to be all the same, to mince biographies
to some exact phrases, some
exact and toxic genealogy

III

One year she sat at the television weeping,
no reason,
the whole time

and the next, and the next

the wars' last and late night witness,
some she concluded are striving on grief
and burnt clothing, bloody rags, bomb-filled shoes

the pitiful domestic blankets
in the hospitals,
the bundles of plump
corpses waiting or embraced by screams,
the leaking chests and ridiculous legs

the abrupt density of life gone out,
the manifold substances of stillness

nothing personal is recorded here,
you must know that, but
one year the viciousness got to be too much

the news was advertisement for movies,
the movies were the real killings

the baked precipitous ditches,
twisted metal hulks of things that used to be,
fires intense as black holes, voids in schoolyards
and hotels, in kitchens and prophetic boys

all this became ordinary far from where it happened

the Arab faces were Arab faces after all,
not even the western hostages were hostages,
the lives of movie stars were more lamentable,
and the wreckage of streets was unimportant

what confidences would she tell you then,
what would possibly be safe in your hands

but never mind that, here is the latest watchful hour

—twenty-seven in Hillah, three in fighting in
Amariya, two by roadside bombing, Adhaim,
five by mortars in Afar, in firefight in Samarra

two, two in collision near Khallis, council member
in Kirkuk, one near medical complex, two in
Tal Afar, five by suicide bomb in Kirkuk, five

by suicide in Shorgat, one in attack on police
chief, Buhurz, five by car bomb in Baquba,
policeman in Mosul, two by car bomb, Madaen

five by mortars in Tal Afar, Sufi follower
near Baghdad, twelve by suicide bomb in
restaurant, bystander in Dora, in Mishada,
in Hillah, twenty-seven again, twenty-seven—

she's heard clearly now, twenty-three,
by restaurant bomb near green zone, Ibn Zanbour,
and so clear, syntonic, one, threading a needle

three beating dust from slippers, anyone looking
for a newspaper, an idea in their head like figs will soon
be in season, four playing dominoes, drinking Turkish coffee

seven by shop window, with small girl, in wading pool,
twelve half naked by river, nine shot dead in

Missouri shopping mall, possible yes, in restaurant
in Madison, three nephews, one aunt in Nashville fire bomb,
six by attack near hospital in Buffalo, two listening to radio

sixteen by bomb at football stadium, one reading
on bus "the heart is enclosed in a pericardial sac
that is lined with the parietal layers of serous membrane . . ."

three with the electricity gone since Thursday,
still fumbling for candles then finding the matches

beating on the tympanic bone, by suicide bomb,
by suicide bomb, by car bomb, by ambush, any
number by sunlight, in daylight, by evening

still on those safe streets, amber alerts go out
by television, by puppetry, in sessions of paranoia,
in heavy suits with papers in cool hands as if staring at fools

there are announcements of imagined disturbances,
of dreads and sometimes it must be play, surely,
and the peculiar fragility of power

where it's the safest they use yellow and amber
and red pretending like the movies that there's
a bad guy every sixty seconds, and a car chase
coming and a hero with fire power

still in June,
in their hiatus eight killed by suicide bomb at
bus station, at least eleven killed in Shula at
restaurants, at least fifteen by car bomb, Irbil

At least someone should stay awake, she thinks,
someone should dream them along the abysmal roads

twenty-three by suicide bomb at Ibn Zanbour kebab
restaurant, no need to repeat this really, just the name
of the kebab place is new, isn't it

enough numbers still to come so twenty
outside bank in Kirkuk, the numbers so random,
so shapeless, apart from their shape, their seduction of infinity

the ganglia and meninges, the grey matter
of the cerebrum, the viscous peritoneal cavity

did she say two listening to the radio, to Nancy Amriq perhaps
any, any, preferring by sleep, by magic, in hallucinations

but here it is in rush hour, in traffic, a queue near the scarf
seller, in a moment's inattention, injured by petals of nails,
and hot wire, fugitive valves, a rain of small glittering teeth

and bones beatific, sharpened with heat, at least

it was sudden if not predictable at any rate
not on Sunset Boulevard, Potsdame Strasse,
Oxford Circus, Rue du Faubourg St. Honore and
all those streets

of reasonable suspicion, of self-fulfilling
dread, charred by home improvements,
self-makeovers, what goes for conscience now

what foundations, what animus calms, we're
doing the best we can with these people,
what undeniable hatred fuels them, what else
can we do, nothing but maim them,

we do not deserve it, it's out of the blue,
the sleeplessness at borders, the poor sunlight,
the paralyzed cars, they hate our freedom,

they want the abominable food from our mouths

“It is worst during the night
when the bombardment is most intense”

look, where are the matches, no, don’t light a fire,
the tap’s dripping precious,
the electricity will soon come back, how far
away is it now, the phosphorescent bodies,

the tremulous wounded hallways

she has to keep watch at the window
of the television, she hears what is never shown,
the details are triumphant,
she’ll never be able to write them in time

the paper now, and where’s the hair oil,
the butter’s gone rancid,
remember that cat we used to have,
it disappeared the first day,
lemons, remember to buy lemons

there's another life, she listens, each hour, each night,
behind the flat screen and the news anchor,
the sleek, speeding cars, the burgers, the breaking

celebrity news, unrealities of faraway islands,
bickering and spiteful,
each minute so drastic, they win a million dollars

the waiting, she can't bear the waiting,
the metal, metal, metal of waiting,
she sits devoted, the paring knife close
to a harvest of veins

now everything is in her like ends and tastes,
the loosening clasp of affinities
everyone grows perversely accustomed,
she refuses

If they're numb over there, and all around her,
she'll gather the nerve endings
spilled on the streets, she'll count them like rice grains

she'll keep them for when they're needed

for music and the ornaments of air without bombing,
for bread and honey, the kilos of figs
in December and baked yams from burnt

fingered vendors, the washing to be done,
the sewing, the bicycles to be repaired,
the daily lists to be made of mundane
matters, like the cost of sugar, or the girl losing
her new pencils again

and not to say, for the memories of the forgetful, the
spinners of silences,
the teethed impasto of broadcasts

she'll gather the passions of women,
their iron feet, their bitter hair, their
perpetual nuptial assignment

to battered kitchens and rooms
radiant with their blood vessels

their waiting at doors
at night in the universe, such waiting

the mind surpasses, the bones are a failure,
the pregnancies wretched again, and again

she'll store the nerves' endings in glass
coloured bottles on a tree near the doorsteps,
for divine fierce years to come

when the planet is ruined, the continent
forlorn in water and smoke

till then
where are the packages of black pepper,
the oil for the lilac bore, the shovel

if she wakes up tomorrow and things are still this way,
then the shovel for the ice
in the garden, the winter-eaten sidewalk

someone died leaving her a basket,
she'll fill it with the overflow,
line it with day lilies and the wine
she makes sitting there
pressing and pressing these bundles of dried blooms

the bus stations are empty and sobbing,
the unemployment lines are runny
like broken eggs, the construction sites
pile up endlessly, nothing is finished

she is a woman who is losing the idea
of mathematics,
the maximum is so small, the
crushed spines of vehicles fly in the air,
all September, all October

where's the flour, the nighttime stories, where's
the sugar for the tongue's amusement, muscle
and likeness,

now she wishes she could hear
all that noise that poets make about
time and timelessness

come throw some water on her forehead,
look for the butterflies so wingless,
the oven is freezing with a steady, steady cold

Stay now, she's written a letter,
an account of her silence,
its destination all the streets
beginning with Al Kifah, Al Rashid,
Abu Nuwas, Hafa, Mansur, and the 14th of July

beginning—what door are you looking through now,
still what door are you looking through,
what sound does the world make there,
the sound you must have heard
before these disasters, the sound
you must keep

don't pray it only makes things worse, I know,
think instead of what we might do
and why, why are only the men in the streets,
all over the world

the houses are on the edge of rotted dreams,
all the dictators' palaces are made of the same wood

if I say in this letter, I'm waiting
to step into another life,
will you come then and find me

without rivers, without hopes, without nails,
without anything we now know, without
bruises, without bullet-holed walls

will you come without news of confessions
of serial killers and lost brides?

let us forget all that, let us not act surprised,
or make coy distinctions among mass
murderers, why ration nuclear weapons,
let us all celebrate death

when you come though we'll listen
to Coltrane's *Stellar Regions*, to water,
to rain, again, anywhere, and to Betty Carter

to caterpillars gnawing at leaves,
to gira cooking in oil, to all the songs
I love and have forgotten like Smokey
Robinson's "Ooh Baby Baby" and Roaring Lion's
"Caroline," we'll just listen

the ear is so valuable, it is like sleep

to Dinah Washington and Leonard Cohen,
to Fairuz, to yawning and to one bee eating fruit

what time do you like best, whenever,
the best thing then is the Atlantic, wherever
you find it, then you don't need music,
it is the beginning of music

Cecil Taylor knows this, and Kathleen Battle
and Fateh Ali Khan, and Abdullah Ibrahim,
then just watching that ocean evens out the world

all I can offer you now though is my brooding hand,
my sodden eyelashes and the like,
these humble and particular things I know,
my eyes pinned to your face

understand, I will keep you alive like this,
the desolate air between us is no match
for the brittle orchids we are destined to eat together,
the ashen tulips we will devour voraciously

take this letter, put it on your tongue,
sleep while I keep watch,
know that I am your spy here, your terrorist,
find me

Days, moored to the freight of this life,
the ordnances of her brooding hands, the
abacus of her eyelids

thirteen drowned off the coast of Italy,
nine by car bomb in Amarah, twenty by
suicide in Baghdad, child on bicycle by bomb
in Baquba

why does that alliterate on its own, why
does she observe the budding of that consonant

demonstrator shot dead in Samarra,
woman in mortar attack in Mosul,
five poultry dealers shot dead in Yusufiyah

two men and child by car bomb,
TV news director in Sayyidiyya, twenty-one
cockle pickers by drowning at Morecambe Bay

by malaria, by hemorrhagic fevers, by hungers,
by fingerprint, by dogs and vigilantes

by arrests near the tunnel,
in arrest by La Migra in Brewster County,
Hidalgo County, Dona Ana County, and Zapata County

by asylum
in Traiskirchen, at Brussels, at Helsinki,
in deportations to Buenos Aires, Ricardo Barrientos

in childhood at Pagani, at Lampedusa and Regina
Pacis, at Safi army barracks, in three hundred
and ninety-five terrible villages in Darfur—Sisi,
Mangarsal, Artala, Mukjar, Jabel Moon

in documentaries, in liquid surfaces,
in oceanic blue screens, in disappearances in
the secret seas of living rooms here

where's their sweet life of green oranges,
of plums and dates, of papayas ripening

forget it, we can't speak of nature in that breath any more,
the earth is corroding already with cities

then where the cafés with students plotting
rebellion,
wreathed in thin cigarette smoke and flagrant lust,
the brains angry and lovely with doorways

where she lives they go about their business,
carry umbrellas against the drizzled rain of evidence,
the tattoo parlours are full as if making
warriors, but nothing happens

the wealth multiplies in the garbage dumps,
and the quiet is the quiet of thieves

there are cellphones calling no one,
no messages burn on the planet's withered lungs

all that koltan from Kahuzi-Biega, the landslides,
to carry nothing

what about the love notes, what, the absolution of airplanes

it's all empty, she thinks, but then again
that's not news

the mollient burdens carried in knapsacks,
all the footwear and headgear and SUVs,
the anodyne poets of jingles,
the drugstores of painkillers are for this

what next, everything is touched,
the train stations not the least with massive
explosions, and the mind limps to its tribal
impulses

Let us not invoke the natural world,
it's ravaged like any battlefield, like any tourist
island, like any ocean we care to name,
like oxygen

let's at least admit we mean each other
harm,
we intend to do damage

then she may stop this vigil for broken things,
then she can at least sit down
to eat the chrome muscles of grocery carts,
the hearts of ubiquitous concrete barriers

we,
there is no "we"
let us separate ourselves now,
though perhaps we can't, still and again
too late for that,
nothing but to continue

the underground subways are hysterical with gurneys,
and yellow tape and smoked saliva,
the cities wear bandages over the eyes

the conversation is over except,
"we won't change our way of life for this savagery
against civilized nations . . . murders when we talk peace"

whatever language we might have spoken
is so thick with corrupt intentions,
it persuades no one

she's fearful, yes, like anyone,
explosions in Jakarta, the same day,
Ayodhya two days before,
a hurricane moving toward Guantanamo

seems harmless enough
and merely like the hand of God

though ominous rain, the blue seas' limning screens
are saturated with experts on terror

where did they learn this,
where you wonder did such men, ruddy with health,
cultivate this wicked knowledge

then you realize they have an office,
a new industry for the stock exchange
and an expense account, an ardour for subterfuge

they're traders, like anybody else these days,
in what's obvious,
and skilful in half-hourly repetitions
of the same shameless verses

day and night

It was not coincidence then that the day
was beautiful, the highways roaring,
the sky that blue which is deeply ordinary
and infinite

perhaps in this city she was distracted
for a few seconds by the open blinds,
the living room's clarity, the kitchen's decisions,
she'd thought then of going, going somewhere

the six lanes hummed, scratched under the wheel,
the windows of houses going by blinked vacant
through the speed and noise

machine and body, shield and tissue,
the highway worked itself into her shoulders
and neck, now she was trembling, tasting
all the materials the city stuffs in its belly

now she was concrete and car, asphalt and oil,
head whirring like any engine,
becoming what they were all becoming

sunny and hot, sunny and hot, the radio chirped

the same in London, Chicago, Tours, Barcelona,
some rain in St. Elizabeth, Port-au-Prince deluge,
floods in Matanzas, regular day in Melbourne, São Paulo

the physical world is not interested in us,
it does what it does,
its own inventory of time, of light and dark

not faith and doubt, not malice or charm,
inexplicable then our certainty
in the fame of politicians and the blackmail of priests

memory will tell us this was foolish,
only, we're not there

there's laughter on some street in the world, and a baby,
crying same as any street, anywhere, and some say
the world is not the same, but it is you know

now, same as anywhere, still, a baby crying here
may not be about hunger, not that kind of hunger

eating years into the cheeks, making puffed bellows
of the abdomen, ah why invoke that, we know about it

we don't care beyond pity, so the thing is straight and simple,
the suburbs, the outskirts are inevitable

Aulnay-sous-Bois, Jane-Finch, the faithless hyphens,
the electrical yards, the unsociable funereal parking lots
with transparent children and their killing play,
that ravaged world is here

and the day is always beautiful somewhere

does she care "about the human species
spreading out across the cosmos"
no, God forbid, stop them, and forgive her this one
imprecation to a deity

then the expert on the radio said, "It would be
like how they spread across the New World"
the glee and hedonism in his voice

and the man who killed Van Gogh, Mohammed
Bouyeri, said to Van Gogh's mother,
"I have to admit I don't have any sympathy for you,
I can't feel for you because I think you are a non-believer"

That's not a revolution you want, ever, to win,
the theory of nothing, theories of nothing in return

These maples that now sentinel her thoughts
know that, and that river with its irregular susurrus

a highway sighing from its aches at 3 or 4 a.m.
she hears this too,
even Martha's lion with its marble eyes, frozen
of course this north in stone

the evening hummingbird's beak spiralling
through the derangement of a spider's web,
the various last calls of day birds she cannot
name, her left hand, its involuntary tensing,
the city's summer heat at bay in this forest
after hours of driving

the newspapers dishevelled on the floor,
her lover bathing up the stairs,
the cobalt destiny of all skies,
a telephone call to another hemisphere

how is it, how's the coming hurricane,
it's passed, the hurricane just came, yawned
and left

we're here, a bomb went off,
two days ago though, you didn't hear, no,
a dry run they think, a small device, a lady
got hurt

how is it there, only hysteria,
nothing really, okay then, well

the ripples of resignation there, the lightning
bolts, the salt to take with life
though it was always like this somewhere

the border guards endlessly increase,
like those hard-bodied ants she watches,
hatching, moving, leaving their radioactive
shells strewn on the floor

like those spiders patrolling the windowpanes,
building quadrants of belligerent silk,
more and more ruthlessly, across
the hummingbird feeder,
the gateway to the stairs,
pincering traceries between trees,
the mouth of the river

the path to the lake,
furiously
modernizing their barbed wire every breached hour

Eight hundred every month for the last year

it was July then, a decent month at any other
time, a month of heat and water, beer and
friends, beaches and parks

little pain usually

bandages of sunlight salving the eyes,
and somewhere
in someone's life it's still true

they'll look forward to the cafés till late,
and talk till sleep,
and sobering up tomorrow to begin again
the romance with streets and sidewalks, jubilant
immortal electricity

yet, this figure, eight hundred every month
for the last year, and one hundred
and twenty in a brutal four days,
things, things add up

IV

i

At Al Rifai Mosque,
the Shah of Iran lies on an onyx floor

entering the mihrab,
the guard offers to sing so we can hear
the perfect acoustic of the burial chamber,
then cups the most beautiful music
from his throat, the call to prayer,
you would think the onyx would break,
or melt away,
the Shah awake and beg forgiveness
for all the despicable years

but no,
the guard releases his face
from his hands,
and returns to the commerce of such an exchange,
his sweet voice for baksheesh,
we paid him gladly,
how much would be enough
for the ruin of his life,
singing to the Shah, hourly

we told him he was beautiful,
at least that

ii

Something else, more happened there

once among the silversmiths,
among the old work of ornamentation,
the shining pain of metal and hammer,
a voice called to me, "Welcome back, Cousin,"
familiar like the sound of water,
rain on a roof or the sea outside a door,
"Welcome, Cousin, it's been a long time,
we have a lot to talk about,
you could be a spy from Upper Egypt

come back alone tomorrow,
we have a lot to say to each other,"

and yes, he could have been my cousin,
and was

In that whole place with everything
for sale

he tried to sell me nothing,
only our genealogy
needing to be polished,
spun over so much suspicion and time,
the silver on the shelves was worthless between us

he smelled of some perfume,
some secret room that thunder makes
when it claps and moves across skies,
of dust that ants accumulate
going about the long business
of gnawing the world away,

and sand so fine it's air

I wanted to go back, take

his hand, eat from it, but,
that was, would be, another life,
and all our rumours would collide and
take that moment away from us when
he called me "Cousin," when cousin
came from both our mouths
and was a warning and a lie, and
a soft meeting and a love

all the time I remained in Cairo,
his papery voice
caressed my cheek,
though I never returned to his small

silver place

and then I think he might have disappeared,
never existed

or never called me "Cousin"
that word is more than father sister brother
mother, clasping what is foreign whole,
all the time nevertheless,
I left him to himself

the ringing metal of his shop, the
bracelets, anklets, rings done, he said,
in the old ways,
the speckles of argentum on his tongue and brow,
his slippers on the wooden floor, the time
you know, when something falls so perfectly
from your hands

I needed nothing from the market

after that, no scarves, no perfume bottles,
no nuts, no directions to all the gates of Cairo,
no souvenirs of ancient Egypt
other than the time we'd spent in some life,
before and since,
this charm of ours as I've said before

it meets you sometimes
on a hot mountain road or in a cool silver shop,
its startling purposes,
its imperishable beckoning grace,
so unexpected,
so merciful

iii

The day you left the air broke
into splinters,
all night before the tree outside
held its breath,
the windows ached,
the newspapers whimpered unread,
old lovers, unknowing, staggered
in doorways,
We should gather rivers for you,
the Layou, the Niger, the St. Lawrence
should weep now,
we should call storms,
our grief will dry lakes,
this city should spring hibiscus
in late winter when your name
is said, full subways and streetcars
should sprout wings and fly
urgently to your side,
You knew the world,
its weather scraping our skins,
we hear you in our sleep, wild
as verses of autumn maple

We should carry you
to that country you dreamed
for us, where your liquid voice
is astonishing
If we sing here like crickets,
as perfectly, if we fill all rooms
with silence, you would return then,
or tell us how it is where you are,
how we could dilute bitter things
and acrid cities; how
to strain sorrow through our hands,
then mount demonstrations against
your death,
will you send word
in letters, in goldenrod leaflets
in spiders' threads or how we used to
at night—with buckets of glue—
on light posts,
till then Marlene,
we will fix petals of you to our eyes

to Marlene Green

iv

Everywhere,
out the window the muezzin singing
reaches the upper leaves of deserted
Cairo trees,
heard too the cheery stupidity of cellphones,
it was another December, dusty, late, the Sahara sprays,
the men, all men, heads bruised
with passion, or grief or conviction
or failure at noticing absences,
such deliberateness

noticed only men,
except one night in Khan el-Khalili,
a sexual thing,
covered in the film of a garment

blind, held, and desired

the man smiling, his own small hand
strong on hers, his own small frame,
a cage,
she, of course she, small too, red,
if that colour can be more burdened in the carnal,
so, red, why waste another one,
her urgency too, to become,
wanted, the poise in being wanted,
the market, lit as it is at night,
not that creation of light bulbs and wires,
but Cairo, awake,
then their incandescence, desire and desired
defeating each other, his hand again
on the ephemera of her, she dragged and willing,
everywhere

modernity for everything but this

V

i

so you find yourself anywhere
selling toys, fake roses, in the Piazza della Scala,
to the privileged, among them
a poet
you find yourself anywhere
reading Neruda, ventriloquist, to the second
millennium, *we exhausted so much on useless destruction*

always three policemen haunt our piazzas,
interpretazione simultanea, ola preti

it's better, the elliptical roses,
mechanical universes,
some escaped
could share life on the surface

she needed someone like that, elliptical,
and as usual the fucking Americans came,
strafing her meditation on things,
wanting, wanting, a chair, a space,
the two of them so fragile and alone in Europe,
talking loud,
arguing about the wine

you find yourself, any one,
anyone
you say it's all bullshit, it all
doesn't matter, *U.S. engagement in*
Afghanistan ribbons its way along TV screens,
you wonder, was this the same telecast
so many years ago,
uranium enriching in your stomach,
delicate postules

these monuments that survive
everywhere, in essence signs of the most brutal
among us, look at the cornices,
the fretwork, evenly taken for love
or reverence, if we sum it up,
if what we have now is the result,
what else was it but something hard,
some small-mindedness

hollowing out the steeples, the domes,
scarring the minarets
look now, the hordes of us collecting
at the windows,
the sermons of politicians,
their corporate benedictions

ii

Sarkozy will say, in months to come,
they must "pressure clean" the "rabble"

everywhere they say, "We come to work
with our coffins on our backs,"
at the Indian ports where they break ships,
the poor holes in Poland digging coal
for the black market

I wish I had beautiful legs
to get me to another planet,
to run in the lustrous substances of all that's left out,
all that may have,
to wake up at 5:25 a.m. to the business of birds,
the discredited physics of Christianity and Islam

iii

the gruesome things that settle
at the bottom of the brain,
there are children whose hearing's
been ruined already by the noise
of this,
she heard one today, veiled, on her cell-
phone say, "Tell that dumb bitch to get it."

sick modernity ciphers sick tribalism
everywhere

over in St. Elizabeth the sea was boiling
over the rocks, the unreplenishing coral
waking up, driving again, this time through a dawn
turned over, burning cars,
the same three policemen, a road,
the rain two nights before, eternal

iv

She's travelled such hours,
sat in the merciful transience of trains
hurrying,
each hotel room she checks
the news, and again that useful colour
of fire leapt to her bed from cars incinerated
in a market this morning,
from these rooms she sorts out the bodies
on Iraqi streets, this time
forty, then in Milan twenty-four
and in Florence thirty or so, with
sixty wounded, then twelve, then two,
in all one hundred or so in one week,
no television back in Venice, the damp
room distracted her from the inventory

v

The men here are plasma,
they collapse into video games, Palm Pilots,
remedies against dreams

let us simply recognize
happiness as soon as it shows itself

they declare themselves innocent of all events,
those that have happened and those to come,
everything
they examine the evidence against themselves
and suggest the victims cunning

they found themselves good,
down to the last general and secretary
of state

vi

rain fell,
the seas on the south coast rose,
one suicide bomber on Hafa Street smoked a cigarette,
one took care of an itch over his right eye,
not as a final act but a simple one,
reflexive

vii

the body keeps thinking it will return
to its vigour, it will receive phone calls,
and run to the corner with pamphlets,
a headband and a leather-stringed jacket,
to spread the news

tomorrow then she'll buy a mirror,
hang it in the room where the woodcuts
hang, the manifestations of the poet
in Chinese opera, two warriors, one musician,
one six-armed spear-bearing tumbler,
pendant,
in paper, the inability to fall or for that matter
hang on to bone, to crushed ear, to banked light, to ease

viii

She's afraid of killing someone today,
picked up the laundry, ate pasta,
and a citrus tart,
bought a book, drove a street,
all the while, sun in her left eye,
its usual butter of fall lindens,
maple bleeding, her hand
on the wheel,
looking back, in case it was someone
she'd killed, someone she'd hit,
infected with the afternoon

your sources are compromised. didn't you
read my note. A spare room, a talkative
and secretive friend, a map out of
hell . . . not inured either, only one day a week . . .
the news is always
exaggerated. Cut it in half, divide it by four,
and subtract it from itself.
Information all has to do with location,
you know that. so tired of reading
for good signs. the chatter, chatter, chatter,
the applause for nothing. I sleep
with Sun Tzu
under my pillow. But if you don't have a room
well okay then
tell me of a pretty
place near the end of May
much love

x

Consider then the obliteration of four restaurants,
the disappearance of sixty taxis each with one passenger
or four overcrowded classrooms, one tier of a football
stadium, the sudden lack of, say, cosmeticians

or mechanics, a pedestrian intersection at lunchtime,
ostentatiously
vanished, two or three hospital waiting
rooms, the nocturnal garbage collectors gone

tearful kindergartens perhaps two or so, a city
of window washers, the mournful feast of Catholics
who march for Senhor Santo Cristo dos Milagros

tenacious too the absence and impossibility of names

let us all deny our useless names in solidarity
with these dead dinner guests and pedestrians,
and anonymously dead mechanics, and desultory
children and passengers, and those faceless cosmeticians

xi

she's never liked twilight, you know,
when it comes, it only confirms
we've failed at everything
again,
it only arrives to insist,
what a waste,
it says, I at least end things, I
understand perfection, deep
at its source it isn't power,
nothing so small, so edible
there, it is immaculate possibility

VI

It's August now, the light is deeper,
the sky explosive with rains,
a turning, turning the body of the world
toward a darkness, a sleep, no,
sleep would be forgiving

last night, late August,
Katrina's wet wing flapped, dishevelled
against the windows like great damp feathers,
she brushed the alleyways, the storm shutters,
I felt the city she had carried away,
drowned and stranded New Orleans,
anyway, she was finished,
a ruffed foot, a quilled skirt trailing off

like what billions of rainless universes do we kill
just stepping through air, what failing cultures
submerge under a breath

word on the street is that God sent Katrina
as a lesson in destruction,
lucky I'm not any kind of believer,
a taxi driver told me this, then the hairdresser,
then the old Italian ladies who peddle Jesus

when I tell them I'm an atheist they see
an opportunity for conversion

they want some single story, the story of my life,
I say this big world is the story, I don't have any other,
they offer me the immured peace
of Christianity,
and an address in Pennsylvania to send money,
they always win, these soothing ladies,
I haven't the courage to tell them we're fucked,
and they, unfortunately, will have a reason for that

though the birds of the world know this,
the banded pitta, the mangrove pitta, the bulbul,
the iora, the red-naped and scarlet-rumped

trogon, the fire-tufted barbet, flame back, philentoma,
the rufous-throated wren babbler, I tell them,

they, the birds feel this, the wingbeat,
the feathered work of greed,
this shorn planet,
the hoary-throated barwing, the greater adjutant,
the crake, the alliterative blue-bearded bee-eater,
it's clear to them,
they all must set a fire to the earth,
you see, they're saying, what would it be without birds,
what if we spread extinction, transform blood
to other tender fluids

listen to all the laughing thrushes,
striated, white throated, orange headed, all
the plain backed, blackened, chestnut, cocoa,
summoning oblivions, raining disasters

after all, how many vows of death or endless death
for endless peace have I heard from the wingless,
the flightless? The gulls, the owls, the grouses

the stalks, the larks, the finches have had it too,
with sightlessness, such clarity,
the scientists
are intent on dreamy financial answers,
but I know the suicidal skill of insurrection,
self-slaughter hunched in veins, the skull's
fever, the tissues' elations,
I too am waiting for the flutter of another century,
treading water near that meagre strip of land,
stooping there, the noise even closer

VII

On reading this someone will say
God, is there no happiness then,
of course, tennis matches and soccer games,
and river song and bird song and
wine naturally and some Sundays

and some highways with the relief of water
and wild flowers at the end,
and fresh snapper and wild salmon,
though that all depends on killing something,
and the eagerness of children and their certainty,
look how they try to walk straight

the surface of the earth, how it keeps springing back,
for now, and the irregular weather of hurricanes,
tsunamis, floods, sunlight on any given day,
anywhere, however disastrous at least magnificent

and moments when you rise to what you might be,
bread,
the girls and boys you saw in Cairo,
their hands and mouths
full, and the way a woman stands
when you meet her at an unexpected corner,

anywhere, the one that blue morning in Les Coteaux,
the one on the way
to Firenze with the baby on the train,
and the flight and dive of pelicans, the scent
of sandalwood and the scent of mangoes
when they grow black,
great ravens lifting north

and sand again, the day you realize it's stone
worn down, how long that must take,
yes, of course, there's sitting still,
and reading or merely cleaning the steps
to the little veranda,
observing the certain movement of great ants

the longitude of hours, their roiling ascent and fall,
or the latitude of palms, what makes them
appear at certain temperatures, and

men, at 5 a.m. with lunch boxes waiting,
in cool mornings at intervals of domestic road,
to go do some mindless work, how they crouch
in their clothes,
willing the truck to arrive or meet
with catastrophe, let this be the morning of the end
of the world, they pray,
there's something of a beauty there

at how one flees at the appearance of mosquitoes,
all right, the nightclubs, the bars, the dancehalls,
we all know, keeping in mind
the drunk recrimination on a life wasted,
that's common, no matter where you are,
and people who somehow make a music

come out of nothing,

yellow, there's a thing,
and something edible in a desert, or perhaps
the inedibility of deserts,
an engine on a vacant road, someone who says,
don't worry, when you need it, rain,
rain is the happiest of weathers

bicycles, great inventions even if you never
learned to ride, and coffee,
plain and hot, again at 5 a.m.
a boat, even a wrecked and wretched boat
still has all the possibilities of moving

a stick, when you're walking through
an unknown forest, so defensive, so stable,
yet blithe like a feral dog

the dancehalls, were
the dancehalls mentioned before, their capacities
for joy, the way you can't be false there

it shows, because dancehalls want nothing,
do what you like, pretend if you want, it
doesn't matter, no one to lie to there,
you can either dance or you can't

feet, their innovativeness, look how
many things they do and how open-minded

sleep, sleep is infinitely this, and waking
up, involuntary both, outside one's help,
circadian and residential, the body must,
weighed down
only by the revolutions
of the earth's incandescence and gloaming

safety pins, time and time again, time and time again
dirt, very solid whatever it is, then periwinkle,
it flourishes regardless, mimosa, most of all,
needled, flowering, vigilant, every resistant thing
in one

so yes, there's that and parcels addressed
to you from foreign countries, their smell,
of dresses and books and someone's thoughts

speaking of drunk recrimination, nothing
wrong with that,
at least it's an examination
of things past,
pity it's only fools that do it,
caught, unlike the powerful, in the immediate
effects of their ego or anger or greed

where do they spit up, those others, whatever
bile they have, so dangerous it burns the world
to dust, it devastates hospitals and scant dreams,
ask them
about happiness, not me, why should
I know how to dance and sing in the middle of it all,
okay, okay this list is not so exhausted yet

guitars then, like Hendrix and Santana,
Kongar-ool Ondar and Tanya Tagaq, throat
singing
Jali Nyama Suso playing kora, Mariza again,
singing fado,
Fela, immortal, the whole of music, the whole of it

the off-key voices in church basements and showers,
the always misinterpreted sounds of popular songs,
five Indian boys in a car listening to bangara,
the traffic jam
where we met this summer,
in the middle of all that killing

the scratching of a needle on a record,
a sample of James Brown and the Fatback Band,
squirrels in the eaves of a house going about
their business,
ground doves fluttering from tree to lemon tree

all this, black butterflies and flying ants,
rain ants, the many times that rain is mentioned here,
candle flies, poui falling

this composition that nature makes, the theories
of hummingbirds and beavers,
agoutis
and armadillos, morrocoys and one-inch pandas,
all different, don't be mistaken, they're not simple

not simple as the ways to kill them, far more
complicated,
but let's leave nature for a while
how can we, yes, let's not essentialize the only
essential thing, it doesn't work, it fails often,
fails, fails whom

and so, barrios and slums, crazy, crazy places,
violent too sometimes but there happiness
is a light post, a scar, stigmata, blazing
in every hand and water, a passport

being screams there, the jangling of intense limbs,
the expiration of any breath, its succeeding intake,
the surprised and grateful lungs

you have to measure this also there, the degrees
of the eyelashes, the width of the thumb and forefinger,
going over old newspapers, old clothes, old cans,
the wreckage of other people's lives
which is your boon,
when a day ends again the body's exhaustion,
if it comes, that's success

grackles, to return, and the yellow-crested
oropendola's chromatic notes, a flock of
dragonflies so blue you think, a dizzy spell

exquisite and contiguous, never alighting
in one place too long, the unsteadiness
of strangers, driftwood, one coastline

Marigot,
very long ago, unbathable, impassable,
smudged ochre, redundant to say rock, and yes

coastlines in general, especially from the ferry
between Vancouver and Galiano, one woman
Marlene, living, her hand pulling the strands of hair
at her temple, unravelling all the political
questions

four devotees mourning Nina Simone,
drinking wine and listening to "See-line
Woman," recalling where they were in their life
when she sang this, which city, which club, when
they first saw her as if they'd seen themselves

some lovers of course, the way they made you
laugh, the way they held their heads,
then too the relief of their leaving, of course

slowness, weeding gardens if you
have them, if not a small vinous plant, portable,
to place on a trellis when you get one, both naturally
if working in a field is not your regular job

in that case it's backbreaking, arthritic, a foul aura
surrounds you
then, standing, that move perfected by another species
one million years ago, is perfect, and gardens an eyesore

some words can make you weep,
when they're uttered, the light rap of their
destinations, their thud as if on peace, as if on cloth,
on air, they break all places intended and known

soft travellers

happiness is not the point really, it's a marvel,
an accusation in our time,
and so is this, Monday, February 28th, one
hundred and fourteen, Tuesday, August 16th, ninety
Wednesday September 14th, one hundred and eighty-
two, Friday November 18th, eighty
these were only the bloodiest days in one year,
in one place

there are atomic openings in my chest
to hold the wounded,

besides the earth's own
coiled velocities, its meteoric elegance,
and the year still not ended,
I have nothing soothing to tell you,
that's not my job,
my job is to revise and revise this bristling list,
hourly

OSSUARIES

(2010)

OSSUARY I

I lived and loved, some might say,
in momentous times,
looking back, my dreams were full of prisons

in our narcotic drifting slumbers,
so many dreams of course were full of prisons,
mine were without relief

in our induced days and our wingless days,
my every waking was incarcerated,
each square metre of air so toxic with violence

the atmospheres were breathless there,
the bronchial trees were ligatured
with carbons

some damage I had expected, but no one
expects the violence of glances, of offices,
of walkways and train stations, of bathroom mirrors

especially, the vicious telephones, the coarseness of
daylight, the brusque decisions of air,
the casual homicides of dresses

what brutal hours, what brutal days,
do not say, oh find the good in it, do not say,
there was virtue; there was no virtue, not even in me

let us begin from there, restraining metals
covered my heart, rivulets
of some unknown substance transfused my veins

at night, especially at night, it is always at night,
a wall of concrete enclosed me,
it was impossible to open my eyes

I lived like this as I said without care,
tanks rolled into my life, grenades took root
in my uterus, I was sickly each morning, so dearly

what to say,
life went on around me,
I laughed, I had drinks, I gathered with friends

we grinned our aluminum teeth,
we exhaled our venomous breaths,
we tried to be calm in the invisible architecture

we incubated, like cluster bombs,
whole lives waiting, whole stellar regions,
discoveries of nebulae, and compassion

from the cities the electric rains pierced us,
the ceaseless bitter days folded like good linen,
the phosphorous streets gave off their harmful lights

we bit our fingernails to blue buttons,
we staggered at the high approach of doorways,
plunged repeatedly to our deaths only to be revived

by zoos, parades, experiments, exhibits, television sets,
oh we wanted to leave, we wanted to leave
the aspirated syllables and villages, the skeletal

dance floors, the vacant, vacant moons that tortured us,
when the jailers went home and the spectators drifted
away and the scientists finished their work

like a bad dog chained to an empty gas station,
for blue blue nights,
I got worse and worse, so troubling

I would fall dead like a specimen,
at the anthropometric spectacles
on the Champ de Mars, the Jardin d'Acclimatation

the mobile addresses of the autopsy fields,
though I could see no roads,
I was paid for losing everything, even eyesight

I lived in the eternal villages, I lived like a doll,
a shaggy doll with a beak, a bell, a red mouth,
I thought, this was the way people lived, I lived

I had nights of insentient adjectives,
shale nights, pebbled nights, stone nights,
igneous nights, of these nights, the speechlessness

I recall, the right ribs of the lit moon,
the left hip of the lit moon,
what is your name they asked, I said nothing

I heard the conspiratorial water,
I heard the only stone, I ate her shoulder,
I could not hear myself, you are mistaken I said to no one

the chain-link fences glittered like jewellery,
expensive jewellery, portable jewellery,
I lost verbs, whole, like the hull of almonds

after consideration you will discover, as I,
that verbs are a tragedy, a bleeding cliffside, explosions,
I'm better off without, with vermillion, candles

this bedding, this mercy,
this stretcher, this solitary perfectable strangeness,
and edge, such cloth this compass

of mine, of earth, of mourners of these
reasons, of which fairgrounds, of which theories
of plurals, of specimens of least and most, and most

of expeditions,
then travels and wonders then journeys,
then photographs and photographs of course

the multiplications of which, the enormity of this,
and drill-bits and hammers and again handcuffs,
and again rope, coarse business but there

some investigations, then again the calculations,
such hours, such expansions, the mind dizzy
with leaps, such handles, of wood, of thought

and then science, all science, all murder,
melancholic skulls, pliant to each fingertip,
these chromatic scales, these calipers the needle

in the tongue, the eyes' eye, so
whole diameters, circumferences, locutions,
an orgy of measurements, a festival of inches

gardens and paraphernalia of measurements,
unificatory data, curious data,
beautiful and sensuous data, oh yes beautiful

now, of attractions and spectacles of other sheer forces,
and types in the universe, the necessary
exotic measurements, rarest, rarest measuring tapes

a sudden unificatory nakedness, bificatory nakedness,
of numbers, of violent fantasms
at exhibitions again, of walks, of promenades

at fairs with products, new widgets, human widgets,
with music, oh wonders,
the implications

then early in this life, like mountains,
already pictures and pictures, before pictures, after pictures
and cameras

their sickness, eye sickness, eye murder,
murder sickness, hunger sickness,
this serendipity of calculators, of footprints

with fossils, their wingspan of all time,
at crepuscules' rare peace time, if only,
like water, in daytime, no solace, so, so different

from solitude, all solitude, all madness,
so furious, so numerous, the head, the markets,
the soles of the feet, so burnt, so thin

and the taste, so meagre, so light-headed,
the cloud flashes, the lightning geometry,
the core of reflectivity so vastly, vastly vast

the wait now, lumens of aches, such aches,
the horizontal and the vertical aches of lightning,
its acoustics, loud pianos, percussive yet

strings and quartets, multicellular runnels yet and yet,
the altitude of the passageway, its precipitation
and grand arithmetic, the segments

the latitudes of where, where and here,
its contours, its eccentric curvatures,
so presently, angular and nautical, all presently

just fine my lungs, just fine,
hypothesis absolutely, but just fine,
why lungs, strange theory

oh yes and the magnitude of jaundice, trenches,
like war, continuous areas and registers, logarithms
so unexplainable, rapid scales, high notes

besides, anyway so thermal, atmospheric,
wondrous aggressions, approximately here,
elaborate like radiation and seismic, yes all over

the bodies' symptoms of algebraic floods,
tiredness for one, weariness actually,
weary with magnetic embryos

petals, yes petals of sick balm please, now yes,
for my esophagus, analgesics of indigo,
of wires, of electric shocks, why eucalyptus leaves

of course lemon grass, labernum, please, lion's claw,
remedies of cloves, bitter bark,
still birdless though, worldless

asthma with blueness, then music,
gardens truthfully, truthfully nauseous with
tonsured numbers, volumes of fibres, embroidery

and hair nets of violence, blue,
like machine guns, of course knives, extensions
of blueness, all right then wherever

same radiations, lines in the forehead,
tapers, electrodes, invisible to the eyes,
official hammers and corkscrews, official grass

official cities now for appearances after all this,
all these appearances, generous, for certain
scraggly, wan, and robust appearances

assignments and hidden schedules of attendance,
a promise of blindness, a lover's clasp of
violent syntax and the beginning syllabi of verblessness

OSSUARY II

to undo, to undo and undo and undo this infinitive
of arrears, their fissile mornings,
their fragile, fragile symmetries of gain and loss

this is how she wakes each day of each underground year,
confessions late and half-hearted pour from her sleeping
mouth, beginning in the year of her disappearances

the grateful rooms had to be gathered into their temporal
shapes, the atmosphere coaxed to visible
molecules, definite arrangements of walls and doors

solidity lies beside her in its stigmatic shreds,
I, the slippery pronoun, the ambivalent, glistening,
long sheath of the alphabet flares beyond her reach

how then to verify her body, rejuvenate the blood-dead
arm, quell her treacherous stomach, its heaving solar
jumps, or seduce the preposition, where and where

her neck crackles to the radio voice, that coastal beacon,
last night she exchanged one set of keys for another,
her palms, branched, copper basins outstretched

now one numb finger, one thumb searched,
through all their known grammars for which room, which
dewy bed, and then what fateful day

nearsighted she needs her glasses yes, to summarize
the world, without them she's defenceless,
that's why they're always at the precipice of the bed

some violent drama was as usual surging,
on the airwaves and "plane" she heard, the usual
supercilious timbres hysterical, a cut larynx

she thought of splinters, slivering boards,
scooped the glasses from her abdomen to align
her brain, here notice, notice what is false from true

what is possible, and where's the doorway of this room,
kinetic news breaking sunlight,
but where was she, which city, what street

Albany, Buffalo, Havana, back tracks, Algiers,
to the swift boat ride from the south of Spain, back when,
the brief embossed room, a reversal, a body at sea

then, the short wave asserted, Manhattan,
Yasmine's tingling hand summoned the volume
in its circumference of black plastic, she

could not be in Manhattan, though the radio insisted,
her back alert like paintings to its usual ache,
some mornings she could return to sleep even

in the middle of the most gruesome news,
caught,
caught, every comrade caught

she could delay events with this groggy chemistry
of spasms and refusals,
a drowning, that second sleep, in lists of the undone

ungiven, unsought, the nausea could last days,
this room took shape now in yellow and brown,
a window lay behind a wilting curtain, tepid sunlight

the radio veered once again toward her, speeding,
"explosion," it mourned,
a kitchen knife, spanner, tweezers, skill saw

she felt a joy innocent like butter open her,
blinding stratus, ants, tongs, bolts, rust,
the whole ionosphere bounced into her mouth

glancing against her teeth, exceeding her nostrils, her
heart burrowed,
in corks, broken bottles, nails, finned incendiaries

she flew like shrapnel off the bed,
felt her way blind, as fire with slender strands,
as glaze, sand, starch caps, uniforms, and bracelets

the prepositions are irrelevant today, whichever house,
which century, wherever she was,
the bruised wires, severed, this they only ever dreamed

she would love, love to talk to them today,
though the dreaming had come to little and no end,
and less, there in the grey blood of the television

the spectacular buildings falling limpid, to nothing,
rims, aluminum, windowless, fragile staircases,
she wanted, wanted to whisper into telephones

it's done, someone had done it, someone,
had made up for all the failures,
she looked, pitiless, at the rubble, the shocked

the stumbling shattered dressed for work,
the powdering towers, the walls and windows
stuck to their skins like makeup and grease

look, the seared handbags, the cooked briefcases,
wheels, clocks, the staggered floors,
the startled one-winged orioles

the flights of starlings interrupted,
the genocides of September insects,
the disappearances after of sugar bees and quick footsteps

it was just past nine in any city,
but a glass of wine would do, a beer, a toke,
here's to the fatal future

how many times they'd asked each other,
you are ready to die but are you ready to kill,
she had been willing once

a jealousy orbiting her skull, its brittle calcium,
outside everywhere burned skin,
would she have flown into that willing skin

what equations she wondered of steel's pressure,
and concrete, matter and vacuum and terrible faith,
of sacred books, of tattooed foreheads, of small knives

she believed in nothing too, not broken hearts,
not blood with wine, not beloveds,
not the weight of her eyelids nor her own intentions

not even people whom she'd once admitted
were her hopes, and what she'd calculated
all her acts against

but failure is when they describe what you've done,
and she lives in that description hand to mouth,
outside the everyday, in refugee shafts

and tiny rooms, and in other people's passports,
in mathematical theorems of trust,
in her vigilant skin and feathery, feathery deceit

it is not enough to change the bourgeois state,
this sentence slumbered in her, sleek,
you have to bring it down, winched to this

each dawn's lurid ambivalence,
the chest fire flaring on any sofa, any chair, any bed,
the calculus of infidelity on each forehead kissed

she read the periodic table of elements in an eyebrow,
the length of patience in love,
this moment to depart in coffee's taste

fall crept now in the rind of deciduous stems,
and she could read it seconds before it arrived,
and hear birds and their music head south like musicians

packing up kit, decamping stale beer-smelling
halls, the floors' sly self-serving penitence,
the dismissive flutter of high-speed wings

it was sunny, a pale sunny, and the lindens down
three storeys spun their leaves tipped yellow,
grim joy overtook her

come the true fall here, come the fall, the romance
with the air is over but now,
now, who has such mortal imagination

her joy was not grim, her knuckles knotted in her lap,
insisted, yes she is aware that joy is grim, how these
two make a marriage, how long their courtship in her

house finches in the eavestroughs
went about their fall business, remorseless,
their urban quickness, their rapid knowledgeable song

and she had mourned enough for a thousand
broken towers, her eyesight washed immaculate and
caustic, her whole existence was mourning, so what?

OSSUARY III

I loved and lived, as I said, for a time,
looking up from water like sea shells,
I arrived where the sonorous oceans took me

washed and washed, coral overcame my feet, my hands,
the shocks of immobility, the stung tendons,
the clamped Achilles, the enamel vocal cords

I did well they say, given the circumstances,
the spiked municipalities rationed their handouts
of free breads, free bicycles, free bracelets

free sugars, free plastics, free razor blades,
free bullets, free coverings, free enclosures,
free fences, free, free, absolutely free freeness

still they required performances,
one needed licences and stamped forms, and masks,
and stickers and worse of all transparent veins

to be frank most of my time was spent
sleeping in one courthouse or another defending
charges of one thing and another

larcenies, robberies, trespassing,
loitering, intimidation, resisting arrest, vagrancy,
but fundamentally existence

I took my case everywhere, naturally,
all continents, several unknown galaxies, some as yet
unarmed moons, needless to say, nameless to count

the prodigious silence, the thunderclaps of
salutary ignorance,
so as I said momentous, ravenous, ugly times

I am aware how this looks, like pins
and fractile glass, and after a time anyone could see,
the futile jurisdictions and all my waterlogged paper

lived and loved, common oxymoron,
if I have lived, I have not loved,
and if I have loved, I cannot have lived

it was difficult to live and love at the same time,
you see what I mean,
since to live is to be rapacious as claws, to have

the most efficient knives and broken beer bottles,
needles, powers of attorney,
nonchalance, indifference, negligence

to love is an impediment to this hard business
of living
so I cannot have loved, not me

do not think this of me, do not think
I did not try to breach the fluorescent streets,
to admit the long-disillusioned sandbanks, do not think it

I rented secretive rooms to see what it was like,
no denying, I spread prickling sheets on narrowing beds,
stretched out beside one person and then another

the night dew we collected at our throats, cackling,
the cardamon aroma of our breaths, the cinnamon
we rubbed in our hands before touching

the basil leaves with which we covered ourselves,
obviously my rainy rainy eyes, my earth-filled hair,
all this I brought across sticky bitumen highways

to the dim-lit ambiguous approaches of these stanzas,
their permanences, their impermanences,
we wore in our heavy, heavy coats

the dried lavender flowers I crushed in my palms
before opening the doors,
my coastal limbs carrying shells and seaweeds

the full ocean in my mouth, oh I longed, longed
for the deepest suicidal blue waters, I craved the seas,
where what was on earth could not scar me

I gave all this to lovers, I gave them too my glasses,
we looked through windows from hotels off
freeways, off the industrial parks, off garbage dumps

we saw demolitions that stung our eyes rheumy,
indefinable liquids passed through our indefinable
souls

here I am then, goodbye, again and again,
how we left these rooms fully clothed twigs,
and branded bones again

do not say, do not say it was my fault,
do not say I could have gathered blue dragonflies,
or the showering sunlight

the ashes of volcanoes or the residue of songs
from the cups of saxophones
I could not, I could not, I could not

have raised ferned cadavers, thistles, tabebuia rosea,
anthurium horses,
could not, tribes of tigers and ginger lily

cartridges,
I tried love, I did,
the scapulae I kissed, I did

the flat triangular bones I filled with kisses, spumes
of kisses, gutters of kisses, postponed kisses,
and early new-born kisses

the curve of clavicles, I dug artesian wells of kisses there,
utensils of kisses,
spoons of kisses, basins of kisses, creeks of kisses

the jugular notch I ate in kisses,
I devoured in kisses,
teeth-filled kisses, throat-filled kisses, gullet-stuffed kisses

so don't tell me how love will rescue me,
I was carnivorous about love, I ate love to the ankles,
my thighs are gnawed with love

still and yet I cannot have loved,
since living was all I could do and for that,
I was caged in bone spur endlessly

eye sockets ambushed me,
I slept with harassment and provocations,
though I wanted to grow lilacs, who wouldn't?

to know the secrets of spiders, who wouldn't?
yet the rumours of newspapers persisted, the pained sighs
of the waiting rooms of existence were called good music

I could not leave my house without plans,
a perfect stranger's thought, and bone would sprout
on my heart like a lantern trapping a light

OSSUARY IV

oh heart, oh heart, blind like daylight,
when they came back, it was Albany and clear,
1977, from Algiers and Cairo and she's forgiven him

he had of course never asked for forgiveness, she
had not forgiven him publicly, not to his face,
that is she had not said, "I forgive you"

though a deep hatred like forgiveness erupted in her,
that year, that year, fractious like parchment,
she grew lavenders in small clay pots, read *The Origin*

of the Family and *The Eighteenth Brumaire*, "The tradition of all
dead generations weighs like a nightmare on the brains of
the living . . ." nursed the air of their small apartment

gave it patchouli incense, marijuana, eucalyptus oils,
the smoke of three thousand cigarettes, one after another,
the clatter of wooden beads around her neck and wrists

a front door painted red then black then red again,
she found her true mind drifting on the ceiling,
soaring away from him on the loosening tether of Engels

“You’re nothing, Yas,
I made you something by fucking you,
other that that, you’re nothing.”

his motionless face, redundantly handsome,
condescending,
as if this truth should give her comfort

comrades, speechless, as if
this rhetoric twirling from his tongue,
corkscrewed across the room

has struck them dumb like some edict,
outrageous and extravagant,
as if from a god

as if she should hear instead Monk’s
“Crepuscule with Nellie,” its deliberate
and loving notes scoring her back

Yasmine slips out the room, a volcanic mist,
molten through the doorframe,
brain on fire, "Give her a break, huh?"

finally finds a tongue "We got work to do." But
she's gone, a low hum, a bacteria, incubates in her left ear,
Charles Mingus recovers her, "Pithecanthropus

Erectus," and he does, then she was
three and her mother lifted the needle on the record,
the rushing out and out her feet tingling

bare on the pavement the day is finished,
her planet's already spun one millennia around the sun,
and the world as she knows it is vanished and

she's sitting on the unpolished floor of the boarding
house with her mother and the record player, and the true
meaning of things, run, run, as far as after yourself

she reads later that Mingus said the last movement
suggests the "frantic burst" of "a dying organism,"
and there with her mother, her feet bare on the floor

the planets already spun for months and years, she's
run out in 1977, past the loose hysterical trills of wood
winds, past the small ambitions meant for her

she looked then at the beacon of the record player,
to lead her out of the intuitions of gloom
and penury, but more, a science of incalculable waste

gleaming on every body in every boarding house they'd
lived, a glistening powder, an iridescent toxin,
whose only antibody was music and all she learned later

as early she knew she'd get up off that floor and walk,
right out beyond the broken parts, beyond her mother's
skirt, her brother's preacherly advice, his certain god

going over the realizations of Cairo, holding the faithful
in a future year in this Albany apartment,
Miles's "Bitches Brew" on the stereo and Fanon

like a double-edged knife in her teeth,
she's been wearing its ambivalent jewel like a tongue
ring, a gag it's true, it's true what Owusu said

"Pharoah's Dance" had been playing for thirteen
of its twenty minutes, Owusu lies on the floor digging
Miles, he loved Miles, the thin mean horn she hated

and Cairo, he called to her in the bathroom again,
about Cairo, the crossings of revolutionaries,
the bottle of sickly wine they drank was almost finished

the cynicism and who gives a fuck trumpet, that
should have been her first warning, now see,
the desert dust she'd missed seeing this December

when he opines, of their great mosques,
their cool stones, their great light signifying,
nothing between god and the human

she says maliciously who hefted the stone,
who carried the water, who fed the fires,
who opened the gates, who washed the clothes

who cut the wood, crushed the olives and palm into oils,
who bore the weight of all these gods,
whose eyes were put out to make their light

"when these people are in the world . . ." Engels ran
around her skull ". . . that will be the end of it . . ."
like water around the washed rim of a bowl

here's the difference, she told him,
between Miles and Bird,
Miles kept living, till life was rancid, Bird flew off

next dawn she paces the cobalt path,
from kitchen to living room, blue black,
living room to blue black kitchen until light

came through the blinds, light
as it is here murky and hesitant, she
drank espresso after bitter espresso

the base of her head flaming with small fires,
she waits for the grey air to lift its caution,
impatient for the window's slow morse

to time her shower,
hot water to hit her shoulder,
then she dressed for any type of weather

conscious as bees,
to the finest changes of sound,
and shadow, sweat and heat, she knows what she is to do

OSSUARY V

I must confess, I must, that early on
it was nothing to me, believe me,
you could dip your dingy hand in my chest

and it was nothing, I had enough bandages,
enough salves and enough razor blades,
I had a grin like jagged stone, like baleen plates

and then like sharks' teeth serrated, oblique,
hairs would tear you apart brushing against me,
but all the shifting wore me down, the efferent blood

petitions, I gave here, I gave there, I allowed,
of course here's my innocence, my shivering
never bothered me, much, I thought, it will pass

it will pass, but of course it didn't so here I am,
down to the last organ and happy to be there,
tired with it, exhausted to be there, bone dry

without walls, without embrasures, no height at all,
scatter bones, losing all relation to myself,
reified, common really, common the powdery skulls

the imponderable orbs in my forehead,
a lantern, around a light, what light,
the waxing crescent, the waning crescent come and go

unrelieved, along the coast, caustic sodas
stiffen the vertebrae rigid in the bristled winds,
blindness first, corroded lungs next

it was the same, the transparencies I thumbed,
for this for that, innumerable defences,
I drowned in vats of sulphurous defences

the crate of bones I've become, good
I was waiting to throw my limbs on the pile,
the mounds of disarticulated femurs and radii

but perhaps we were always lying there,
dead on our feet and recyclable,
toxic and imperishable, the ways to see us

I could hear music somewhere though, somewhere
in a distance backward or forward,
time split like willows

vague music that couldn't yet be music surely,
or was already music anyway,
it rushed ahead until it was a granule of light

the moon lay on the floor alone with us,
it drank the tiles,
it ate what we ate, it cupped our breath

the body skids where the light pools,
each bone has its lost dialect now,
untranslatable though I had so many languages

in the rooms above,
the hours spin their bangles,
supine, we listen

if I broke my chest open now,
with a small hammer,
I assure you, there would be nothing there

there would perhaps be a powder, a long thread,
a needle perhaps a photograph
of what I was to be to someone

I once saw "Lucia Monti" shine,
on the canvas of Jose Villegas Cordero,
in a museum, summing up

the black ages before her,
gleaming beyond
the aesthetic of sin and purgatory

will my bones glitter beyond these ages,
will they burn beyond the photographs'
crude economy

OSSUARY VI

this genealogy she's made by hand, this good silk lace,
Engels plaited to Bird, Claudia Jones edgestitched
to Monk, Rosa Luxemburg braids Coltrane

as far as she's concerned these names reshaped time
itself though time seems somehow set itself,
in time

in so few rooms that Yasmine herself is caught
and trapped in its coarse drenched net,
a blue crab angling and articulating

sideways, these names would help
here, but
such, such did not create the world or fix time

in that bulbous concentration,
of what matters,
what appears

Yasmine knows in her hardest heart,
that truth is worked and organized by some,
and she's on the wrong side always

she scrubs the tables till they're raw,
alive,
this she's done for three exact years

in this exact city,
whose exact location must remain vague,
here she is a polyglot, wise, too wise, silent like time

two hours before the onslaught of children,
their ferile enthusiasms,
the snow still falling over in Buffalo

that band of weather would not arrive
here,
before afternoon, before

what was the absence of weather,
and it always seems to be snowing in that city,
south of her exile, crouched as its name in winter fur

the children mattered, or so she told herself,
a platitude, people at base are craven,
more so children, their spongy senses

some days she spared them the sight of her,
the talk of her, except eat, sleep,
for fear of ruining them

where was she, that again, which city now,
which city's electric grids of currents,
which city's calculus of right and left angles

which city's tendons of streets, identical,
which city's domestic things,
newspapers, traffic, poverty

garbage collections, random murders,
shoplifting, hedge
cutting

all these coincidences,
the death of Robert Creeley, the bombing in Peshawar,
the habit of biting the lip

beginning to read *The Year of the Death*
of Ricardo Reis
for the twentieth time

and the light slow drizzle outside,
not to mention another ruin of all accords,
events happening in their order

a certain regularity,
which leads you to believe fancifully,
in coincidences

but which situate you at the apex of every
trajectory, composed irresolutely by you,
yet, only dimly recalled as consciously made by you

calculated, this flickering of light
in a specific meter of four four two,
the lone last light post on the street

the raised back of the stray cat,
at eleven every day,
resigned to hunger and random death

the same tiredness and stillness of the windy day,
when all the exercise instructions flew to the floor,
the day she decided to change places with Owusu

change chords, the four-note ending of her love,
slipped, dispassionate,
flared off, like Bird's exits

he had been right, how she'd become,
some receptacle for his spit, his sperm, his combed-out
hair, the shavings of his fingernails, each liquid phrase

he had uttered, she had drowned,
in the shell of her ear,
until his voice seemed to come from her

all because of attention to the wrong thing,
the still unknown-unknown she'd been, she'd pinned
her life to his existence when what she wanted was to be

at the crossing, when I am in the world,
she did not often think of that part of her life,
except of course

the way one remarks a low-grade fever,
a river that never recedes,
a chronic headache immune to narcotics

except it was always there,
struck, harder, the lack of self-forgiveness,
aluminum, metallic, artic, blinding

OSSUARY VII

venus, I could walk there on the ragged edge,
full of broken glass, ripped steel,
its ridge of bee stings

don't take me in from the window,
please,
don't remind me of my sweet voice

the water in my nostrils still,
the industry of birds, so busy,
in a hurry, hurry

going out in a stellar taxi,
querulous, smoking,
the year is two hundred and twenty-four days short

what force or will collected,
in that walking figure, erectus,
what fierce bright timbals

and which ambitious cells,
and which collisions of molecules,
reach their outer space sounding

don’t take me in from the window, please,
I hear the crackle of the oceanic crust,
the fracture of extraterrestrial plains

I’ve got no time, no time, this epistrophe, no time,
wind’s coming, no time,
one sunrise to the next is too long, no time

the heart lays cloaked and clawed,
its axial tilt jittery,
I’m using up all my light

all my light, don’t pull me close,
in pools of pebbled water,
I hear thumbs plangent with string and air

I’m leaning out of my skull,
don’t distract me,
I’ve never been here you know, you know

OSSUARY VIII

Havana, Yasmine arrived one early evening,
the stem of an orange dress,
a duffle bag, limp, with no possessions

the sea assaulted the city walls,
the air,
the birds assaulted the sea

she's not coastal,
more used to the interiors of northern cities,
not even their ancillary, tranquil green-black lakes

though nothing was ever tranquil about her,
being there out of her elemental America
unsettles her, untethers her

being alive, being human, its monotony
discomfited her anyway, the opaque nowness,
the awareness, at its primal core, of nothing

a temporary ache of safety,
leafed her back like unfurling fiddleheads,
she glimpsed below the obdurate seduction of Atlantic

and island shore,
when they landed, a contradiction,
a peppery drizzle, an afternoon's soft sun

the oiled air of Havana pushed its way onto the airplane,
leavened, domestic,
the Tupolev cabin like an oven darkening bread

she was alive in this place,
missing forever from her life in the other,
a moment's sentimentality could not find a deep home

what had been her life, what collection of events?
these then, the detonations,
the ones that led her to José Marti Airport

so first the language she would never quite learn,
though determined, where the word for her,
nevertheless, was *compañera*

and there she lived on rations of diction,
shortened syntax, the argot and tenses of babies,
she became allegorical, she lost metaphora, irony

in a small room so perfect she could paseo its rectangle,
in forty-four exact steps,
a room so redolent with brightness

cut in half by a fibrous bed,
made patient by the sometimish stove,
the reluctant taps, the smell of things filled with salt water

through the city's wrecked *avenidas*,
she would find the Malecón, the great sea wall
of lovers and thieves, jineteras and jineteros

and there the urban sea washed anxiety from her,
her suspicious nature found,
her leather-slippered foot against a coral niche

no avoiding the increment of observation here,
in small places small things get their notice,
not just her new sign language

oh yesterday, you were in a green skirt,
where's your smile today,
oh you were late to the corner on Tuesday

don't you remember we spoke at midday,
last week near the Coppelia,
you had your faraway handbag

your cigarette eyes,
your fine-toothed comb
for grooming peacocks, anise seeds in your mouth

you asked for a little lemon water,
you had wings in your hands,
you read me a few pages from your indelible books

what makes your eyes water so,
I almost drowned in them on Friday,
let me kiss your broken back, your tobacco lips

she recalled nothing of their encounters,
but why,
so brilliant at detail usually

the green skirt, the orange dress, the errant smile,
the middays all dissolved into
three, five, ten months in Havana

one night she walks fully clothed, like Bird,
into the oily pearl of the sea's surface,
coral and cartilage, bone and air, infrangible

and how she could walk straight out, her dress,
her bangles, her locking hair, soluble,
and how despite all she could not stay there

OSSUARY IX

what can I say about the storms,
the suns, the evenings, the moons
which have left the skies

the clouds' soft aggressions,
the seas leadening,
to brilliant slate

what is left of the winds' hoarse hands,
eclipsed by farms, the latitudes
hulahooped to the bottom of the stratospheres

the floors of oceans raked with backhoes,
the sea beds gutted,
the sheets of coral ripped by toenails of trawlers

the human skin translucent with diesel,
the lemon trees' inadvertent existences,
the satellite whales, GPS necklaces of dolphins and turtles

what can I say truly about the lungs alveoli
of plastic ornaments,
erupting, without oxygen

OSSUARY X

detonations, bullets,
there is the amber frisson of charged particles,
gravitational force so extravagant it is silence itself

the car ostentatiously broken down,
brown, wingless,
a wiry sweat down her backbone

Albany, snow outside, redundant,
two comrades glide, slip, slink toward
the bank's bronzed doors, they enter

then nothing, she is supposed to drive,
east of the bank there's a carwash,
an emaciated tree, a fire hydrant

he hums his coolness,
fills the car with himself, his sweet cigarettes,
then opens the door joint

she sees all the naive difficulty of their plan,
first the pathetic car under her gloved hands,
the tree, scabies on its bark, its obvious question mark

the winter hanging on, and hanging on,
its grubby sidewalks deserted,
the ramshackle street

"Cool," he says,
"Cool," she says,
"Power to the people." She. "Al hamdu lillaahi." He

he moves now, the same slinking gait,
as the two before,
the walk he'll use to disappear, later

as she, underground, will wait
for things to cool, though she confirms it to herself,
forever

for now he'll walk into the bank, for now
they are encircled by their beautiful predictions,
justice pumped through their veins, history will see

in the grizzled winter light,
she unlocks her finger from the steering wheel,
before he reaches the door she's at his shoulder

"I'll go, comrade." That last formality,
ground as though she'd quarried that sentence,
for the whole of their erogeny

this way she ends things and begins them,
a give in his muscles, as his assent,
"Power . . ." he begins, "to the people." She ends

you would think, you would think,
she felt fear,
none of them did

what was behind them was more fearsome,
than that ahead,
so no, no fear, what could that be today

a shelf of pigeons speculates,
first on the day,
then on the business below

the man halted in slippery stride,
the woman, gloved secretive hand on his shoulder,
they uncouple, the pigeons lose interest

the woman saunters under the puff of feathers,
the shelf shifts,
sets off a round of cooing and cuckling, resettling

the man turns to confront the reluctant car,
they must depend on its industry,
the lace of rotten rust that hangs on the doors

and fenders,
the open back windows that compensate
for the carburetor

the woman, she, Yasmine they call her,
her gloved right hand claws the metal at the bank's door,
her left nestles in her coat's reassuring pocket

it's over, one life, these two hands, this face
and what falls now,
the skies, the mornings, let them fall

the day, the withering in mirrors,
she cannot help but notice the years to come,
the door swings open

they are brilliant, those calendars spread out ahead,
and he might, or might not, be in them,
but she will

the small talon of her right hand sets to the massacre,
of her old life
its whingeing place, its spattering wavelengths

the cap of snow sky, the wedge
of fixed time that seals the body,
this new way she enters the bank, fatal

the door swings, cuts, her arm
rises to its lethal axis
"Don't anyone . . ."

and nothing here defies her stillness,
not the morning commerce, the sandy scrape
of paper, the count of dollars, the surprise of tellers

the manager in the middle of his grey dominance,
nor the rickety guard who will betray his class
by putting up a fight

the planetary swivel of her head,
the comrades descending as angels to her goodness,
cicada swift, they echo her signal

the vault pried open from the manager's head,
the angels swoop into its vacuum,
swoop out to find the incidental guard

face crushed into gristle
by the butt of her avenging gyre,
they stop, newly awakened to her violence

it could be for anyone, them too, they know,
and quick too like living,
they show her their feathers and veins, open

and all retreat out the door,
past the prone, the urinated, the supine
to money, and now Yasmine

the hulk of brown rust shudders toward them,
the pigeons shuffle on the ledge,
garbage fattened through autumn for just this day

their beaks compacted into stone,
their feet the crud of tree bark,
they mind their own business, as they should

a drizzle of tiny ice pellets begins,
begins to fall,
the car coughs its reluctance, its indecisions

in vain, they tumble in, and without a word,
before the bank door erupts, or the supplicants of its
marble floor rise from their prayers, or sirens mewl

their syrup song,
they drive, drive, drive, drive, drive,
you would think it elegant the bucket of a rusted car

fleet, it understands occasion, urgency,
there might have been noise, there might not have been,
someone might have said something

or perhaps not,
it's all the same to her now,
that replete silence is what she heard

quiet they have, as, in some twilights,
and some mornings, that cool green
silence, like the one in books

and the one on days when you are home,
alone,
in rural houses, with fields or forests

the brown dragonfly, rusted wings,
flies along the highway out of town in long leaps,
it defies its cratered flanks, its overheated gasket

the earthbound metal of its thorax,
its compound eyes survey each angle of the flight,
for cops, patrols

OSSUARY XI

In the museum I sat with Jacob Lawrence's war,
his "victory," red and drenched, looked like defeat,
of course

he lifts these paintings from their ultraviolet vats,
from the Venusian winds that blow only west,
so much like him, or me, so much faster than our planet

such stillness, such stanzaic and raw elations,
when light appears on his paper,
he is already gone

I cried with him, held his lovely heads,
his angular gentle faces as my own, his bodies,
driven with intention, attack their catastrophe in gouache

"shipping out"
who could not see this like the passage's continuum,
the upsided down-ness, the cramp, the eyes compressed

to diamonds,
as if we could exhume ourselves from these mass graves,
of ships, newly dressed

if we could return through this war, any war,
as if it were we who needed redemption,
instead of this big world, our ossuary

so brightly clad, almost heroic, almost dead,
the celebratory waiting, the waiting,
the smell of wounds

the raw red compartments,
and the sharecropping, city-soothed
hands, big to kill something else

"another patrol" those three,
it could be any year then or now or in the future,
it could be home, dense clouds of carbon

and what border are they patrolling,
the thin diagonal between then and now,
and for whom their determination to mount

the fragile, fragile promise of humanity,
their painter knew the rimlessness of any hopes,
the limitless vicinities

which made all land perilous,
but patrol yes, of course for those who think
there's country to be gained

or any place that could be made safe,
the aeronautic spheres of raincoats,
the three valises, the chasm below them

prepared for any year, when will we arrive,
the steep gradient
of nothing

"beachhead" the arms wide as Olaudah Equiano,
the teeth fierce, bayonets for self-inflicted wounds,
suicides, and riots when the end of the day

is another precipice, another hill,
the imaginary line moving like revolving latitudes,
the heart then is an incendiary

the guitar strings of veins play a future
music still unheard, the bayonets
do their sacrificial work, close

that crucifix, that crucifix,
for those who believed,
it would take them to the other shore

by then, they were scarecrows
to the world, the wind whiffing through
ribs, the sound of air through paper and straw

though some element, iron perhaps or simply
the reflexive throws of a body losing
oxygen

beating out its last gushes,
of a living thing,
said, rest, place is somewhere

"going home" the wounds, hand, shoulder,
head, in gauze and blood,
fragile like eggs

an arm electrified and supplicant, spiked
with nuclear tips, its transmutation
in the verdant shoulder of penitentiaries

to come, who would mistake these wounds,
who call these declarations nothing,
these tender anatomies

love should meet them, nothing short,
these broken heads and propitiatory arms,
clean love should meet them

povertous dowries wait at the landings,
scapegoat necklaces ring harbours,
felonies of buses, and bars, and schools

and toilets, pocked laws will address
one hand, one foot, one ringlet of hair,
recant and harden, lapse, forget

this boat should remain out there,
will remain out here, ghosting in its watery solitude, praying
never to make shore

life rafts above and below the decks,
blue, blue as blue always anticipates
the football stadiums flooded, the defenceless hurricanes

"reported missing" again, missing again,
missing, again missing,
a body out of time, moving at a constant angle

its paths through space under these forces,
flights impossible to correct,
the unnecessary barbed wire's twisted crosses

horizontal and flimsy, these reports
reach no one,
satellites pick up eroded gigabits, in decades to come

perhaps but not now, cracked and crystalline,
this news lays on the soul's floor,
like numberless calendars

what does it matter, dates
by any reckoning dates don't count,
nor the sight of lilies that must bloom beyond the lines

to be missing in all hemispheres,
is a great feat for some, disappearances are not
uncommon, for the figure in the foreground

beyond this there must be oceans, there must be
telephones, there must be notebooks with data,
there might be the curve of snows and rains

the bends in roads, the horizons or the sunrises,
that is our hope behind this wire,
gravity must give up its hold on us

surely, gravity the jail guard, the comandante
of surfaces,
might relent someday, unpin us

surely it will unhook our hearts,
from us, anchorless we will scale our faithless
legs, shed jealous hours

someone will find us brittle-winged,
beyond the punishments of leaves, of docile trees,
of windows, of our own skeletons

someone, beyond the insatiable forecasts,
the small retinas, the heart's disease,
the tattered filaments

here we morph as twig and ice and bark
and butterfly, weed and spider, vespids,
hoping against predators

convergent mimesis, all means,
stand still and hope it passes, the diatonic,
ragged plumage of our disappearances

OSSUARY XII

one will leave at Corinth, one will make a way at Utica,
one at Syracuse, one split another highway,
she'll take Utica, deluged in a thousand years of silt

it doesn't exist anymore, she knows
its vertigo, its river sickness, its wars,
its sodden coordinates

37 degrees, 3 minutes, 28. 6 seconds,
North,
10 degrees, 3 minutes, 45.35 seconds East

and all its conquerors, up to the Vandals,
its last walls devoured by esparto
grass, and silt

she knows sulphur and iron and pumice stones,
what's buried near the house of treasures,
there's an archway there

and this is how she disappears, this is where,
into an ancient city, since no city here could offer
anything but brutal solitudes, ashen mirrors

fitting, phantom limbs, intermittent hearts,
they'll all return to start this epoch again,
catastrophes will swing their way

she'll take Utica, pawn her bangles,
her earrings, her school ring,
the gun, welded to her grip and furtive

no one mentions it, still hanging between them,
no one until she chooses Utica,
the man at the wheel, who doesn't know he cannot speak

her language anymore,
or touch her sisal robes, her skin, her votive throat,
the urn in her hand, which is a good urn for water

her new plan for the river's erosions where she is,
she knows what no one here will know
how in four millennia only one wall or two will survive

and so she will enter an earlier time,
contrive to change the river's course,
the forensic circumstances of her own

she's turned all directions in the car,
the one who leaves at Corinth will burrow,
become a diviner of aquifers

sniff sandstone and limestone where he's left, she'll
pass him in some market,
sometime. They'll know and not know each other

in Utica the day is different already by anticipation,
the cap of snow sky pried loose,
a stark white shaft of road declares itself here

there she answers, commands the car to stop,
the brakes embrace, the wretched muffler hacks,
helpless, the gas tank is exhausted anyway

the driver, dumbstruck for once,
she is leaving, will leave it to her angels to explain,
she will float out on the winter's breath

two months from now, one dares to say, maybe more,
at the safe place, we'll meet,
now she laughs without leaving, short, deep leaves

safe place, she laughs, safe,
safe place, she is in stitches, the Syracuse teenager
giggles. You're righteous, Yas, stoned righteous

she takes to leave, the man they all consign
to Corinth begs through their hysteria,
but what was I here, what

and is this far enough away, a far enough way,
or are we still slaves in this old city,
back then, back then, always back then

drive, man, I'm sick of back then,
fucking straitjacket, man,
then and still now, get me to another country

another time when time isn't measured
like now, look, man, this ain't for me,
let's go on, find another world, find some elevation, cool?

this is our bed, the driver says, the first time he says
anything, since all events that rearranged
their lives occurred, since the axis of the day

regraphed his authority, and snow outside
took root in all their hearts against him,
this is our bed, he said it like it was inevitable

like it was some sour juice, some medicine,
they had to take and admit,
or the second vertebra of the neck, the pivot

now they know how hopeless he is,
now they hear what once seemed like courage,
what once hung out of his mouth, like his swagger

they'd envied in hallways when they were frightened,
his languor and that added ingredient of daring,
those outrageous shoes and hats

his time in the penitentiary,
when he'd read Marx and Lenin
and took the nickname Trotsky, from a brother

how he said once he was tired of seeing his mother's
heart broken, no word that he was the one who broke it,
she could have handled all the ache of America, save him

and a gun exposed, the faults he laid in all their plans,
not wilful but like this bed talk,
careless, or heading to some unexpected doom

and then this rattled ride from one old town,
to another, the bald tires skidding
on these hard diamonds of ice, the passing worlds

of forest and farm deserted now like their lives,
though perhaps not, their lives were always deserted,
always factional in the soul, always divided

so against themselves, their cells split,
their laughters bleached, blanched,
and this is what they were trying to lose, or gain

and now he'd said, this is our bed,
not mine, says Yas, not yours either, she
tells the man from Corinth, not yours

raze Corinth, every pot, every ugly thing,
make alphabets extinct,
there's the silence that is to come for her

her gun leans in his chest,
its letter O burns as if he's shot,
and she might as well, he thinks, his life will sink

anyway, phyllite fathoms
we'll never meet again he says, missing
her fire, her new violence, her charm

the way she is vapour already,
hot dances, a steel mallet, a stone axe,
he sees her wet feet, meteoric heart

what was I here, he asks her,
she, he should have followed, known her,
rather than the avatar with his hands on the winter road

everything to me more everything than most,
he can feel his face on icy decades to come,
this small damp town, this bald meridian of his life

sedimentary, limestone, dolostone,
tell me again I was something to you,
tell me, so afraid he would fade away from this new Yas

in shale, having never known her,
the car is full of all their last possibilities,
all the spherical tumult of former fears return

the ones in childhood tenements,
in gazes through low hallways,
food smells, in their oily jackets

the ever-peeling walls, the idiosyncratic
hobbies of eating chalk, kicking doorstops,
bouncing balls, of every circumference

and here no dreaming except to jump off,
rooftops, fall twelve or twenty storeys,
to the pavement below, intact

to observe some rites of Sunday churches,
or more radically Saturdays with straight-backed
mothers, their arms like ramparts spiked

to hold back the inevitable concrete storms,
of waste
and drift

too much for them this job of catching air,
with butterfly nets,
of stopping water with bottomless jars

too much collecting the sloughed skins
of this world's eyelids,
too much shattering the squares of caged fingers

it's a wonder they don't burst open on the road,
here the mildewed roof of the car is the sky,
here their bones erupt like skeleton over skeleton

and going on seems like their curse,
until they hear the inevitable sirens in the dull foggy
distances, behind them, they turn

the hoary road rolls away, the one who will leave
at Syracuse, his chin feathered in nineteen-year-old down,
he is afraid of nothing

not troopers, not dogs, not bullets, not knives,
not jail, already most of his short life has been
enclosure, institutions, so what, he thinks

he'll take the vacant road, he'll take it on foot,
if he has to, bare foot
he loves the fog closing in, the clouds shutting the sky

the day, like every day for him, an emergency not a life,
he grins with tension, bitter dog, he says,
I could use some bitter dog, some reefer too, good reefer

they suddenly see their wounds in him,
the gashes in their skins, the gouging, scraping
places left, open raw cavities of their long, long losses

history will enter here, whistling like train wheels,
boat winches,
the road will either end or won't, the cops catch up or not

they will arrive wherever,
they will be at war with their veins,
at war with all accounts, at war, so what

and, look, anyway, they're all composed in bony anchors
at the feet, they'll escape or they won't,
those are eternal cops behind them, glacial and planetary

yeah, Yas repeats, some bitter dog,
they laugh for him, that laugh, so prodigious,
the car's got endless fuel, they drive on

OSSUARY XIII

if only I had something to tell you, from here,
some good thing that would weather
the atmospheres of the last thirty years

I would put it in an envelope,
send it to my past life,
where someone would open it and warn the world

though, this news would arrive corroded,
you would still read it, its rust blooding,
its oxygen asperous and brittle

I'd hope you would still understand it
from here, what and how, I've been wasted,
these metal glyphs, falling and then

as if I'm gone, fingernails
peeled back in salt,
what it is, to lie down in water each night

to feel the mouth full like drowning,
the lungs like pinned butterflies,
and then as if the heart was eaten out, cored

this would do you no good to hear,
that from one January to the next,
nothing happened much that was not the same

arteries of stone,
capillaries of desolate cement,
and no kisses

rather I should say nothing, leave you to it,
make your own vain flights,
see how it goes, I can't tell time anyway

what is the sense then in sending this envelope,
porous as it is, don't worry,
look out, that's all it will say, but go on

go on, the brilliant future doesn't wait,
forget this,
I've been wasted, look, the chest like a torn bodice

ripped the guts right out of me, go,
go, my toes are eaten away by frost and rubber,
some chemical has boiled my eyes

the rest of me's been stolen,
I should say wrecked, well let's say,
I never knew it, like wire

full of jealousies, red coils,
like swallowing powder above everything,
the throat of broken glass and thorny sprigs

the falling slabs of skies in each deluged year,
I'd like to know how my assassination took place,
only why go over the summer

it was whatever it was,
one day a certain breeze, a certain
humidity, a fan of spirea waving

the sure thought that life would not be lived
here, like other people, a sickness
of uncertainties, of shifts

how to say I wish for permanence,
then I cast it off as dullness, stupidity,
then wish again for certainty, to be

in life, sitting at a bar,
cigars hanging from my fingers, I'd tip
the waitress half the cost of everything

to inhabit whole,
which is to exist simply, the bone
is an organ like any other

this was the chance, but everything can
be discussed, except that we are predatory
so on we go, take no note of what's been said here

the presumptive cruelties,
the villages that nursed these since time,
it's always in the lyric

the harsh fast threatening gobble,
the clipped sharp knifing, it's always,
in the lyric

and how I'm never left to take the sun,
to take my ease, or sleep
in the transparent parts of the day

but I'm one of the ones who likes to think,
of humankind,
I read that one can be morally exhausted

what fool said that,
what enemy of conscience,
after all this time, I'm naive as wrinkled babies

it may be useless now, to say
the awkward life, the hovering life, the
knowing life, born so early in me

known so deeply, the palm,
the sepal, unopened,
the calyx knotted, and what couldn't matter

now that we are speeding on
our atrocious axis,
the lost streets, the crashed doorsteps

the so much sorrow that cracks eyes,
such perpetual belittlings,
a woman is lying sideways on her arms

a grandfather is drifting,
into the roadway again,
a hoarse laugh outside the windows

cosmic orange flowers are waving
in their distance, what of
the patent-leather shoes hanging

from legs near the ice-cream bench,
what species of ants live in sugary maple trees
that are about to die in a former year

who will see the bedraggled gawping doorways,
the solitary deaths of finches that winters strand,
before smiles were wire, and before knives

were food and teeth were asphalt,
before sunlight was acid, on cedar porches
and hair was exiled beneath gas stoves,

the shawls strewn everywhere, sightless
walks in cities, the bony sands, the acidic
shorelines of skyscrapers, the seething airwaves all over

the starving boats and lithic frigates,
stingless bees, the canvas shirts,
the bright darkness, the clotted riverbeds

the flaking skins, the second thoughts,
the afterthoughts, dry timbre of air pockets,
the inabilities to live, the inabilities to live

right or fully, not live right,
the liveried skin, the flesh thickened with cancers,
tumours of sightlines, readjusted

ankles, fenced mouths,
mechanic vulva, plastic toenails,
pincered knee, nib of palms, wire
lifelines, elongated radius, cellular

disintegration, *dedos destruidos*
swollen tongues, *espalda goteando*,
snowy pubis, stone aorta

leathered skin, gelatinous skin,
threnodic skin, shrugged hands, you see,
I've sat here all this time being reasonable

like this, in the eye-filled years, the wall-filled years,
the returning years, the formaldehyde years,
the taxidermy years, the dishevelled years

the years of viola and mahalia and tamasine,
and gangadia and white shirts,
and sightlessness, flatsight, only sight

and coarseness,
leapy calves, leaden breath, sodden
leaden sicklyness, baked songs

I've prolonged skin bits, powdered, ashed
notebooks, copybooks,
nicks of hearts, cardboard spleen

runny veins,
husks of knuckles, the eclogite tibias,
some parts that went missing, April 19

if only someone opens this in that year,
I hope they won't understand all of it,
it should be dust too, it will, it will

look for nothing it will say, the cataclasite sacral crest,
the gutted thorax, except the schistic rib cages,
the feldspar wrists, the hyoid bone, what's left

the prosthetic self and all the broken bodies,
collapsed chest caves, will appear dressed, clattering
down streets, in all fashions of all years,

no one suspected the inventions,
I felt my own acid hand on the knee joints,
some gritty fluid on the mandible, the letter-writing finger

OSSUARY XIV

not until April did she make her way,
across the Niagara River,
the drop from rail to water, decisive and honest

the train, trolling the back of gluttonous
small cities,
dead vehicles slackly gathered, heaped

rickety and disorderly, to watch her,
spectacle, sheathed in a guiltless dress,
a new passport, a razor-bladed photo

the woman died in a car accident, she was
Caucasian, but the forger's razor blade fixed that,
and the year she died, six and counting

and the state, way south, and the family,
all perished too, all concentrated now
in Yasmine, in the train's window pane

rattle, piled truck dross, old bus carcasses,
ripped plastic with sonar senses passed,
then the ice-sweet grapevines greeted her

apple trees, collecting their bare bones
for another bearing,
and acres of desultory brick houses

gearing up for quixotic summers,
cemeteries, their solitary collections of meagre
stone biographies go by, lumber in waiting

bales, frightful garbage,
but the sky, the sky,
air glass, lung-widening sky

if she could remain suspended
between that steel, that river's gush,
this bridge, this brief relief

the only thing that amazes her now is the earth,
its ubiquitous snows and lights,
and waters, its combustible air, its nocturnal

screeches and beeps, its miraculous
colours,
what to say about that, everything

that hasn't been said, no names
for those, only ineffective attempts,
but the eyes know better, know this failure

not before April, not before joints disentangled,
their instinctual fears, could she get clear,
of a grey translucent feeling, to trust the forger

take the train toward the river's bridge,
toward the electric fields the diagonal bungalows,
graveyards of car tires, and still vines, marsh

keeps struggling up, waste like costal cartilage,
bandages the limbs of sumach, underwears the shoots,
ropes their feet, she's tired of struggling up

too, along the train's ridged centipedal back,
the spring sweats, the wind snaps
insects in two, the deserted

willows lean, inhale the tentative air
of this April,
supine, cunning month, or perhaps

fickle, or perhaps out of control,
or perhaps this damp new month will
share out its thirty days, in its usual rain

and gasps of sunlight,
and occasional blisters of snow,
its incipient lilac, her new-washed intentions

to be someone else, to be, that infinitive
that, for instance, set her on this train,
she talked to no one, found and kept a lone seat

her legs like a gate, her chin
steady on its elegiac stem, and that hand,
its history spread like spider orchids across her lap

what did this arriving city know of her,
her recumbent violence, her real
name like a music, with perfume on the end

Yasmine, some long-fingered horn player,
could blow confessions over those two cool syllables,
she'd take the teeth grit of the brusking train wheels

a wheeling bird outside, an anonymous bird,
call it oriole, call it flycatcher, more than likely,
seemed to follow her window for a while

she slept head bobbing on that alert filament,
and somehow six or so other passengers know,
to stay away, stay clear from the woman in her rookery

the woman whom the bird outside was following,
call it crow, call it hawk, call it peregrine falcon,
call her brooding even in sleep

it left when she woke up fully, call it
magpie then, her eyes its diamond, its brilliant metal,
call it heron, great blue, long-legged migrating alone

north, it broke off, it took air,
flew into an apostrophe,
heading to the wet marsh of another lake

Yasmine gathers her legs, her perfunctory luggage,
scythes the train car with her lethal gait,
stands first at the door when the wheels stop

she steps into another country, another
constellation of bodies,
her compass reset to what reckonings

at the Maple Leaf farms, Yasmine signs
to get in, signs to get out,
this is not a nuclear installation but a killing farm

for chickens,
she lines up, as each woman does,
on a steel plank, each woman with a knife

to dissect, as each woman knows how,
viscera, fat, muscle, tendon,
this daily killing, daily flesh eating

water dripping from the tables,
waterlogged to their feet, arthritic and cold,
to cut a particular part out

each woman knows what part,
their hands,
are deadly

OSSUARY XV

they ask sometimes, who could have lived,
each day,
who could have lived each day knowing

some massacre was underway, some repression,
why, anyone, anyone could live this way,
I do, I do

anyone, I'm not unique, not shy,
someone goes out for milk and butter,
and returns with gashed face, wrung larynx

practically ancient,
I'm not fooling myself, I've tried,
this regime takes us to the stone pit every day

we live like this,
each dawn we wake up, our limbs paralyzed,
shake our bones out, deliver ourselves

to the sharp instruments for butchering,
to appease which rain god,
which government god, which engine god

I don't know,
I know the abattoirs for carving, the everyday chemical
washes, and the fissile air in any regular sky

so here we lie in our bare arms,
here the ribs for a good basket, a cage,
the imperishable mandible, the rhetorical metatarsals

the hip's alertness, the skull's electricity
firing, the lit cigarette tip of the backbone
leans for its toxic caresses

here we lie in folds, collected stones
in the museum of spectacles,
our limbs displayed, fract and soluble

were this a painting, it would combust canvases,
this lunate pebble, this splintered phalanx,
I can hardly hold their sincere explosions

NOTES

These notes are re/assembled and revised from the original volumes—the gratitude to all my interlocutors, and the literary debts, are eternal.

PRIMITIVE OFFENSIVE

In respecting the original, I felt that *Primitive Offensive* needed some tightening, some weeding of lines from the original text.

WINTER EPIGRAMS AND EPIGRAMS TO ERNESTO CARDENAL IN DEFENSE OF CLAUDIA

These poems are in part a small homage to the epigrams of the Nicaraguan poet Ernesto Cardenal. On hearing of them, via the writer Stephen Henighan, Cardenal so graciously wrote in his memoir, *Vida Perdida: Memoria I*, "Nothing has remained except for a few epigrams that many have read, especially young men and women, and a little poetry book written by the Canadian poet Dionne Brand, *Epigrams to Ernesto Cardenal in Defense of Claudia*, in which, with a charming feminism, she pretends a few reproaches from Claudia to me. Fictions of a fiction because God willed the story I have told here to be a fictitious reality."

CHRONICLES OF THE HOSTILE SUN

For *Chronicles of the Hostile Sun*, in respect of the original work, I have added some punctuating control, some recess from the strong emotions that produced the work, although even at this remove from the events, the last sections resisted editing.

The three volumes, *Primitive Offensive, Winter Epigrams and Epigrams to Ernesto Cardenal in Defense of Claudia* and, *Chronicles of the Hostile Sun* were published first by Williams-Wallace Publishers. They were collected later in *Chronicles, Early Works* with a preface by the literary scholar Leslie Sanders, and published by Wilfrid Laurier Press 2011. Eternal thanks to publisher Ann Wallace and editor Roger McTair.

NO LANGUAGE IS NEUTRAL

The title of this book *No Language is Neutral* is taken directly from Derek Walcott's *Midsummer*. The poems are deeply indebted to that work.

Thanks to Ted Chamberlin for his advice and readings. My sisterhood to the Toronto Black Women's Collective for listening to it.

Thanks also to Michael Ondaatje who facilitated the first edition of this work with Coach House Press 1990. The second edition was published by McClelland & Stewart 1998.

LAND TO LIGHT ON

Thanks to Ted Chamberlin for his editorial acuity.

Much gratitude also to Adrienne Rich and Michael Ondaatje, who read early drafts of the book.

THIRSTY

My deepest thanks to Ted Chamberlin for reading this work, and to Leslie Saunders, Rinaldo Walcott, and Kwame Dawes for doing the same. Also to the Women's Studies Department, Simon Fraser University, without whose support this book would not have been possible.

INVENTORY

The lyric fragments on page 418 are from the following songs: "The Times They Are A-Changin'" by Bob Dylan; "Say It Loud, I'm Black and I'm Proud" by James Brown; "Revolution" by The Beatles; "We Shall Overcome" by Zilphia Horton, Frank Hamilton, Guy Carawan, and Pete Seeger; "Mercedes Benz" by Janis Joplin; and "Inner City Blues (Make Me Wanna Holler) by Marvin Gaye.

The lyric fragments on page 420 are from "Te recuerdo Amanda" by Víctor Jara.

The list of reported civilian deaths on page 427 is from the Iraq Body Count Project.

The lines from Pablo Neruda's "The Masks" on page 467 and "Spikes of Wheat" on page 473 are taken from *2000* by Pablo Neruda, translation by Richard Schaaf.

OSSUARIES

The following works were instrumental during the writing of this volume.

Theory: *The Eighteenth Brumaire of Louis Bonaparte* by Karl Marx; *The Origin of the Family, Private Property, and the State* by Friedrich Engels; *Endless Forms Most Beautiful* and *The Making of the Fittest* by Sean B. Carroll; *Human Zoos*, eds. Pascal

Blanchard, Nicolas Bancel et al.; *Everyone Talks About the Weather . . . We Don't: The Writings of Ulrike Meinhoff*, ed. Karin Baur, preface by Elfriede Jelinek; and *Long Time Gone* by William Lee Brent.

Music: "Epistrophy" by Thelonious Monk; "Ornithology" by Charles "Bird" Parker, Jr.; "Venus" by John Coltrane; and "Pithecanthropus Erectus" by Charles Mingus.

Paintings: *War Series* by Jacob Lawrence and *Lucia Monti* by Jorge Villegas Cordero.

Thanks to Ellen Seligman and Anita Chong for their patience, Heather Sangster once again for her commas; Don McKay for the hike in Banff.

ACKNOWLEDGEMENTS

Effusive thanks to Jared Bland (M&S publisher) for producing this new and collected work. And, for reading the new long poem *Nomenclature for the Time Being*, with insight. I must mention here too, my gratitude, and respect for him for our years of collaboration at McClelland & Stewart, making the work of many poets happen.

My profound gratitude to Christina Sharpe for her generous introduction to this new and collected volume. To have a thinker of her capaciousness work through, contextualise, and expand these labours of mine is an honour.

Torkwase Dyson, I am a dedicated admirer of her sculptures and paintings and now to have her work enclose mine I am thankful and in her debt.

Thank you to Suzanne Gardinier for her sharp poetic attention to the new work.

To Kelly Joseph (Senior Editor) and Ruta Liormonas (Publicist) of whom nothing I ask is ever impossible; to Chimedum Ohaegbu who read and reread these pages; merci, gracias, obregada, ase.

And before I run out of ways, let me extend my deep appreciation to Ken Wissoker of Duke University Press for his graciousness, prescience, and literary advocacy.